ExamKrackers MCAT

PHYSICS

6TH EDITION

OSOTE PUBLISHING

ISBN 1-893858-38-3 (Volume 5)
ISBN 1-893858-42-1 (5 Volume Set)

6th Edition

To purchase additional copies of this book or the rest of the 5 volume set,
call 1-888-572-2536 or fax orders to 1-859-255-0109.

examkrackers.com

osote.com

audioosmosis.com

Inside layout design: Saucy Enterprizes (www.saucyenterprizes.com)

Cover design: Scott Wolfe, Visible Theory (626) 795-1885

Inside cover design consultant: Fenwick Design Inc. (212) 246-9722; (201) 944-4337

Illustrations by the ExamKrackers staff.

Acknowledgements

Although I am the author, the hard work and expertise of many individuals contributed to this book. The idea of writing in two voices, a science voice and an MCAT voice, was the creative brainchild of my imaginative friend Jordan Zaretsky. I would like to thank Scott Calvin for lending his exceptional science talent and pedagogic skills to this project. I also must thank five years worth of ExamKrackers students for doggedly questioning every explanation, every sentence, every diagram, and every punctuation mark in the book, and for providing the creative inspiration that helped me find new ways to approach and teach physics. Finally, I wish to thank my wife, Silvia, for her support during the difficult times in the past and those that lie ahead.

READ THIS SECTION FIRST!

This manual contains all the physics tested on the MCAT and more. It contains more physics than is tested on the MCAT because a deeper understanding of basic scientific principles is often gained through more advanced study. In addition, the MCAT often presents passages with imposing topics that may intimidate the test-taker. Although the questions don't require knowledge of these topics, some familiarity will increase the confidence of the test-taker.

In order to answer questions quickly and efficiently, it is vital that the test-taker understand what is, and is not, tested directly by the MCAT. To assist the test-taker in gaining this knowledge, this manual will use the following conventions. Any term or concept which is tested directly by the MCAT will be written in **bold and underlined.** To ensure a perfect score on the MCAT, you should thoroughly understand all terms and concepts that are in bold and underlined in this manual. Sometimes it is not necessary to memorize the name of a concept, but it is necessary to understand the concept itself. These concepts will also be in bold and underlined. It is important to note that the converse of the above is not true: just because a topic is not in bold and underlined, does not mean that it is not important.

Any formula that must be memorized will be written in **large, red, bold type**.

If a topic is discussed purely as background knowledge, it will be written in *italics*. If a topic is written in italics, it is not likely to be required knowledge for the MCAT but may be discussed in an MCAT passage. Do not ignore items in italics, but recognize them as less important than other items. Answers to questions that directly test knowledge of italicized topics are likely to be found in an MCAT passage.

Text written in this font is me, Salty the Kracker. I will remind you what is and is not an absolute must for MCAT. I will help you develop your MCAT intuition. In addition, I will offer mnemonics, simple methods of viewing a complex concept, and occasionally some comic relief. Don't ignore me, even if you think I am not funny, because my comedy is designed to help you understand and remember. If you think I am funny, tell the boss. I could use a raise.

Each chapter in this manual should be read three times: twice before the class lecture, and once immediately following the lecture. During the first reading, you should not write in the book. Instead, read purely for enjoyment. During the second reading, you should both highlight and take notes in the margins. The third reading should be slow and thorough.

The 24 questions in each lecture should be worked during the second reading before coming to class. The in-class exams in the back of the book are to be done in class after the lecture. Do not look at them before class.

Warning: Just attending the class will not raise your score. You must do the work. Not attending class will obstruct dramatic score increases. If you have Audio Osmosis, then listen to the appropriate lecture before and after you read a lecture.

If you are studying independently, read the lecture twice before doing the in-class exam and then once after doing the in-class exam. If you have Audio Osmosis, listen to Audio Osmosis before taking the in-class exam and then as many times as necessary after taking the exam.

A scaled score conversion chart is provided on the answer page. This is not meant to be an accurate representation of your MCAT score. Do not become demoralized by a poor performance on these exams; they are not accurate reflections of your performance on the real MCAT. The thirty minute exams have been designed to educate. They are similar to an MCAT but with most of the easy questions removed. We believe that you can answer most of the easy questions without too much help from us, so the best way to raise your score is to focus on the more difficult questions. This method is one of the reasons for the rapid and celebrated success of the Examkrackers prep course and products.

If you find yourself struggling with the science or just needing more practice materials, use the Examkrackers 1001 Questions series. These books are designed specifically to teach the science. If you are already scoring 10s or better, these books are not for you.

You should take advantage of the bulletin board at www.examkrackers.com. The bulletin board allows you to discuss any question in the book with an MCAT expert at Examkrackers. All discussions are kept on file so you have a bank of discussions to which you can refer to any question in this book.

Although we are very careful to be accurate, errata is an occupational hazard of any science book, especially those that are updated regularly as is this one. We maintain that our books have fewer errata than any other prep book. Most of the time what students are certain are errata is the student's error and not an error in the book. So that you can be certain, any errata in this book will be listed as it is discovered at www.examkrackers.com on the bulletin board. Check this site initially and periodically. If you discover what you believe to be errata, please post it on this board and we will verify it promptly. We understand that this system calls attention to the very few errata that may be in our books, but we feel that this is the best system to ensure that you have accurate information for your exam. Again, we stress that we have fewer errata than any other prep book on the market. The difference is that we provide a public list of our errata for your benefit.

Study diligently; trust this book to guide you; and you will reach your MCAT goals.

TABLE OF CONTENTS

PHYSICAL SCIENCES

DIRECTIONS. Most questions in the Physical Sciences test are organized into groups, each preceded by a descriptive passage. After studying the passage, select the one best answer to each question in the group. Some questions are not based on a descriptive passage and are also independent of each other. You must also select the one best answer to these questions. If you are not certain of an answer, eliminate the alternatives that you know to be incorrect and then select an answer from the remaining alternatives. Indicate your selection by blackening the corresponding oval on your answer document. A periodic table is provided for your use. You may consult it whenever you wish.

PERIODIC TABLE OF THE ELEMENTS

1 H 1.0																	2 He 4.0
3 Li 6.9	4 Be 9.0											5 B 10.8	6 C 12.0	7 N 14.0	8 O 16.0	9 F 19.0	10 Ne 20.2
11 Na 23.0	12 Mg 24.3											13 Al 27.0	14 Si 28.1	15 P 31.0	16 S 32.1	17 Cl 35.5	18 Ar 39.9
19 K 39.1	20 Ca 40.1	21 Sc 45.0	22 Ti 47.9	23 V 50.9	24 Cr 52.0	25 Mn 54.9	26 Fe 55.8	27 Co 58.9	28 Ni 58.7	29 Cu 63.5	30 Zn 65.4	31 Ga 69.7	32 Ge 72.6	33 As 74.9	34 Se 79.0	35 Br 79.9	36 Kr 83.8
37 Rb 85.5	38 Sr 87.6	39 Y 88.9	40 Zr 91.2	41 Nb 92.9	42 Mo 95.9	43 Tc (98)	44 Ru 101.1	45 Rh 102.9	46 Pd 106.4	47 Ag 107.9	48 Cd 112.4	49 In 114.8	50 Sn 118.7	51 Sb 121.8	52 Te 127.6	53 I 126.9	54 Xe 131.3
55 Cs 132.9	56 Ba 137.3	57 La* 138.9	72 Hf 178.5	73 Ta 180.9	74 W 183.9	75 Re 186.2	76 Os 190.2	77 Ir 192.2	78 Pt 195.1	79 Au 197.0	80 Hg 200.6	81 Tl 204.4	82 Pb 207.2	83 Bi 209.0	84 Po (209)	85 At (210)	86 Rn (222)
87 Fr (223)	88 Ra 226.0	89 Ac† 227.0	104 Unq (261)	105 Unp (262)	106 Unh (263)	107 Uns (262)	108 Uno (265)	109 Une (267)									

	58 Ce 140.1	59 Pr 140.9	60 Nd 144.2	61 Pm (145)	62 Sm 150.4	63 Eu 152.0	64 Gd 157.3	65 Tb 158.9	66 Dy 162.5	67 Ho 164.9	68 Er 167.3	69 Tm 168.9	70 Yb 173.0	71 Lu 175.0
†	90 Th 232.0	91 Pa (231)	92 U 238.0	93 Np (237)	94 Pu (244)	95 Am (243)	96 Cm (247)	97 Bk (247)	98 Cf (251)	99 Es (252)	100 Fm (257)	101 Md (258)	102 No (259)	103 Lr (260)

Lecture ①

Translational Motion

Whether they realize it or not, any good physics student has a system to solve physics problems. Some problems are so trivial that the entire system is done in the mind in a fraction of a second. Other times, each step is given careful and deliberate consideration. The following is my system that you should use to solve every single physics problem on the MCAT. For easy problems you will be able to do the entire system in your head in seconds or less, but, the moment you feel any hesitation, you should begin writing with your pencil.

<u>Salty's Own Never Fail 5-Step-System</u> for solving MCAT physics problems:

Step 1: Be Confident. Don't be intimidated by any MCAT question. Remember the MCAT only tests basic physics. After reading this manual, you will know <u>all</u> the physics necessary to handle any MCAT problem.

Step 2: Draw a well-labeled diagram. A good diagram takes the question out of the 'MCAT environment', and puts it on <u>your</u> terms. Also, the act of drawing a diagram allows you to think about the problem in different ways.

Step 3: Narrow your focus to only the system of bodies in which you're interested. This may be the most obvious step in physics but it is the one most often forgotten. You must learn to concentrate upon only the body or bodies about which the question asks, and ignore all extraneous information.

Step 4: Find a formula that uses the variables in your diagram. Write down several formulas, and then eliminate until you find the useful one. Actually write your formulas out on the test booklet. It doesn't take much time and it increases accuracy.

Step 5: Plug in values and calculate the answer. *Note: This last step is often unnecessary on the MCAT.*

1-1
Solving a Physics Problem

1) **C**onfidence
2) **D**iagram
3) **S**ystem
4) **F**ormula
5) **P**lug-n-**C**hug

1-2
Vectors and Scalars

Appreciating the difference between vectors and scalars will help you solve MCAT physics problems. A <u>scalar</u> is a physical quantity that has magnitude but no direction. A <u>vector</u> is a physical quantity with both magnitude and direction. A vector can be represented by an arrow. The direction of the arrow reveals the direction of the vector; the length of the arrow reveals the magnitude of the vector.

A vector has magnitude and direction; a scalar has magnitude only. Changing the magnitude or direction of a vector creates a new vector.

1-3
Adding and Subtracting Vectors

In order to add vectors, place the head of the first vector to the tail of the second vector, and draw an arrow from the tail of the first to the head of the second. The resulting arrow is the vector sum of the other two vectors. Notice that the magnitude of the sum of two vectors must be smaller than, or equal to the sum of their magnitudes, and greater than, or equal to, the difference of their magnitudes. In other words, the sum of two velocity vectors that are 10 m/s and 7 m/s will be greater than or equal to a velocity vector of 3 m/s, but smaller than or equal to a velocity vector of 17 m/s.

To subtract vectors place the heads of the two vectors together and draw an arrow from the tail of the first to the tail of the second, or add the negative of the vector to be subtracted. The new vector is the vector difference between the two vectors.

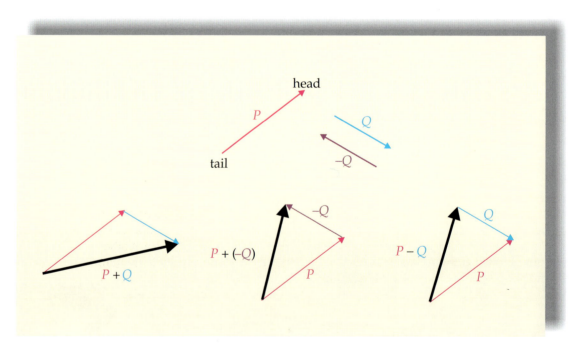

1-4
Multiplying Vectors

Vectors cannot be added to, nor subtracted from, scalars, or vice versa. However, vectors can be multiplied or divided by scalars. When a vector is multiplied or divided by a scalar the direction of the original vector is retained but the magnitude changes in proportion to the scalar.

Technically, one vector cannot be multiplied by another. Instead there is something called *dot product* and *cross product*. Although neither product is required by the MCAT, you will be required to predict the results when certain vector quantities are multiplied together. When multiplying two vectors, first check to see if the resulting physical quantity is a scalar or vector. If a vector, then the vector must point perpendicularly to both of the original two vectors, and the magnitude of the new vector is the product of the magnitude of the original vectors times the sine of the angle between them. ($V_{product} = V_1V_2\sin\theta$). There will always be two possible directions that are perpendicular to both of the original two vectors. *Right Hand Rule* is used to decide between these two directions. Although the MCAT Student Manual lists the Right Hand Rule as being tested by the MCAT, it is unlikely that it will be. If the product of the two vectors is a scalar, the magnitude of the scalar is equal to the product of the magnitudes of the two vectors times the cosine of the angle between them. ($S_{product} = V_1V_2\cos\theta$). Since there are only a few instances on the MCAT that require multiplication of vectors, students often prefer to memorize each case separately rather than memorize the above rules. This manual will cover all possible MCAT occurrences of vector multiplication on a case by case basis.

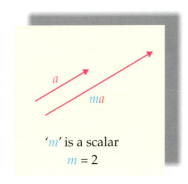

'*m*' is a scalar
$m = 2$

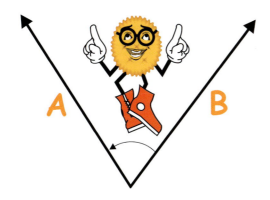

A vector times a scalar is a vector. The product of two vectors may be either a scalar or a vector. For instance, if we multiply vectors A and B as shown and the product is a vector, it will point into or out of the page depending upon Right Hand Rule. For the MCAT you just need to know that the vector will point perpendicularly to both A and B. The magnitude of the product vector will be ABsinθ. If the product is a scalar, it will have a value equal to ABcosθ.

1-5
Component Vectors

Any vector can be divided into two perpendicular **component vectors** whose vector sum is equal to the original vector. This is often convenient, since vectors acting perpendicularly to each other sometimes don't affect each other, or affect each other only in a limited fashion. We shall examine this more closely in projectile motion, circular motion, and other areas. In addition, any vector has an infinite number of possible component vectors, offering great versatility in solving vector problems.

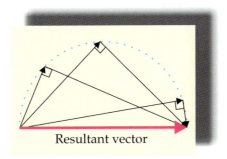

Resultant vector

The diagram on the left shows three possible pairs of components for the resultant vector. Each component is perpendicular to its partner and sums with its partner to equal the resultant. Each of the infinite number of points on the semi-circle represents a pair of possible component vectors.

The lengths of the component vectors are found through simple trigonometry such as the **Pythagorean Theorem** and **SOH CAH TOA**.

Any vector can be replaced by component vectors. Component vectors are always at right angles to each other and their sum is equal to the vector being replaced.

Pythagorean Theorem:
$$A^2 + B^2 = C^2$$

SOH CAH TOA

$$\sin\theta = O/H$$
$$\cos\theta = A/H$$
$$\tan\theta = O/A$$

As long as we're thinking about the Pythagorean theorem, we might as well remember one of the most common triangles used on the MCAT: the 3-4-5 triangle, and a less common cousin: the 5-12-13 triangle.

PythagoSaltoras

By the way, SOH CAH TOA is a little bit slow for the MCAT. You should memorize the following:

$$O = H\sin\theta$$
$$A = H\cos\theta$$

The MCAT will provide the values of sine and cosine when needed (and, more often, when not needed).

1-6
Distance-Displacement, Speed-Velocity, Acceleration

Distance and displacement are scalar and vector counterparts, as are speed and velocity. In other words, displacement is distance with the added dimension of direction, and velocity is speed with the added dimension of direction. The definitions of speed and velocity are given by the following formulae:

$$\text{speed} = \frac{\text{distance}}{\text{time}} \qquad \text{velocity} = \frac{\text{displacement}}{\text{time}}$$

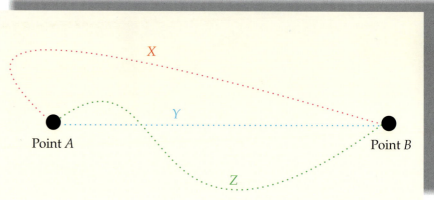

If a man walks from Point *A* to Point *B*, his distance traveled can be measured by the number of steps that he takes. His displacement is his position relative to his starting point or his *net* distance. If Point *A* and Point *B* are 10 meters apart, the man's displacement is 10 meters to the right; however, the distance that he has traveled is unknown, because he may have taken path *X*, *Y*, or *Z*. If the entire trip took 100 seconds, the man's average velocity is his displacement divided by the time or 0.1 m/s to the right. Notice that the average velocity is independent of the path chosen. The man's average vertical velocity during the trip was zero. Since the man's distance is unknown, his speed or instantaneous velocity at any moment during the trip is unknown. Even if the man took path *Y*, he may have covered the first half of the trip in 99 seconds and the second half in 1 second, thus, not maintaining a constant velocity or speed.

Acceleration is a vector, and is defined as the rate of change in velocity.

$$\text{acceleration} = \frac{\text{change in velocity}}{\text{time}}$$

Any change in velocity, in either magnitude or direction, is acceleration. This means that a particle must accelerate in order to change the direction of its motion. An object traveling at 10 m/s north one moment and 10 m/s east the next moment has accelerated even though it is moving at the same speed. This also means that a particle moving at constant velocity has no acceleration.

You have a natural intuition about velocity, but not about acceleration. For instance, we all know what it feels like to move at a velocity of 55 miles/hour, but what does it feel like to accelerate at 55 miles/hour^2? Are we thrown to the back of our seats, or do we become impatient waiting to reach a good speed. We can understand 55 miles/hour^2 as a change in velocity of 55 miles/hour every hour. In other words, starting from zero by the side of the highway, it would take us one hour to reach a velocity of 55 miles/hour, and still another hour to reach 110 miles/hour. Now you know what it feels like to accelerate at 55 miles/hour^2.

Outta the way Kracker boy!

Sorry, no can do. Science experiment in progress.

One more point about acceleration: Velocity and acceleration do NOT have to be in the same direction. A particle can be moving to the left while accelerating to the right, or moving up while accelerating down. For instance, a ball thrown upwards is accelerating downwards even while moving upwards. In fact, it is even accelerating the moment it reaches its maximum height where its velocity is zero.

1. A weather balloon travels upward for 6 km while the wind blows it 10 km north and 8 km east. Approximately what is its final displacement from its initial position?

    A. 7 km
    B. 10 km
    C. 14 km
    D. 20 km

2. Which of the following gives the average velocity of an athlete running on a circular track with a circumference of ½ km, if that athlete runs 1 km in 4 minutes?

    A. 0 m/s
    B. 2 m/s
    C. 4.2 m/s
    D. 16.8 m/s

3. A man entered a cave and walked 100 m north. He then made a sharp turn 150° to the west and walked 87 m straight ahead. How far is the man from where he entered the cave? (Note: sin 30° = 0.50; cos 30° = 0.87.)

    A. 25 m
    B. 50 m
    C. 100 m
    D. 150 m

4. The earth moves around the sun at approximately 30 m/s. Is the earth accelerating?

    A. No, because acceleration is a vector.
    B. No, because the net displacement is zero.
    C. Yes, because the speed is not constant.
    D. Yes, because the velocity is not constant.

5. An airliner flies from Chicago to New York. Due to the shape of the earth, the airliner must follow a curved trajectory. How does the curved trajectory of the airliner affect its final displacement for this trip?

    A. The displacement is less than it would be if the airliner flew in a straight line to New York.
    B. The displacement is greater than it would be if the airliner flew in a straight line to New York.
    C. The displacement is the same as it would be if the airliner flew in a straight line to New York.
    D. The final displacement of the airliner is zero.

6. An automobile that was moving forward on a highway pulled over onto the exit ramp and slowed to a stop. While the automobile was slowing down, which of the following could be true?

    A. The velocity was positive and the acceleration was positive.
    B. The velocity was negative and the acceleration was negative.
    C. The velocity was positive and the acceleration was negative.
    D. The velocity and acceleration had the same sign, either positive or negative.

7. All of the following describe the magnitude and direction of a vector EXCEPT:

    A. 10 m/s West
    B. 10 m/s in a circle
    C. 20 m to the left
    D. 20 m straight up

8. An elephant runs at a speed of 36 km/hour. Based on this information, how far can the elephant run in 10 seconds?

    A. 10 m
    B. 50 m
    C. 100 m
    D. 200 m

STOP.

Uniformly accelerated motion is motion with constant acceleration. Since acceleration is a vector, constant acceleration means that both direction and magnitude of acceleration must remain constant. A particle in uniformly accelerated motion will accelerate at a constant rate regardless of the path traveled by the particle. The most common example of uniformly accelerated motion on the MCAT is a projectile. However, before we examine projectile motion we will examine the rules for the simpler case of uniformly accelerated motion along a straight line.

For a particle in uniformly accelerated motion on a linear path, there are four basic variables that will describe its motion completely: displacement (x), velocity (v), acceleration (a), and time (t). The first three of these are vectors and the last one is a scalar. The values for these variables can be found through three basic equations. These equations can be derived with calculus, but it is far better for you to memorize them. We will refer to these equations as the linear motion equations. However, remember that constant acceleration is required for all of them. The equations are:

$$x = x_o + v_o t + \frac{1}{2}at^2$$

$$v = v_o + at$$

$$v^2 = v_o^2 + 2ax$$

In order to use these equations, there must be constant acceleration and linear motion. When choosing which equation to use, pick the one for which you know the value of all but one of the variables.

The velocities above are instantaneous velocities, or velocities at a given moment in time. Another concept that is useful on the MCAT is average velocity. Average velocity in a uniformly accelerated motion problem is given by:

$$v_{avg} = \frac{1}{2}(v + v_o)$$

1-7
Uniformly Accelerated Motion and Linear Motion

The equations on this page require constant acceleration.

1-8
Graphs of Linear Motion

Most graphs of linear motion will be plotted as displacement, velocity, or acceleration, versus time. For these graphs, you should know the significance of the slope, the line, and the area under each curve.

On a displacement versus time graph, the slope at any point is the instantaneous velocity at that time. An upward slope indicates positive velocity; a downward slope, negative velocity (velocity in the reverse direction). A straight line indicates that the slope is constant and, thus, the velocity is constant as well. A curved line represents a changing slope, which indicates a changing velocity and thus acceleration. (Acceleration is the rate of change in velocity.) The area beneath the curve has no meaning for a displacement versus time graph.

Sometimes students look at these graphs and imagine that the particle follows a path that somehow resembles the line. This is incorrect. On the displacement versus time graph, if the slope is positive, the particle is moving in the positive direction (let's say to the right). If the slope is negative, the particle is moving in the opposite direction. Notice also that the graph tells us nothing about any perpendicular motion (up or down, in or out) that the particle may have.

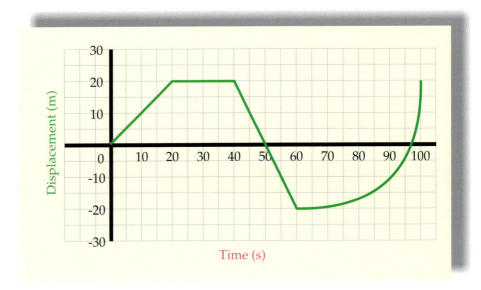

If the graph above describes the position of a particle confined to a horizontal line, and we arbitrarily choose the rightward direction as positive, then between zero and 20 seconds the particle's velocity is 1 m/s to the right. Between 20 and 40 seconds the particle is stationary at a position 20 meters to the right of its initial position. At 50 seconds the particle is back where it started but moving at 2 m/s to the left. Also at 50 seconds it has traveled a distance of 40 meters, yet its displacement is zero. At 60 seconds the particle changes directions and begins accelerating to the right. The average velocity of the particle after 100 seconds is 20 m/100 sec or 0.2 m/s to the right. If you just read through this very quickly, go back now and examine the graph at each step, and try to derive the values for yourself.

The linear motion equations can be used on any of the straight-line sections of the displacement graph, because acceleration for those sections is a constant zero.

On a velocity versus time graph, the slope at any point is the instantaneous acceleration at that time. An upward slope indicates positive acceleration; a downward slope, negative acceleration. Negative acceleration is not necessarily slowing down. It is acceleration in the reverse direction, which means slowing down if the velocity is already in the positive direction, or speeding up if the velocity is already in the negative direction. A straight line indicates that the slope is constant and, thus, the acceleration is constant as well. A curved line represents a changing slope, which indicates a changing acceleration. The area beneath the curve can represent distance or displacement. If we label all the area between the curve and zero velocity as positive, the area represents distance. If we label the area below zero velocity as negative, the total area represents displacement.

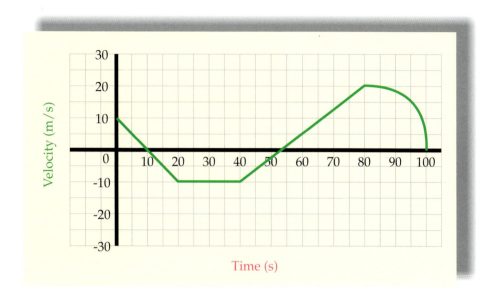

If, again, we assume that the above graph is of a particle moving horizontally with the positive direction to the right, we see that the particle began with a velocity of 10 m/s. The particle is constantly decelerating for the first 20 seconds. At 10 seconds, the particle has traveled 50 meters to the right (not zero meters). At 20 seconds the particle has a total displacement of zero from its starting point but it has traveled a distance of 100 meters. Between 20 and 40 seconds the particle has no acceleration and is moving at a constant velocity to the left. At 80 seconds the particle begins decelerating to the right or accelerating to the left (either is correct, think about it). This deceleration is not constant, however, as is indicated by the curved line. At 100 seconds the particle has a positive, nonzero displacement. Calculating the displacement would require subtracting the area under the x-axis and above the curve from the area above the x-axis and under the curve. To find the total distance traveled would require adding these areas, because distance is not dependent upon direction. Although, when the curve is below the x-axis, the displacement is negative, the entire area between the curve and the x-axis represents positive distance traveled. (Distance has no direction.)

Want a fast, easy way to solve projectile motion problems without using the equations? Use a v/t graph as follows. Draw a line and label the left end with the initial velocity and the right end with the final velocity. If the acceleration is constant, this line represents the line on a v/t graph. The exact middle of the line is always the average velocity. Since the displacement is the average velocity times the time, you know the displacement. If you don't know the time, it is the change in velocity divided by the acceleration, or the difference between the two ends of your line divided by the rate of change in velocity. Remember to always think of acceleration as how fast velocity is changing.

It's not as complicated as it sounds. Watch.

What is the distance traveled by a particle that starts at 30 m/s and accelerates to 50 m/s in four seconds? What is the acceleration?

50 m/s

30 m/s

1) draw and label your line

50 m/s

40 m/s

30 m/s

2) find the average velocity
   exactly at the middle

3) average velocity times time is 160 m.

4) the acceleration is 50 minus 30 divided by four = 5 m/s^2

An object is dropped from a plane and falls for 5 seconds. How far does it fall?

1) Vertical velocity for a projectile changes by 10 m/s each second
   so final velocity is 50 m/s.

50 m/s

0 m/s

2) draw and label your line

50 m/s

25 m/s

0 m/s

3) find the average velocity
   exactly at the middle

4) average velocity times time is 125 m.

9. Which of the following graphs best represents a particle with constant velocity?

A.

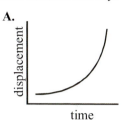

C.

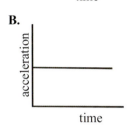

B.

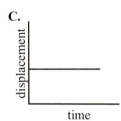

D.

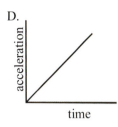

10. The graph below represents a particle moving along a straight line. What is the total distance traveled by the particle from $t = 0$ to $t = 10$ seconds?

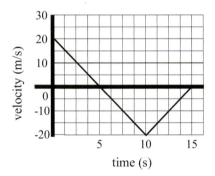

A. 0 m
B. 50 m
C. 100 m
D. 200 m

11. Which of the following is the most probable description of the motion of the object depicted by the graph below?

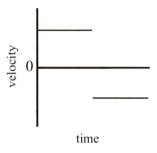

A. A person on a bike accelerating in a straight line, and then decelerating.
B. A baseball thrown by a pitcher and hit by a batter.
C. A planet in orbit.
D. One swing on a pendulum.

12. A car accelerates at a constant rate from 0 to 25 m/s over a distance of 25 m. Approximately how long does it take the car to reach the velocity of 25 m/s?

A. 1 s
B. 2 s
C. 4 s
D. 8 s

13. A particle moving in a straight line slows down at a constant rate from 50 m/s to 25 m/s in 2 seconds. What is the acceleration of the particle?

A. -12.5 m/s^2
B. -25 m/s^2
C. -50 m/s^2
D. -100 m/s^2

14. The graph below shows the displacement of a particle over time.

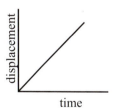

The particle exhibits increasing:

I. displacement
II. velocity
III. acceleration

A. I only
B. II only
C. I and II only
D. I and III only

GO ON TO THE NEXT PAGE.

15. A driver moving at a constant speed of 20 m/s sees an accident up ahead and hits the brakes. If the car decelerates at a constant rate of –5 m/s², how far does the car go before it comes to a stop?

    A.   10 m
    B.   20 m
    C.   40 m
    D.   100 m

16. The graph below represents a particle moving in a straight line. When $t = 0$, the displacement of the particle is 0.

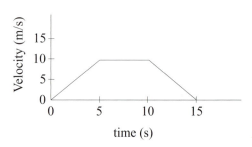

All of the following statements are true about the particle EXCEPT:

    A.   The particle has a total displacement of 100 m.
    B.   The particle moves with constant acceleration from 0 to 5 seconds.
    C.   The particle moves with constant velocity between 5 and 10 seconds.
    D.   The particle is moving backwards between 10 and 15 seconds.

_____

STOP.

Projectile: a body projected by an external force and continuing in motion by its own inertia. Because projectile motion is not linear motion, we cannot apply the linear motion equations directly. However, we can separate projectile motion into perpendicular components and analyze it as two distinct linear motion problems. Separate the motion into vertical and horizontal components. For the vertical motion, acceleration is constant and due to gravity (10 m/s²). For ideal situations with no air resistance (as on most MCAT problems) the horizontal acceleration is a constant zero.

1-9
Projectile Motion

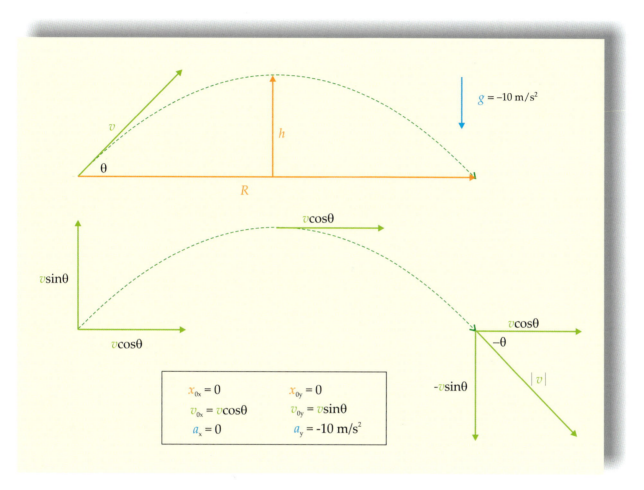

In the diagram above a projectile experiencing no air resistance is launched with a velocity v at an angle θ. In order to describe this motion with the linear motion equations, we must separate the motion into perpendicular components. For convenience we choose the horizontal and vertical directions. Using SOH CAH TOA we find that the initial vertical velocity is always $v\sin\theta$ and the horizontal velocity remains constant at $v\cos\theta$. Notice that there is no acceleration in the horizontal direction, and therefore no change in horizontal velocity throughout the flight. Notice that the vertical acceleration throughout the flight remains constant at g. At its peak height (h), the projectile has no vertical velocity but is still accelerating downwards at 10 m/s².

The peak height of the projectile can be found from the equation:

$$v_o \sin\theta = \sqrt{2gh}$$

where g is positive 10 m/s². By substituting $v\sin\theta$ for $v_o\sin\theta$, this equation gives the final velocity v of a projectile when dropped from a height h. It can be derived from special cases of the third linear motion equation and, by doing so, you can see why positive g is used.

Projectile
Salty

Notice that the path of a projectile not experiencing air resistance is independent of the mass of the projectile. In a vacuum, a bowling ball will follow the same path as a ping pong ball if their initial velocities are the same.

You should also know that vertical velocity alone dictates the time of flight for a projectile. The range (horizontal distance) is the horizontal velocity times the time in flight; thus the range is dictated by both horizontal and vertical velocities.

Finally, a projectile exhibits symmetry: its path upward is the mirror image to its path downward. This means that for a projectile over a flat plane time is the same for both halves of the flight, and initial speed is equal to final speed.

Understand projectile motion qualitatively and quantitatively. In other words, don't just rely on the equations. Stop right now and contemplate projectile motion. Even though the projectile moves both up and down in the same flight, its acceleration is constant. Even while the projectile is motionless at the instant it reaches its peak, acceleration is still g. How can a motionless object have acceleration? The answer lies in the definition of acceleration.

Use the symmetry of projectile motion to help you solve problems. For instance, if we use only the second half of the trip, vertical v_o will always equal zero, making calculations easier.

Understand that vertical velocity dictates time of flight. If two projectiles leave the earth with the same vertical velocity, they will land at the same time, regardless of their horizontal velocities. For example, a bullet shot horizontally from a gun and a rock dropped from the same height will both land at the same time.

And, of course, always remember that, in the absence of air resistance, mass does not affect projectile motion.

1-10
Air Resistance

Air resistance is created when a projectile collides with air molecules. Air resistance is a type of friction. We will discuss friction in Lecture 2. Air resistance takes away energy and slows a projectile. For the MCAT, you need to understand air resistance only qualitatively. In other words, you don't need to memorize or be familiar with any formulae.

Large **surface area** increases air resistance because it allows for more collisions with air molecules.

Factors that change air resistance are: speed, surface area, and shape.

Shape also affects air resistance. Streamlined objects with smooth surfaces experience less air resistance than irregularly shaped, rough objects.

Generally speaking, the higher the **velocity**, the greater the air resistance.

Mass doesn't change the force of air resistance, but it does change the path of the projectile experiencing the air resistance. Since the force of air resistance remains constant for any mass, then, from $F = ma$, we see an inverse relationship between mass and acceleration; acceleration must decrease as mass increases. This acceleration is not g; it is only the deceleration due to air resistance. Thus, larger masses experience less deceleration due to air resistance because they are less affected by the same force of air resistance.

To understand how air resistance affects a projectile, compare a bowling ball (a massive projectile) with a volley ball (a less massive projectile). Propel both of them down a bowling alley at bowling pins. The bowling pins represent the air molecules that create air resistance. Both experience the same resistance, but the volley ball is deflected to the side while the bowling ball moves through the pins like they're not there. Air resistance has less effect on a more massive object.

Mass changes the effect of air resistance, but does not change air resistance.

1-11
Equation Summary

$$v = \frac{d}{t} \qquad \vec{v} = \frac{\vec{d}}{t} \qquad \vec{a} = \frac{\Delta\vec{v}}{t}$$

d = distance $\qquad \vec{d}$ = displacement $\qquad t$ = time
v = speed $\qquad \vec{v}$ = velocity $\qquad \vec{a}$ = acceleration

a must be constant.

$$x = x_o + v_o t + \frac{1}{2}at^2$$

$$v = v_o + at$$

$$v^2 = v_o^2 + 2ax$$

$$v_{avg} = \frac{v + v_o}{2}$$

$$v = \sqrt{2gh}$$ v_o must be zero.

t = time
x = displacement
h = height
v = velocity
a = acceleration

17. If an apple that is dropped from an altitude of 100 m reaches an altitude of 80 m after falling for $t = 2$ seconds, what altitude will it be at in $t = 4$ seconds?

   A.   60 m
   B.   40 m
   C.   20 m
   D.   0 m

18. Two skydivers are playing catch with a ball while they are falling through the air. Ignoring air resistance, in which direction should one skydiver throw the ball relative to the other if the one wants the other to catch it?

   A.   above the other since the ball will fall faster
   B.   above the other since the ball will fall more slowly
   C.   below the other since the ball will fall more slowly
   D.   directly at the other since there is no air resistance

19. If an antelope is running at a speed of 10 m/s, and can maintain that horizontal velocity when it jumps, how high must it jump in order to clear a horizontal distance of 20 m?

   A.   5 m
   B.   10 m
   C.   20 m
   D.   45 m

20. Ignoring air resistance, if the initial height of a body in free fall is increased by a factor of 4, the final velocity when it hits the ground will increase by a factor of:

   A.   2
   B.   4
   C.   It depends upon the value of the initial height.
   D.   The velocity will remain the same.

21. A projectile is launched at an angle of 30° to the horizontal and with a velocity of 100 m/s. How high will the projectile be at its maximum height?

   A.   100 m
   B.   125 m
   C.   250 m
   D.   500 m

22. Two balls are dropped from a tall tower. The balls are the same size, but Ball X has greater mass than Ball Y. When both balls have reached terminal velocity, which of the following is true?

   A.   The force of air resistance on either ball is zero.
   B.   Ball X has greater velocity.
   C.   The Ball X has greater acceleration.
   D.   The acceleration of both balls is 9.8 m/s^2.

23. A hiker throws a rock horizontally off a cliff that is 40 meters above the water below. If the speed of the rock is 30 m/s, how long does it take for the rock to hit the water? (ignore air resistance, g = 10 m/s^2)

   A.   3 sec
   B.   4 sec
   C.   5 sec
   D.   6 sec

24. A golfer hits a ball with an initial speed of 30 m/s at an angle of 40° to the horizontal. If the ball is in the air for 6 seconds, which of the following expressions will be equal to the horizontal distance traveled by the ball? (Ignore the effects of air resistance.)

   A. $(15)(6)^2(\cos 40°)$ m
   B. $(30)(6)(\cos 40°)$ m
   C. $(15)(6)^2(\sin 40°)$ m
   D. $(30)(6)(\sin 40°)$ m

STOP.

Whether moving or at rest, all objects tend to remain in their present state of motion. This tendency of an object to remain in its present state of motion is called **inertia**. **Mass** is the quantitative measure of an object's inertia. An object's mass tells us how much that object will resist a change in its motion. On the MCAT, mass is measured in kilograms (kg).

2-1
Mass and Weight

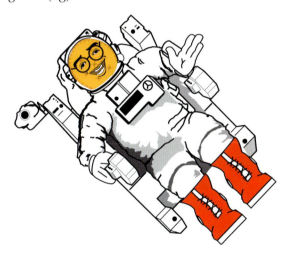

Here in space I am virtually weightless. Yet, my mass is the same as it is on earth. Regardless of where I go, my mass does not change.

Weight is the gravitational force an object experiences when near a much larger body such as the earth. On the MCAT, weight is measured in newtons (N). An object's weight at the surface of the earth is given by the product of its mass and the gravitational constant g. Thus, the weight of any object at the surface of the earth is 'mg'. Weight and mass are proportional to each other, but they are not the same physical quality.

2-2
Center of Mass

When solving mechanics problems it is often convenient to consider an object as a single particle with its mass concentrated at a single point. This can be done without error as long as the point chosen is the **center of mass** and all forces move through the chosen point. The center of mass of a system is the single point at which, for the purposes of a simple mechanics problem, all the mass of that system can be considered to be concentrated. More precisely, the center of mass is the point through which a single force may be applied in any direction causing all points on the system to accelerate equally. For the MCAT it is important that you be able to locate the approximate center of mass of a system. If a system is uniformly dense, then its center of mass coincides with its geometric center. If the system is not uniformly dense, then its center of mass is located toward the denser side from its geometric center. For example, a cube made of one half lead and the other half Styrofoam would have a geometric center at its middle; however, its center of mass would be located toward the lead side of that geometric center. Notice that the center of mass of an object does not have to be located within that object. For example, a ring with uniform density has a center of mass located at its circumscribed center, a point where there is no mass. The **center of gravity** of an object is the single point at which, for the purposes of a simple mechanics problem, the force of gravity can be applied to the entire mass. If gravity is the only force, the result will be the same regardless of the orientation of that mass. The center of mass and the center of gravity will always coincide.

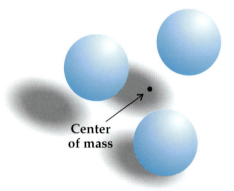

Center
of mass

The center of mass is the point where, if you could hang your system by a string, your object would be perfectly balanced in any orientation. But center of mass isn't limited to systems with only one object. A system with any number of objects also has a center of mass.

For instance, if the spheres in the diagram above were of uniform density, the center of mass would be in the position shown. If these spheres were planets, and if a spaceship were far away, they would appear as a single small dot. The ship would be affected by their gravitational force as if their entire mass were concentrated at the center of mass of the system.

2-3
The Nature of Force

There are only four forces in nature. They are:

1. the *strong nuclear force*;

2. the *weak nuclear force*;

3. **gravitational force**;

4. **electromagnetic force**.

The first two are not on the MCAT. Thus, all forces on the MCAT will be gravitational or electromagnetic. This would make identifying forces very easy except for one problem. Some electromagnetic forces are difficult to identify. For instance, if a person pushes a book with his finger, this force is actually electromagnetic.

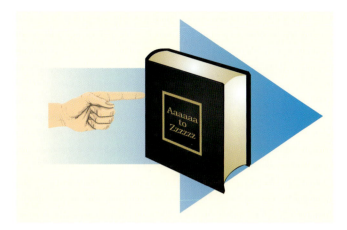

The electrostatic repulsion between the atoms in the person's finger and the atoms in the book create a force that we naturally think of as being created by contact. Since it is difficult to think of such *contact forces* as electromagnetic, we will label all such forces as 'contact forces' instead of electromagnetic.

Thus, for any MCAT problem, there are only three possible forces:

1.   gravitational;

2.   electromagnetic; and

3.   contact.

Only gravitational and electromagnetic forces act a distance. These forces are easy to identify. Gravity is usually just mg. Electromagnetic forces require a charged object or a magnet. In order for any other force to be acting on a system, something must be making visible contact with the system.

Contact forces must act in at least one of two directions:

1.   perpendicular to a surface; and/or

2.   parallel to a surface.

(An exception is tension, which is a contact force that can act in any direction away from the object. Tension will be discussed later in this Lecture.) The perpendicular force is also called the normal force. The parallel force requires friction. Both the normal force and friction will be discussed later in this Lecture.

Let's go back to my 5-step-system. The third step, choosing a system, is what I want to address here. Choosing a system is very important. A system can be any mass or group of masses. Define your system carefully. In other words, make certain that you know what is your system and what is not. When working your problem, consider only the forces that act directly on your system. Ask yourself "Is there gravity acting on my system?" Then label it. Ask yourself "Is my system charged or is it a magnet?" Then label the electromagnetic forces, if any. Finally, look for anything touching your system, and label the contact forces created by those objects. After this, you know that you have included all the possible forces, and cannot include anymore because no other forces are possible.

For instance, if we are interested in the movement of the box in the diagram below, we should consider only the forces acting on the box. The top diagram contains all kinds of force vectors and is nearly useless. The black vectors in the bottom diagram represent only forces acting on the system (the box) and are the only forces that should be considered. So, first draw the weight forces, then any electromagnetic forces, and then any contact forces, which can only be due to something making direct physical contact with your system.

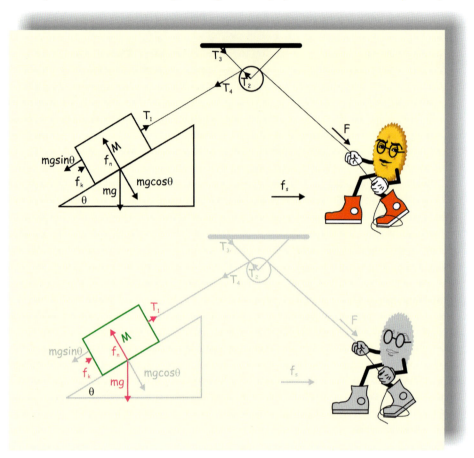

2-4

Newton's Laws

Newton's First Law is the law of inertia: an object in a state of rest or in a state of motion will tend to remain in that state unless it is acted upon by a net force.

Newton's Second Law tells us quantitatively that, when an object is acted upon by a net force, the change in that object's state of motion will be inversely proportional to the mass (m) of the object and directly proportional to the net force (F) acting upon the object. In formula, Newton's second law is:

$$F = ma$$

Newton's Third Law states that, for every action, there exists an equal and opposite reaction. This simply means that when object A applies a force to object B, object A experiences a force of equal magnitude but in the opposite direction. Newton's third law forces never act on the same system.

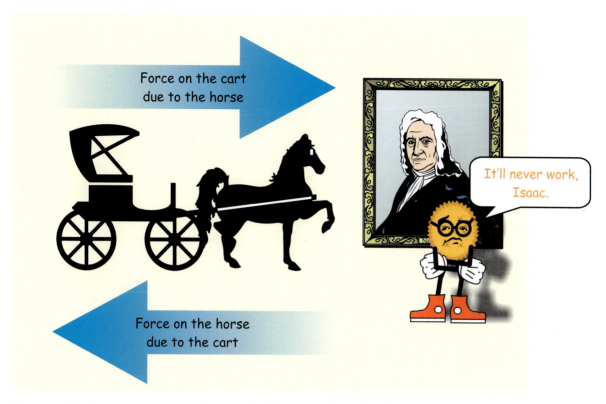

Force on the cart
due to the horse

It'll never work,
Isaac.

Force on the horse
due to the cart

How can the horse accelerate the cart? No matter how hard the horse pulls, the cart pulls back just as hard. How can it possibly move?

For the answer, choose your system to be the cart only and then draw only the forces acting on the cart. Notice that the equal and opposite force to the horse pulling on the cart, is the cart pulling on the horse. When we choose our system to be the cart, we ignore this force because it is acting on the horse. Now we see that there is a net force on the cart.

25. An astronaut on the moon applies a 100 N horizontal force to a 10 kg mass at rest on a table. At what rate does the mass accelerate? (Note: The gravitational constant at the moon's surface is 1.6 m/s². Ignore friction.)

- **A.** 5 m/s²
- **B.** 8 m/s²
- **C.** 10 m/s²
- **D.** 16 m/s²

26. A bottle rocket is launched into the air. The black powder, which propels it, burns leaving an exhaust trail mainly consisting of CO_2 gas. If the force propelling the rocket is constant, the rate of change in its velocity: (Note: ignore air resistance)

- **A.** remains constant.
- **B.** decreases.
- **C.** increases.
- **D.** is zero.

27. A 10 kg mass is in free fall with no air resistance. In order to slow the mass at a rate equal to the magnitude of g, an upward force must be applied with magnitude:

- **A.** 0 N
- **B.** 10 N
- **C.** 100 N
- **D.** 200 N

28. A 50 kg skydiver and a 100 kg skydiver open their parachutes and reach a constant velocity. The net force on the larger skydiver is:

- **A.** equal to the net force on the smaller skydiver.
- **B.** twice as great as the net force on the smaller skydiver.
- **C.** four times as great as the net force on the smaller skydiver.
- **D.** half as great as the net force on the smaller skydiver.

29. If F is the force of air resistance on an object with mass m moving at a constant velocity, which of the following best describes the acceleration of the object when the force of air resistance is reduced by a factor of 4?

- **A.** F/m
- **B.** $\dfrac{1}{2}F/m$
- **C.** $\dfrac{1}{4}F/m$
- **D.** $\dfrac{3}{4}F/m$

30. The system below consists of three spheres of equal mass m.

The center of mass of the system is located at point:

- **A.** 3
- **B.** 4
- **C.** 5
- **D.** 6

31. An airplane's propellers exert a force on the plane of 2500 N to the east. Wind resistance of 500 N acts to the west. If the weight of the plane is 40,000 N, what is the acceleration of the plane?

- **A.** 0.5 m/s² to the east
- **B.** 0.5 m/s² to the west
- **C.** 0.05 m/s² to the east
- **D.** 0.05 m/s² to the west

32. An automobile with a mass of 3000 kg is traveling down a straight flat road at a constant speed of 20 m/s. The coefficient of friction between the tires and the road is 0.5. The net force acting on the automobile is:

- **A.** 0 N
- **B.** 30,000 N
- **C.** 60,000 N
- **D.** 90,000 N

STOP.

Newton's Law of Universal Gravitation states that every mass in the universe exerts an attractive force on every other mass in the universe, and that the force is proportional to both of the masses m_1 and m_2 and inversely proportional to the square of the distance r between their centers of mass. Notice that the distance is from the center of one mass to the center of the other, and not the distance between their surfaces. The formula representing the law of gravitation is given as follows:

$$F = G\frac{m_1 m_2}{r^2}$$

where G is 6.67×10^{-11} m^3 kg^{-1} s^{-2}. This formula gives the magnitude of the force but not the direction. The direction is from the center of mass of one object to the center of mass of the other. According to Newton's third law, both masses experience a force of the same magnitude. Since this is true, the earth pulls you toward its center with a force equal to your weight, and you, in turn, pull the earth toward your center of mass with a force also equal to your weight. When we use the gravitational acceleration constant g, we consider the force that the object exerts on the earth as negligible and assume the earth to be stationary. Of course, due to the large difference in mass, this is a very good assumption. However, if we examined the two bodies below, and were asked to find how fast they would accelerate toward each other, we would have to apply Newton's second law to each mass, and then add the magnitudes of their accelerations.

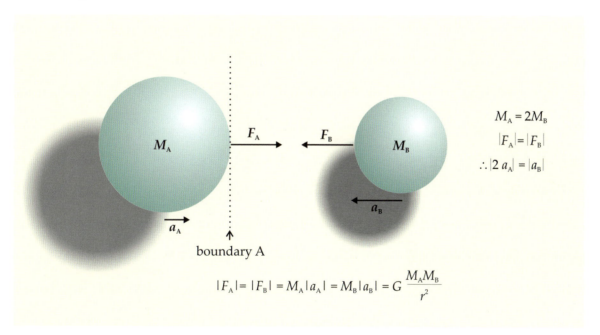

$$|F_A| = |F_B| = M_A|a_A| = M_B|a_B| = G\frac{M_A M_B}{r^2}$$

In other words, suppose that the gravitational force on object A caused it to accelerate 10 m/s^2 in the direction of object B. Assuming object B is half as massive as object A, although the gravitational force on B is of equal magnitude, object B accelerates at 20 m/s^2. These values represent the separate accelerations of the objects, but the two bodies are accelerating toward each other at a faster rate. To find out how fast the bodies are accelerating toward each other, we must add the magnitudes of their individual accelerations for a value of 30 m/s^2. In other words, object B is accelerating relative to object A at 30 m/s^2, but it is accelerating relative to a stationary boundary A at only 20 m/s^2.

Why do things float when in orbit around the earth? Have they gone out of reach of earth's gravity? What is the reach of earth's gravity? By Newton's law of gravity, gravity may become very weak at great distances, but it extends forever. So even things in orbit should fall toward earth at some rate. Besides, look how closely Sky Lab orbited the earth. Could this have been out of reach of earth's gravity? Yet, we know that things floated on Sky Lab. Let's come back to this question when we discuss circular motion.

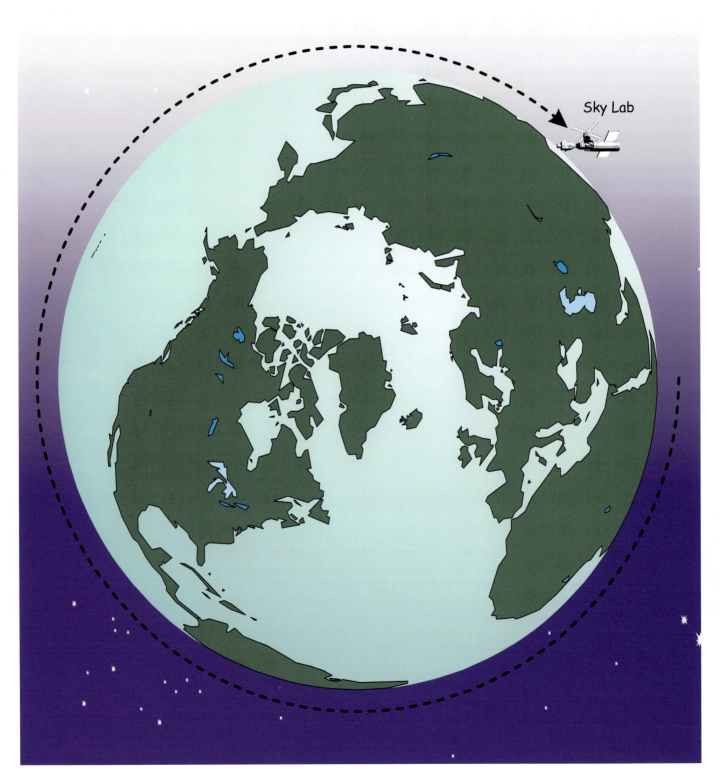

Sky Lab

The **inclined plane** is a specific topic often tested by the MCAT. There are certain basic characteristics that exist for all inclined planes. Once we understand these characteristics, all inclined plane problems become trivial.

In the simplest, ideal case (no friction and nothing attached to the block), the only forces acting on a block on an inclined plane are gravity pushing straight downward, and the inclined plane pushing back. The force of the inclined plane pushing back against the gravitational force is called the **normal force (F_n)**. The normal force is always perpendicular to the surface that applies it. Your diagram of a block on a frictionless inclined plane should look like the diagram on the right.

Since gravity and the normal force are the only forces acting on the block, their sum is called the **net force**. It is the net force that should be plugged into Newton's second law to find the acceleration of your system. Notice from the picture below that vector addition of gravity and the normal force creates a right triangle. Notice also that this triangle is similar to the triangle of the inclined plane. Similar triangles have equal corresponding angles. By SOH CAH TOA we find that the resultant vector has a magnitude of $mg\sin\theta$. Thus the force due to gravity and the normal force of an inclined plane is always equal to **$mg\sin\theta$** for any inclined plane and points directly along the plane.

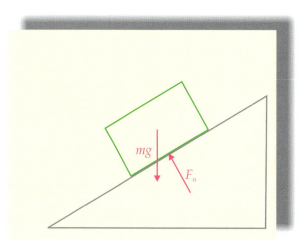

Remember that $mg\sin\theta$ is the vector sum of the weight and the normal force. You may not label your system with both $mg\sin\theta$ and weight or the normal force, since this would be redundant.

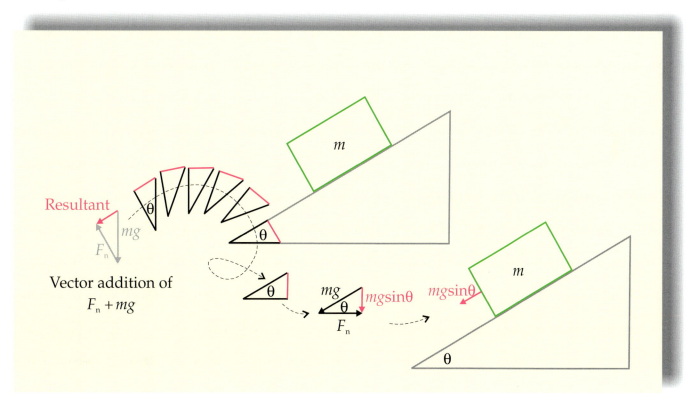

You may also notice from the diagram above that, by the rules of SOH CAH TOA, the normal force is always equal to **$mg\cos\theta$**.

Whenever you see an inclined plane, think mgsinθ. This is always the net force down any inclined plane due to gravity and the normal force. Likewise, mgcosθ is always the normal force. These formulas work regardless of the angle of the plane. Even curved surfaces can be thought of as an infinite number of inclined planes, and the force along the inclined plane at any given instant is as if the mass were on an inclined plane with a surface tangent to the circle.

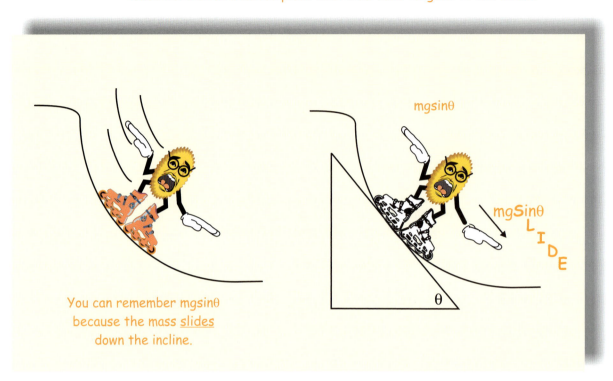

You can remember mgsinθ because the mass <u>slides</u> down the incline.

Be careful: The normal force for a mass moving down a curved surface has two jobs:

1. a portion (mgcosθ) counters some gravitational forces, and

2. the rest (mv^2/r) must create the centripetal acceleration to change the direction of the velocity.

The normal force is therefore mgcosθ plus the centripetal force, which is our next topic.

By the way, the extreme cases of inclined planes are 90° and 0°. At 90°, mgsinθ = mg; at 0°, mgsinθ = 0. Therefore, an object on a frictionless incline with any angle between 0° and 90° will accelerate at some fraction of *g*.

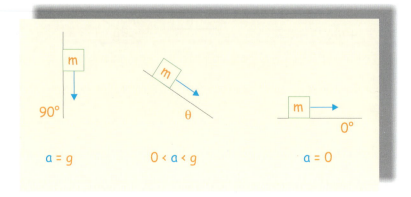

Angular velocity (ω) and *angular acceleration* (α) are not tested on the MCAT. We shall address them briefly for completeness. Angular velocity is a measure of the speed at which an object spins and is given by the equation:

$$\omega = v/r$$

where r is the radius at which the velocity v is measured. Angular velocity is given in radians per second. The following formula converts angular velocity into frequency (*f*):

$$f = \omega/2\pi$$

The frequency is the number of full rotations per second.

Angular acceleration is simply the rate of change in angular velocity and is given by:

$$\alpha = a/r$$

2-7

Circular Motion and Centripetal Force

The equations are given only for clarification and are not on the MCAT. We will refer back to these equations from time to time to improve our understanding of certain concepts that are on the MCAT. Okay, the stuff below is what you really need to know about circular motion on the MCAT.

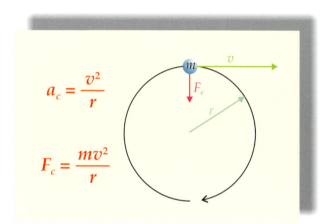

$$a_c = \frac{v^2}{r}$$

$$F_c = \frac{mv^2}{r}$$

Circular motion on the MCAT deals with concepts in translational motion applied to objects spinning or moving in circles. Examine the diagram above. An object moving in a circle at a constant speed has an instantaneous velocity v at any given moment. The magnitude of this velocity remains constant but the direction continually changes at a constant rate. The rate of this change in velocity is acceleration. So, the object's speed never changes, yet the object is continually accelerating. This type of acceleration is called **centripetal acceleration** (a_c). Centripetal acceleration always points toward the center of the circle that is circumscribed by the motion. Since, when an object moves in a circle, the direction of centripetal acceleration is constantly changing, only the magnitude of centripetal acceleration is constant. By Newton's second law we know that an acceleration must be accompanied by a net force. The net force in this case is called **centripetal force**. Of course, centripetal force always points toward the center as well. The formulae for centripetal force and centripetal acceleration are shown in the diagram above.

The thing to remember about centripetal force is that it must be at least one of the three forces: gravity, electromagnetic, or contact forces. Whenever centripetal force exists, there is always some other force responsible for it. Most centripetal force problems on the MCAT can be solved by equating the centripetal force with the responsible force. For instance, the gravitational force of the earth causes the moon to move around it. In this case we simply set the centripetal force equation equal to the Newton's gravitational force equation. We do not add the two forces together. These two forces are the same force, and thus are equal. An object being swung in a circle by a string is another example. Here, the centripetal force is created by the tension in the string. Whenever there is a centripetal force, there will always be a force causing it.

An easy way to remember that centripetal force must be created by another force is by thinking about a car on ice. A car on ice cannot turn or drive in a circle because there is nothing to create the centripetal force. What would normally cause the centripetal force that allows a car to turn on pavement? That is our next topic.

But first, back to "Why do things float when in orbit about the earth?" The answer is that they don't. Something in orbit about the earth is actually constantly falling toward the earth due to gravity. Remember, there must be a force causing the centripetal force. Gravity creates the centripetal force that makes a satellite orbit the earth rather than fly off in the direction of its velocity. So, a satellite is constantly falling toward the center of the earth but its velocity makes it continually miss the ground, and always by the same distance. Thus, to someone falling in a circular orbit with the satellite, the satellite appears to be floating.

Questions 33 through 40 are **NOT** based on a descriptive passage.

33. If *M* is the mass of the earth, *m* is the mass of the moon, and *d* is the distance between their centers, which of the following gives the instantaneous velocity of the moon as it orbits the earth? (The universal gravitational constant is given by *G*.)

   A. $\sqrt{\dfrac{GM}{d}}$

   B. $\sqrt{\dfrac{GMm}{d}}$

   C. $\sqrt{\dfrac{Gm}{d}}$

   D. $\sqrt{\dfrac{GM}{md}}$

34. The owner of a warehouse asks an engineer to design a ramp which will reduce the force necessary to lift boxes to the top of a ½ m step. If there is only room enough for a 4 m ramp, what is the maximum factor by which the lifting force could be reduced.

   A. ½
   B. 2
   C. 4
   D. 8

35. If the radius of the orbit of a satellite orbiting the earth is reduced by a factor of 2, the gravitational force on the earth will:

   A. decrease by a factor of 2.
   B. remain the same.
   C. increase by a factor of 2.
   D. increase by a factor of 4.

36. Which of the following is true of the magnitudes of velocity and acceleration, as the ball rolls down the slope as shown?

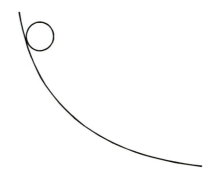

   A. The velocity and the acceleration increase.
   B. The velocity and the acceleration decrease.
   C. The velocity increases and the acceleration decreases.
   D. The velocity decreases and the acceleration increases.

37. A box starts from rest and slides 40 m down a frictionless inclined plane. The total vertical displacement of the box is 20 m. How long does it take for the block to reach the end of the plane?

   A. 1 s
   B. 2 s
   C. 4 s
   D. 8 s

38. An object of mass *m* resting on the surface of the earth experiences a force equal to its weight *mg*, where *g* is the acceleration due to gravity. If *M* is the mass of the earth, *G* is the universal gravitation constant, and *R* is the radius of the earth, which of the following expressions is equal to *g*?

   A. $\dfrac{GMm}{R^2}$

   B. $\dfrac{GM}{R^2}$

   C. $\dfrac{GMm}{R}$

   D. $\dfrac{GM}{R}$

GO ON TO THE NEXT PAGE.

39. A jogger is running on a circular track with a radius of 30 meters. If the jogger completes one trip around the track in 63 seconds, what is her average speed?

A. 0 m/s
B. 1 m/s
C. 2 m/s
D. 3 m/s

40. A box rests on an incline. Which of the following describes the forces on the box as the angle of inclination is increased?

A. The force parallel to the ramp increases and the force perpendicular to the ramp decreases.
B. The force parallel to the ramp increases and the force perpendicular to the ramp also increases.
C. The force parallel to the ramp decreases and the force perpendicular to the ramp also decreases.
D. The force parallel to the ramp and the force perpendicular to the ramp remain constant.

STOP.

Any object that contacts your system may apply forces in two directions:

1. the normal force is always perpendicular to the contact surface;
2. a frictional force is always parallel to the contact surface.

Friction is caused by the attractive molecular forces between contiguous surfaces. Since the forces are attractive, friction opposes the relative motion between contiguous surfaces.

There are two important types of surface-to-surface friction on the MCAT: static and kinetic friction. **Static friction (f_s)** is the force opposing motion when two contiguous surfaces are not moving relative to each other. If you lay a block on an inclined plane and the block does not slide down the plane, it is the static frictional force that prevents it from sliding. **Kinetic friction (f_k)** is the force resisting motion once the two contiguous surfaces are sliding relative to each other. A block of wood sliding down an inclined plane moves more slowly than a block of ice sliding down the same plane, because the kinetic frictional force is greater on the wooden block.

For any two surfaces, there are two **coefficients of friction (μ_s and μ_k),** which represent the fractions of the normal force that will equal the static and kinetic frictional forces. Thus the formulae for static friction and kinetic friction are respectively:

$$f_s \leq \mu_s F_n$$

and

$$f_k = \mu_k F_n$$

Since friction is usually a fraction of the normal force, the coefficients of friction generally have a value less than one. In addition, μ_s is greater than μ_k. Imagine pushing a heavy object. Once the object is moving, it is usually easier to push. This is due to μ_s being greater than μ_k.

When faced with a friction problem on the MCAT, first decide if your system is moving relative to the surface creating the friction. If it is, then use kinetic friction. If not, then use static friction. If you don't know, then calculate the component of the net force (excluding friction) on your system that is parallel to the surface creating the friction. Next, compare that *calculated* net force to $\mu_s F_n$. If the *calculated* net force is smaller than $\mu_s F_n$, then your system is probably* not sliding along the surface; static friction holds it in place. In this case, since there is no acceleration, the static friction is equal and opposite to the *calculated* net force. Notice that the static friction could never be greater than the *calculated* net force. If the *calculated* net force is greater than $\mu_s F_n$, then your system must be sliding along the surface. In the later case, ignore the static friction and subtract the magnitude of the kinetic frictional force from the *calculated* net force to arrive at a new net force that includes friction.

There are other types of friction, such as drag (i.e. air resistance), which is fluid resistance to an object's motion through that fluid, and viscosity, which is a fluid's resistance to motion through itself. On the MCAT these other types of friction will be dealt with only qualitatively or else a formula will be provided for plug-n-chug calculations. We will discuss the qualitative effects of drag and viscosity in Physics Lecture 6.

---

* We say "probably" because if the surfaces were already sliding relative to one another, the calculated net force could still be less than $\mu_s F_n$. Remember μ_k is usually less than μ_s.

2-8
Friction

Friction does NOT oppose motion; it opposes relative motion. Always draw a frictional force vector pointing in the direction that would prevent surfaces from sliding past each other. For instance, the frictional force on the front tires of an accelerating front wheel-drive car points in the direction of motion of the car because the force prevents the tires from sliding backwards on the road.

2-9 Tension

For the MCAT, think of **tension** as a force acting through a flexible object with no mass, such as a string or rope. (We shall refer to all these objects as simply ropes.) Tension is equal throughout a rope as long as there is no friction acting on the rope. At any point in a rope there is a tension force pulling in equal and opposite directions. We only use the force pulling away from our system. Tension requires an equal force at both ends of the rope, and the tension in the rope is equal to only one of the forces, not both. This is tricky, but remember, the rope has no mass. Thus, if a net force were applied to only one end of a rope, it would accelerate at an infinite rate.

Tension is actually beyond the scope of the MCAT. However, they test it in exactly the way explained above. When you see tension on the MCAT, just replace the rope with a force vector acting on your system.

To see where the confusion may result take a look at the mass hanging from the string below. We know that the tension in the rope is mg. But is it really mg, or do we need to add the force of the ceiling pulling up on the rope with a force mg and the box pulling down on the rope with a force mg? And if we add these forces do we get zero or 2mg?

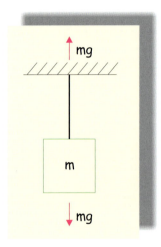

The answer is that the tension in this case is simply mg.

2-10 Hooke's Law

One more important force on the MCAT is the force due to a compressed or stretched object following **Hooke's law**. When deformed, solids tend to 'remember' their shape and reform to it. Hooke's law describes the force applied by most objects against a deforming force. This force is directly proportional to the amount of deformation or, more precisely, the change in position (Δx). Hooke's law is given by the following equation:

$$F = -k\Delta x$$

The most common MCAT questions concerning Hooke's law deal with springs. 'k' is often referred to as the 'spring constant'. The negative sign in the formula can usually be ignored for the MCAT.

where k is a constant unique to a given object. The negative sign indicates that the force is in the opposite direction of the displacement. Most solids follow Hooke's law to some extent. All solids violate Hooke's law at some limit of displacement, unique to that object. The point of violation is called the *yield point*. When an object is deformed beyond its yield point, it loses some of its 'memory' and will not regain its original shape. At some greater displacement, the object will reach a *fracture point* and break.

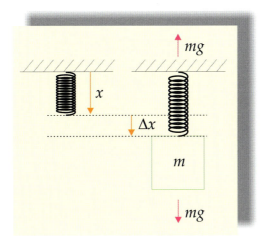

On the MCAT, Hooke's law is most often applied to springs. The force F is really the tension in the spring and Δx is the change from its rest position. For instance: the spring shown above has a spring constant $k = mg/\Delta x$.

Assuming that my head follows Hooke's law, the force that it produces against this vice is equal to the change in its thickness, Δx, times some constant, k_{salty}, which is specific to my head. The change in the thickness of my head is negative because I'm getting thinner. If I were being stretched, the change in my thickness would be positive and the force I create would be in the other direction. According to Newton's third law, the vice applies an equal but opposite force against me. That's the one that hurts.

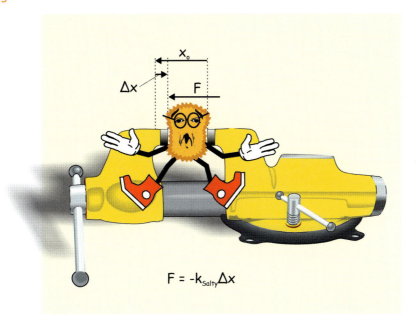

$$F = -k_{Salty}\Delta x$$

2-11
Equation Summary

Newton's Second Law

$F = ma$ The net force applied to the center of mass of a system always equals the mass of the system times its acceleration.

Gravity

$F = G \dfrac{m_1 m_2}{r^2}$ The force of gravity is proportional to the mass of each body and inversely proportional to the square of the distance between their centers of gravity. G is a universal constant.

Inclined Planes:

$F = mg\sin\theta$ The sum of the normal force and the force of gravity is $mg\sin\theta$.

$F_n = mg\cos\theta$ The normal force is $mg\cos\theta$.

Circular Motion

$a_c = \dfrac{v^2}{r}$ An object moving in a circle at constant speed v experiences a centripetal acceleration that is proportional to the square of its speed and inversely proportional to the radius of the circle which it circumscribes.

$F_c = m\,\dfrac{v^2}{r}$ Some force F_c must be applied to an object in order to give that object a centripetal acceleration.

Fiction

$f_s \leq \mu_s F_n$ Contiguous surfaces may exert equal and opposite forces against each other parallel to their contiguous surfaces.
$f_k = \mu_k F_n$ If the surfaces do not slide relative to each other, this force is static friction. If the surfaces slide relative to each other, this force is kinetic friction.

Hooke's Law

$F = -k\Delta x$ When deformed, objects obeying Hooke's Law will exert a force proportional to their deformity. k is a constant unique to the object.

41. If the rear wheels of the truck pictured below drive the truck forward, then the frictional force on the rear tires due to the road is:

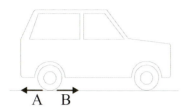

A. kinetic and in the direction of A.
B. kinetic and in the direction of B.
C. static and in the direction of A.
D. static and in the direction of B.

42. If a rope capable of withstanding 900 newtons of tension is attached to a wall as shown, what is the maximum force that can be applied in the direction of F before the rope will break?

A. 300 N
B. 450 N
C. 900 N
D. 1800 N

43. In many harbors, old automobile tires are hung along the sides of wooden docks to cushion them from the impact of docking boats. The tires deform in accordance with Hooke's law. As a boat is brought to a stop by gently colliding with the tires, the rate of deceleration of the boat:

A. is constant until the boat stops.
B. decreases until the boat stops.
C. increases until the boat stops.
D. increases and then decreases before the boat stops.

44. On a particular stretch of wet pavement, the kinetic coefficient of friction μ for a particular car with mass m is 0.08. If the car is moving at a velocity v, and suddenly locks its wheels and slides to a stop, which of the following expressions gives the distance that it will slide?

A. $\dfrac{v^2}{mg\mu}$

B. $\dfrac{v^2}{2mg\mu}$

C. $\dfrac{v^2}{2g\mu}$

D. $\dfrac{v}{2g\mu}$

45. In order to test the strength of a rope, one end is tied to a large tree and the other end is hitched to a team of 2 horses. The horses pull as hard as they can, but cannot break the rope. If the rope is untied from the tree and attached to another team of 2 horses with equal strength, and the two teams pull in opposite directions, the tension in the rope will:

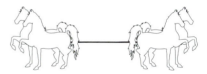

A. decrease by a factor of 2.
B. remain the same.
C. increase by a factor of 2.
D. increase by a factor of 4.

46. A child on a sled is sliding down a hill covered with snow. The combined mass of the child and sled is m, the angle of inclination of the hill is θ, and the coefficient of kinetic friction between the snow and the sled runners is μ. Which of the following expressions gives the frictional force on the sled?

A. $\mu mg\cos\theta$
B. $\mu mg\sin\theta$
C. μmg
D. mg

35

GO ON TO THE NEXT PAGE.

47. The diagram below shows two different masses hung from identical Hooke's law springs. The Hooke's law constant *k* for the springs is equal to:

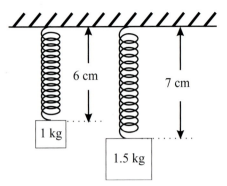

6 cm

7 cm

1 kg

1.5 kg

A. 2 N/cm
B. 5 N/cm
C. 10 N/cm
D. 20 N/cm

48. In a very tall building, an elevator with weight W moves quickly upward at a constant speed. The entire weight of the elevator is supported by a single cable. The tension in the cable is:

A. greater than *W*.
B. less than *W*.
C. equal to *W*.
D. dependent on the speed of the elevator.

Lecture 3

Equilibrium, Torque, and Energy

Equilibrium is a fancy word for no translational (straight line) or angular (rotational) acceleration. Stated another way, a system is in equilibrium if the translational velocity of its center of mass and angular velocities of all its parts are constant (i.e. it is moving and rotating at a constant velocity). If all velocities are zero, then the system is in **static equilibrium.** If any velocities are nonzero, but all velocities are also constant, then the system is in **dynamic equilibrium**. Remember, equilibrium does not mean motionless; it means constant velocity.

**3-1
Equilibrium**

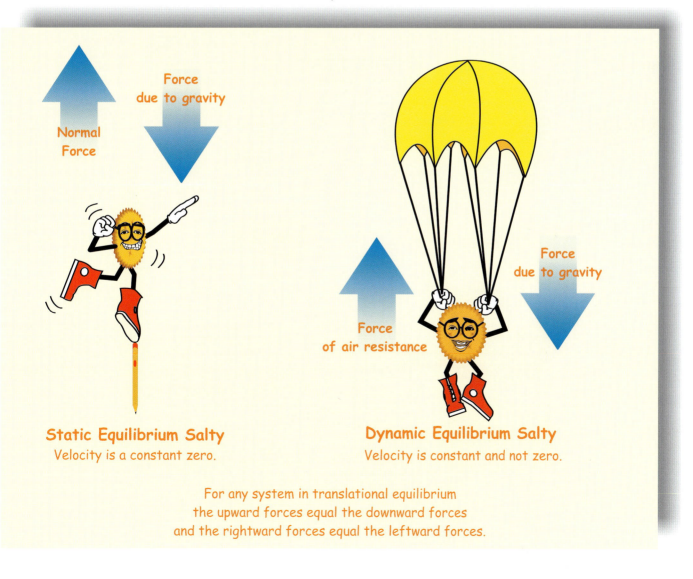

Normal Force

Force due to gravity

Force of air resistance

Force due to gravity

Static Equilibrium Salty
Velocity is a constant zero.

Dynamic Equilibrium Salty
Velocity is constant and not zero.

For any system in translational equilibrium
the upward forces equal the downward forces
and the rightward forces equal the leftward forces.

For all systems in equilibrium, the sum of all the forces acting on the system equals zero. In other words, the net force acting on a system in equilibrium is zero. A reliable and much simpler method of viewing systems in translational equilibrium on the MCAT is as follows: The sum of the magnitudes of the upward forces equals the sum of the magnitudes of the downward forces, and the sum of the magnitudes of the rightward forces equals the sum of the magnitudes of the leftward forces. This method allows you to use only positive numbers for all your forces; it is no longer necessary to decide if g is positive or negative 10. g is always positive with this method.

This is not the method that you learned in physics class, but it is faster and more intuitive for simple problems. More importantly, it is the best method for the MCAT. Thus the formulae that you must know for a system in equilibrium are:

$$F_{upward} = F_{downward}$$

$$F_{rightward} = F_{leftward}$$

3-2
Systems Not in Equilibrium

If a system is not in equilibrium, it simply means that the center of mass is accelerating translationally or its parts are accelerating rotationally. The MCAT does not test angular acceleration, so a system not in equilibrium on the MCAT must be exhibiting translational acceleration. For a system not in equilibrium, the sum of the forces equals the mass of the system times its acceleration or $\Sigma F = ma$. On the MCAT there is a faster and more effective way to solve these problems. When faced with any system not in equilibrium, follow these two steps:

1. write the equations as if the system were in equilibrium;

2. before solving, add 'ma' to the side with less force. Again, this method makes all numbers positive.

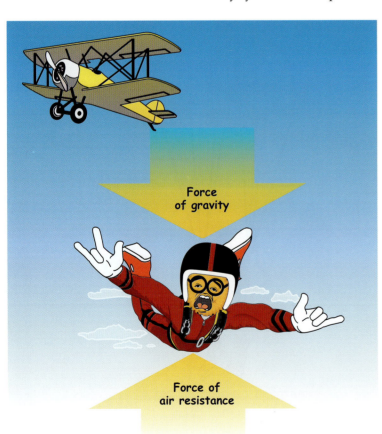

Force of gravity

Force of air resistance

Just after I jump from a plane, I am not in equilibrium. The force upon me due to gravity is greater than the force due to air resistance. In order to find my acceleration, I put all upward forces on one side of the equation and all downward forces on the other. Since I am not in equilibrium, the two sides are not equal.

$$F_{upward} \neq F_{downword}$$

Now I must decide which side has greater force. Since I am accelerating downward, the downward forces must be greater. In order to balance the two sides of my equation, I must add 'ma' to the weaker side.

$$F_{upward} + ma = F_{downword}$$

Now the two sides are equal and I can solve for acceleration.

49. A circus tightrope walker wishes to make his rope as straight as possible when he walks across it. If the tightrope walker has a mass of 75 kg, and the rope is 150 m long, how much tension must be in the rope in order to make it perfectly straight?

   A.   0 N
   B.   750 N
   C.   1500 N
   D.   No amount of tension in the rope could make it perfectly straight.

50. A rescue helicopter lifts a 50 kg rock climber by a rope from a cliff face. The rock climber is accelerated vertically at 5 m/s². What is the tension in the rope?

   A.   350 N
   B.   500 N
   C.   750 N
   D.   1500 N

51. The pulley shown below is old and rusted. When the 50 kg mass is allowed to drop, the friction in the pulley creates a constant 200 N force upward. What is the tension in the rope?

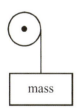

   A.   0 N
   B.   200 N
   C.   400 N
   D.   600 N

52. A skydiver jumping from a plane will accelerate up to a maximum velocity and no greater. This constant velocity is known as terminal velocity. Upon reaching terminal velocity, the net force on the skydiver is:

   A.   zero and the skydiver is in equilibrium.
   B.   zero and the skydiver is not in equilibrium.
   C.   equal to the weight of the skydiver and the skydiver is in equilibrium.
   D.   equal to the weight of the skydiver and the skydiver is not in equilibrium.

53. The arrows shown below represent all the force vectors that are applied to a single point. Which of the following could NOT be true of the point? (Note: sin150° = 0.5; $\cos 150° = -\dfrac{\sqrt{3}}{2}$)

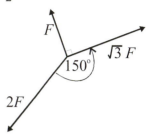

   A.   The point is moving at a constant velocity.
   B.   The point is not moving.
   C.   The point is accelerating at a constant rate.
   D.   The point is not accelerating.

54. There are 3 forces acting on an object. Two of the forces are of equal magnitude. One of these forces pulls the object to the north and one pulls to the east. If the object undergoes no acceleration, then in which direction must the third force be pulling?

   A.   northeast
   B.   northwest
   C.   southeast
   D.   southwest

55. Which of the following describes a situation requiring no net force?

   A.   A car starts from rest and reaches a speed of 80 km/hr after 15 seconds.
   B.   A bucket is lowered from a rooftop at a constant speed of 2 m/s.
   C.   A skater glides along the ice, gradually slowing from 10 m/s to 5 m/s.
   D.   The pendulum of a clock moves back and forth at a constant frequency of 0.5 cycles per second.

56. A child pushes a block across the floor with a constant force of 5 N. The block moves in a straight line and its speed increases from 0.2 m/s to 0.6 m/s. Which of the following must be true?

   A.   The force applied by the child is greater than the force of kinetic friction between the block and the floor.
   B.   The force applied by the child is less than the force of kinetic friction between the block and the floor.
   C.   The force applied by the child is greater than the force due to the weight of the block.
   D.   The force applied by the child is less than the force due to the weight of the block.

3-3
Torque

Torque (τ) is a twisting force (MCAT definition). Although torque is a vector, the MCAT allows you to think of torque as being clockwise or counter-clockwise. Torque is the vector product of both a force vector F and a position vector r. Since this is vector multiplication and the result is a vector, the magnitude of the resultant vector must include the sine of the angle between the original two vectors (see Physics Lecture 1). The magnitude of torque is given by the following equation:

$$\tau = Fr \sin\theta$$

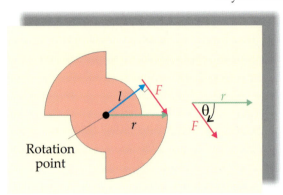

Rotation point

where θ is the angle between the force and the position vectors. In this equation, the position vector is the distance from **the point of rotation** to the point of application of the force. The point of rotation is any fixed point of your choosing. It is convenient to choose the position vector to be from the point of rotation to the point where the force acts at 90°. Such a position vector is called a **lever arm (*l*)**. When the lever arm is used, the equation for torque becomes:

$$\tau = Fl$$

Compare r and l in the diagram to the left.

Any problem on the MCAT involving torque, will be a statics problem. Therefore, use the following three formulas in the order given to solve any MCAT torque problem:

$$F_{upward} = F_{downward}$$

$$F_{rightward} = F_{leftward}$$

$$\tau_{clockwise} = \tau_{counter\text{-}clockwise}$$

In the picture to the right, what is the distance from the left end of a massless board from which I need to hang the weight in order to establish equilibrium?

Let's assume that I'm given the length of the board 'L', the distance from the left end of the board to the hanging string 'x', the mass of the object 'm', and my mass 'm_s'. First, I have confidence that since they asked me, I know that there is a way to answer the problem using only basic science. Second, I draw the board labeling all the force vectors that act directly on it and no others. Third, I choose my system. Since I want the board to be in static equilibrium, I choose the board as my system. Fourth, I choose a formula. Since this is a torque problem (I want to prevent the board from rotating.), I know that I must use the three equations given on the previous page, and use them in the order given. Since there are no horizontal forces, I can throw out the equation with horizontal forces. The equation for the vertical forces leaves me with two unknown variables: d and T.

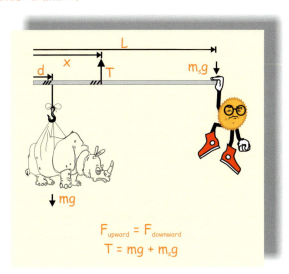

$$F_{upward} = F_{downward}$$
$$T = mg + m_sg$$

Now I go to my third equation. But I need to know the torques on my system. In order to find the torques, I must choose a point of rotation. I can choose any point that I want, but, since I need all the forces to act at 90 degrees to their lever arms, I will choose a point on the board. Let's say that I use the left end of the board as my point of rotation. Now I draw my clockwise and counterclockwise torques.

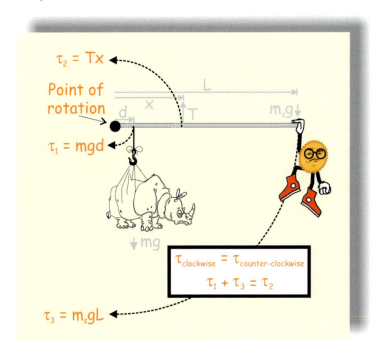

$$\tau_2 = Tx$$
Point of rotation
$$\tau_1 = mgd$$
$$\tau_{clockwise} = \tau_{counter-clockwise}$$
$$\tau_1 + \tau_3 = \tau_2$$
$$\tau_3 = m_sgL$$

To do this, I hold my system motionless only at the point of rotation, and push it around that point in the direction of the force. Finally I set the clockwise and counterclockwise torques equal to each other. Now I have two equations and two variables. I simply plug and chug.

57. A telephone pole stands as shown below. Line A is 4 m off the ground and line B is 3 m off the ground. The tensions in line A and line B are 200 N and 400 N respectively. What is the net torque on the pole?

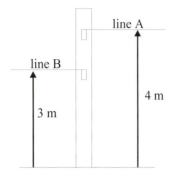

- **A.** 0 Nm
- **B.** 400 Nm
- **C.** 800 Nm
- **D.** 2000 Nm

58. A sign hangs by a rope attached at 30° to the middle of its upper edge. It rests against a frictionless wall. If the weight of the sign were doubled, what would happen to the tension in the string? (Note: sin 30° = 0.5; cos 30° = 0.87)

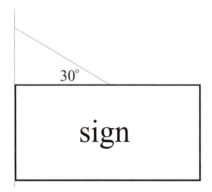

- **A.** It would remain the same.
- **B.** It would increase by a factor of 1.5.
- **C.** It would increase by a factor of 2.
- **D.** It would increase by a factor of 4.

59. If all of the forces below have equal magnitude, which one creates the most torque?

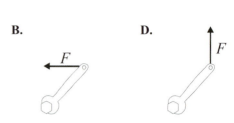

60. A one meter board with uniform density, hangs in static equilibrium from a rope with tension T. A weight hangs from the left end of the board as shown. What is the mass of the board?

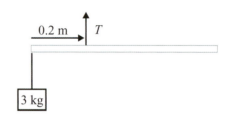

- **A.** 1 kg
- **B.** 2 kg
- **C.** 3 kg
- **D.** 4 kg

61. Boards X and Y are both massless and 4 m in length. A 4 N force F is applied to board Y as shown. Board X is held stationary. The two boards are nailed together at 1 m from the left end of board Y. If the boards do not move, what is the static frictional force between the nail and board X?

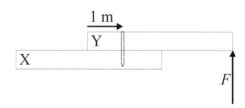

- **A.** 4 N
- **B.** 8 N
- **C.** 12 N
- **D.** 16 N

62. A person pushes on a door and it swings open. Where should the force be applied in order to make the door swing open as quickly as possible?

- **A.** On the edge of the door nearest the hinges.
- **B.** At the center of the door.
- **C.** On the edge farthest from the hinges.
- **D.** A force anywhere on the door will have the same effect.

63. A student with a mass of 40 kg sits on the end of a seesaw with a total length of 10 meters as shown in the picture.

How far to right of the center of the seesaw should a student with a mass of 50 kg sit to achieve the best balance?

- **A.** 1 m
- **B.** 2 m
- **C.** 4 m
- **D.** 5 m

64. A carpenter who is having a difficult time loosening a screw puts away his screwdriver and chooses another with a handle with a larger diameter. He does this because:

- **A.** increasing force increases torque.
- **B.** decreasing force decreases torque.
- **C.** increasing lever arm increases torque.
- **D.** decreasing lever arm decreases torque.

3-4

Energy

Look inside most basic physics textbooks and you will find the statement "**Energy** is the capacity to do work." This statement, which is inaccurate, is an attempt to define energy. It is inaccurate because a system can have energy and still have no capacity to do work. There is no satisfactory definition of energy. Energy is a man-made concept designed to assist us in understanding our universe. The best way to understand energy is to work physics problems. For now, think of energy as you have always thought about it. For instance, you have an intuitive idea of what is meant by the statement "He is full of *energy* today." Use that intuition about energy when you work physics problems.

The units of energy used on the MCAT are the **joule (J)** for macroscopic systems and, for microscopic systems, the **electron-volt (eV).** One joule is one kg m^2/s^2.

Energy is a scalar. Thus energy usually provides the most convenient method by which to solve mechanics problems. Whenever you have a mechanics problem on the MCAT, always check first to see if you can solve it using conservation of energy, which we shall discuss below.

Energy can be divided into mechanical and nonmechanical energies. **Mechanical energy** is the kinetic energy and potential energy of macroscopic systems. A macroscopic system is a system that you can examine without a microscope.

Kinetic energy (K) is the energy of motion. Any moving mass has a kinetic energy given by the equation:

$$K = \frac{1}{2}mv^2$$

Potential energy (U) is the energy of position. All potential energies are position dependent. There are several types of potential energy. The most important types on the MCAT are gravitational potential energy (U_g) and elastic potential energy (U_e). (Electrical potential energy will be discussed in Physics Lecture 7.)

Gravitational potential energy (U_g) is the energy due to the force of gravity. Gravitational potential energy between any two masses is given by $U_g = -Gm_1m_2/r$, where G is the universal gravitational constant, m_1 and m_2 are the two masses, and r is the distance between their centers of gravity. The negative sign indicates that energy decreases as the distance between objects that are attracted to each other decreases. A limited form of this equation, more useful on the MCAT, gives the gravitational potential energy of an object near the earth's surface. This formula is:

$$U_g = mgh$$

where m is the mass of the object, g is the free-fall acceleration at the surface of the earth, and h is the height of the object or system above some arbitrary point.

Elastic potential energy (U_e) is the energy due to the resistive force applied by a deformed object. The elastic potential energy for objects following Hooke's law is given by the formula:

$$U_e = \frac{1}{2}k\Delta x^2$$

where k is the Hooke's law constant for the object, and Δx is the displacement of the object from its relaxed position.

Before we can talk about energy transfer, we need to have some understanding of systems. A *system* is any defined area that we choose to consider separately from the rest of the universe. The rest of the universe is called the *surroundings*. Together, mass and energy define the three basic systems in physics: the *open system*, where energy and mass are exchanged with the surroundings; the *closed system*, where energy is exchanged with the surroundings but mass is not: the *isolated system*, where neither energy nor mass is exchanged with the surroundings. By definition, although the form of energy in an isolated system may change, the energy of an isolated system is conserved. Thus the **Law of Conservation of Energy** states that, since the universe is an isolated system, the energy of the universe remains constant.

Conservation of energy does not say that a certain type of energy (i.e. kinetic or potential) must be conserved; it states that the sum of all energy types must remain constant in an isolated system. In a closed system, the change in the sum of all energy types must equal the energy leaving or entering the system. Energy can enter or leave a closed system only as work or heat. (Work is discussed next. Heat is discussed in Chemistry Lecture 3)

3-5 Systems

Some MCAT questions will be solvable by vectors or with conservation of energy. It will be much faster to solve them using conservation of energy, so always try to solve a mechanics problem first by using conservation of energy.

3-6 Work

There are only two types of energy transfer: work and heat. **Work (W)** is the transfer of energy via a force. **Heat** is the transfer of energy by natural flow from a warmer body to a colder body. (See Chemistry Lecture 3 for more on heat.) Thus all work is energy transfer, but all energy transfer is not work. By 'transfer', we mean transfer from the system to the surroundings or vice versa. Therefore, the amount of work done will depend upon what we choose for our system. [This Lecture will not consider pressure-volume work (*PV* work). *PV* work is discussed in Chemistry Lecture 3.]

Work is a scalar and is measured in units of energy (**joules**).

The work done by any force other than friction is:

$$W = Fd\cos\theta \text{ (for all forces except friction)}$$

where F is the force on some system, d is the displacement of the system, and θ is the angle between F and d. This equation gives the energy transferred into a system due to a force. The force may be one of many forces acting on the system or it may be the net force.

Frictional forces are an exception to the equation above because frictional forces change internal energy as well as mechanical energy. (Internal energy is the energy of individual molecules. Unfortunately, MCAT will probably call this 'heat energy' or, worse, just 'heat'. Internal energy is discussed in Chemistry Lecture 3.)

If the total energy transfer is due to forces and none to heat, the work done on an object is also given by:

$$W = \Delta K + \Delta U + \Delta E_i \text{ (no heat)}$$

If there is neither heat nor friction:

$$W = \Delta K + \Delta U \text{ (no friction, no heat)}$$

where K is kinetic energy, U is any potential energy, and E_i is internal energy. This makes sense in terms of conservation of energy. Since work and heat are the only two types of energy transfer, when there is no heat, work must be responsible for any net energy change, and therefore must equal the sum of all energy changes. If there is no friction, all energy change is in the form of mechanical energy.

In any physics textbook you will also see:

$$W = \Delta K$$

This is the *Work-Energy Theorem*. It is <u>only</u> true when all energy transfer results only in a change to kinetic energy. In other words, it is a very limited case of the previous equations, and is not very useful for the MCAT.

The simplest way to understand work is to remember the first law of thermodynamics: Energy is always conserved, or

$$\Delta E = W + q$$

where q is heat and ^3E is the total change in energy of a closed system. This simply says that there are only two ways that energy can leave or enter a system: work and heat.

Now, if you want to know if work is done, do the following: Define your system. If your system is the same temperature as its surroundings then there can be no heat. Any energy change to such a system must be accomplished through work. Sum the change in energy and you have the work done on the system. If your system is not the same temperature as the surroundings, then heat must be considered and you have a thermodynamics problem. {Caveat: *Change in temperature is not the same thing as heat.*}

3-7
Conservative and Nonconservative Forces

Conservative forces are called conservative because the mechanical energy is conserved within the system. If a force acts on a system as the system moves from point A to point B and back, and the total work done by the force is zero, the force is a **conservative force**. Thus, the net work done by any conservative force on an object moving around any closed path is zero. A second way to recognize a conservative force is that the energy change is the same regardless of the path taken by the system.

It is a necessary but not a sufficient condition that conservative forces be functions of position only. In other words, the strength of a conservative force is dependent solely upon its position. For instance, the conservative force of gravity upon an object is dependent upon its position within a gravitational field; the conservative Hooke's law force is dependent upon the position of the spring or object creating it.

The work done against conservative forces is conserved in potential energy; the work done against nonconservative forces is not conserved.

Conservative forces have potential energies associated with them. Conservative forces do not change the mechanical energy of a system. Thus the **Law of Conservation of Mechanical Energy** states that when only conservative forces are acting, the sum of the mechanical energies remains constant:

$$K_1 + U_1 = K_2 + U_{2 \text{ (conservative forces only, no heat)}}$$

Written another way:

$$0 = \Delta K + \Delta U_{\text{(conservative forces only, no heat)}}$$

Warning: If a question asks, "How much work is done by gravity?" (or any other conservative force), the question itself implies that gravity is not part of the system. There are three methods to answer such a question: 1) use $Fd\cos\theta$; 2) simply calculate the change in ΔU_g; or 3) use: $W = \Delta K + \Delta U + \Delta E_i$ but do not include gravitational potential energy in your calculation of ΔU. Technically speaking, a conservative force doesn't do work because energy is never lost nor gained by the system.

Conservative forces do not change the temperature or the internal energy of an object to which they are applied. Gravitational forces, Hooke's law forces, and electric and magnetic field forces, are the conservative forces that you're likely to see on the MCAT.

<u>Nonconservative forces</u> are forces that change the mechanical energy of a system when they do work. Examples of nonconservative forces are kinetic frictional forces and the pushing and pulling forces applied by animals. For instance, if a human lifts an object from rest to a height '*h*', the total mechanical energy of the object has changed. On the other hand, if an object were propelled by its kinetic energy to a height '*h*', its total mechanical energy would remain constant.

Except for frictional forces, the work done by all nonconservative forces equals the change in the mechanical energy of the systems upon which they are applied. This result is described by the equation:

$$W = \Delta K + \Delta U_{\text{(nonconservative forces other than kinetic friction, no heat)}}$$

Notice that this is the same equation as given for one of the definitions of work. This is because conservative forces don't do work. Compare this equation to the equation for the change in mechanical energy when only conservative forces act.

The work done against conservative forces is conserved in potential energy; the work done against nonconservative forces is not conserved.

This is a tough topic. A famous physicist once wrote "There are no nonconservative forces," meaning that, of the four possible forces in nature, all are conservative. However, on a macroscopic scale, mechanical energy is changed when certain forces are acting. These forces we call nonconservative. It is possible that the MCAT might ask you to identify conservative and nonconservative forces. But the most important thing to understand is how they affect work. If you already understand work, and can do most MCAT problems involving work, then it may be best not to worry too much about conservative and nonconservative forces.

3-8
Work and Friction

Kinetic frictional forces increase the internal energy of the systems to which they are applied. Thus, the entire amount of work done by such a force does not go into changing the mechanical energy. When you rub your hands together to warm them, you are doing work, via kinetic friction, which increases their internal energy. There is no heat because your two hands are at an equal temperature throughout.

In order to find the work done by a kinetic frictional force, we must consider the internal energy. Imagine a box sliding to a stop along a tabletop. Kinetic friction has done negative work on the box; the force decreases the kinetic energy of the box. The mechanical energy change of the box is given by:

$$f_k d \cos\theta = \Delta K + \Delta U$$

However, the box increased its internal energy, so its net energy loss is not $f_k d \cos\theta$. Since the box and table are at the same temperature, there is no heat in this problem; all energy change is due to work. Thus the work done by friction is not $f_k d \cos\theta$. The energy change of the box (the work done by friction) is the change in its kinetic energy, which is negative, and the change in its internal energy, which is positive. The work done on the box is $W = \Delta K + \Delta U + \Delta E_i$. The kinetic energy of the box became internal energy of the box and internal energy of the table.

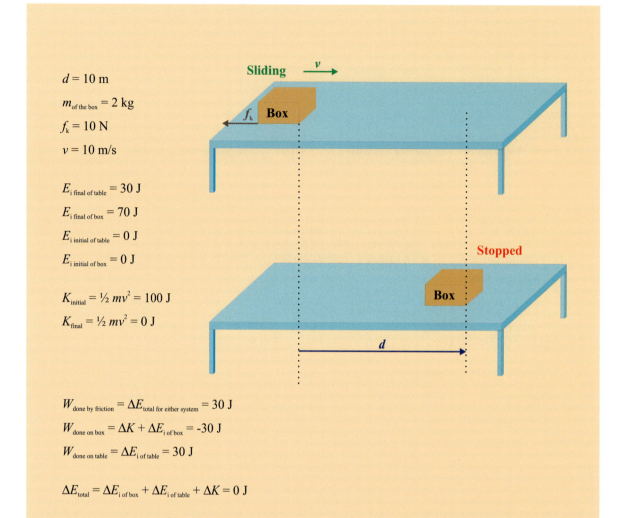

$d = 10$ m

$m_{\text{of the box}} = 2$ kg

$f_k = 10$ N

$v = 10$ m/s

$E_{\text{i final of table}} = 30$ J

$E_{\text{i final of box}} = 70$ J

$E_{\text{i initial of table}} = 0$ J

$E_{\text{i initial of box}} = 0$ J

$K_{\text{initial}} = \frac{1}{2}\,mv^2 = 100$ J

$K_{\text{final}} = \frac{1}{2}\,mv^2 = 0$ J

Sliding $\xrightarrow{\;v\;}$

f_k ← Box

Stopped

Box

d

$W_{\text{done by friction}} = \Delta E_{\text{total for either system}} = 30$ J

$W_{\text{done on box}} = \Delta K + \Delta E_{\text{i of box}} = -30$ J

$W_{\text{done on table}} = \Delta E_{\text{i of table}} = 30$ J

$\Delta E_{\text{total}} = \Delta E_{\text{i of box}} + \Delta E_{\text{i of table}} + \Delta K = 0$ J

Total energy of the isolated system of the table and box is conserved.
The energy transfer into the closed system of the box is equal to the work done on the box.
Notice that work done by friction can only be found if the change in internal energy is known.

Work and Friction

Work done by friction is a subtle point and is explained here only because, without it, the law of conservation of energy is violated and some basic concepts, such as heat and work, are obscured. The MCAT will probably not address these subtleties.

If we look at the diagram below, we have the following:

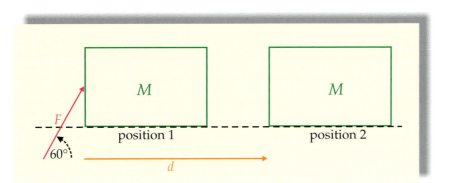

A force *F* acts on mass *M* along a frictionless surface resulting in a displacement *d*. It is important to realize that the force is acting through the entire displacement. The mass moves from position 1 to position 2. Many concepts can be appreciated by this simple display. First, since a force is applied resulting in a transfer of energy from the applicator of the force (whomever or whatever that might be) to the mass, work is done. The vertical component of the force was apparently too small to move the mass off the horizontal line. Thus the vertical displacement is zero, and the vertical force component does no work. Gravity and the normal force are 90° to the displacement and also do no work. The horizontal component of the force, however, moves the mass a displacement of *d*. To find the work done by the force, we would use $W = Fd\cos 60°$. (Notice that $F\cos 60°$ is the horizontal component of the force.) The mass does not change height, so there is no change in potential energy, *U*. Thus, the work done goes completely into changing kinetic energy. The change in kinetic energy is equal to the work.

Consider the physical manifestations of work in the example above. In other words, since work is a transfer of energy, what are the physical changes to a mass as a result of this energy transfer? To test yourself, imagine the same force acting on the box at an angle of 30°. How would this affect the work done on the box? Would one force do more work than the other? If a different amount of work is done in each case, then we should be able to see this difference in physical quantities. What would be the physical manifestations of the difference in work done?

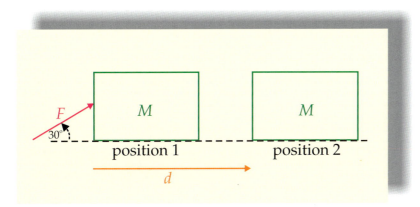

Since the force applied at 30° has a greater horizontal component, it does more work. This greater work would manifest itself in greater acceleration throughout the displacement, greater velocity at the end of the displacement, and less time required to achieve the displacement.

3-10
Summary of Work

When faced with a problem involving work, follow my 5 step system given at the beginning of Physics Lecture 1. Once you have defined your system, decide what energy transfers are taking place. If there is heat or pressure-volume change, you have a thermodynamics problem. See Chemistry Lecture 3. Otherwise, all energy transfer is work. The work done will be W = Fdcosθ unless friction is acting, but can always be found by W = ΔK + ΔU + ΔE$_i$ if information on internal energy change is available. Remember, if you want to consider a conservative force as doing work, you have three methods:

1. Fdcosθ;

2. ΔU;

3. everything but ΔU.

3-11
Power

Power (P) is the rate of energy transfer. The unit of power is the **watt (W)**, which is equivalent to J/s. Do not confuse the unit W with the concept W for work.

Power is given by the following equation:

$$P = \frac{\Delta E}{t}$$

where t is the time during which energy is transferred and ΔE is the energy change of the system, which equals work W plus heat q. A more narrow definition of power, but one that is often used, is the rate at which a force does work:

$$P = \frac{W}{t}$$

The instantaneous power due to a force is:

$$P = Fv\cos\theta$$

where θ is the angle between F and v. We can see by these equations that power is a scalar.

3-12
Equation Summary

Equilibrium
(no acceleration)

$$F_{upward} = F_{downward}$$

$$F_{rightward} = F_{leftward}$$

$$\tau_{clockwise} = \tau_{counterclockwise}$$

Non-equilibrium
(acceleration)

$$F_{upward} = F_{downward} \pm ma$$

$$F_{rightward} = F_{leftward} \pm ma$$

Add ma to the weaker side.

Torque

$$\tau = Fl$$

Energy

$$K = \tfrac{1}{2}mv^2$$

$$U_g = mgh$$

$$U_e = \tfrac{1}{2}k\Delta x^2$$

Work

$$W = Fd\cos\theta \;_{(except\ friction)}$$

$$W = \Delta K + \Delta U + \Delta E_i \;_{(no\ heat)}$$

Power

$$P = \frac{\Delta E}{t}$$

$$P = Fv\cos\theta$$

65. A meteor with a mass of 1 kg moving at 20 km/s collides with Jupiter's atmosphere. The meteor penetrates 100 km into the atmosphere and disintegrates. What is the average force on the meteor once it enters Jupiter's atmosphere? (Note: ignore gravity)

A. 2×10^3 N
B. 4×10^3 N
C. 8×10^3 N
D. 2×10^5 N

66. If 1 kg blocks were stacked one upon the other starting at the surface of the earth and continuing forever into space, the blocks near the bottom of the stack would have:

A. less gravitational potential energy than blocks at the middle or blocks near the top of the stack.
B. less gravitational potential energy than blocks at the middle and the same gravitational energy as blocks near the top of the stack.
C. the same gravitational potential energy as all other blocks.
D. more gravitational potential energy than blocks at the middle or blocks near the top of the stack.

67. Objects A and B are placed on the spring as shown. Object A has twice as much mass as object B. If the spring is depressed and released, propelling the objects into the air, object A will:

A. rise one fourth as high as object B.
B. rise half as high as object B.
C. rise to the same height as object B.
D. rise twice as high as object B.

68. A spring powered dart-gun fires a dart 1 m vertically into the air. In order for the dart to go 4 m, the spring would have to be depressed:

A. 2 times the distance.
B. 3 times the distance.
C. 4 times the distance.
D. 8 times the distance.

69. A 100 N force is applied as shown to a 10 kg object for 2 seconds. If the object is initially at rest, what is its final velocity? (ignore friction: sin 30° = 0.5; cos 30° = 0.87)

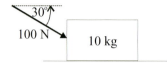

A. 8.7 m/s
B. 1 m/s
C. 17.4 m/s
D. 34.8 m/s

70. A large rock is tied to a rubber band and dropped straight down. As the rock falls, the rubber band gradually stretches, eventually bringing the rock to a stop. Which of the following energy transfers is taking place in this process?

A. Kinetic to gravitational potential to elastic potential
B. Kinetic to elastic potential to gravitational potential
C. Gravitational potential to elastic potential to kinetic
D. Gravitational potential to kinetic to elastic potential

71. Energy consumption in the home is generally measured in units of kilowatt hours. A kilowatt hour is equal to:

A. 3,600 J
B. 6,000 J
C. 3,600,000 J
D. 6,000,000 J

72. A winch is used to lift heavy objects to the top of building under construction. A winch with a power of 50 kW was replaced with a new winch with a power of 100 kW. Which of the following statements about the new winch is NOT true?

A. The new winch can do twice as much work in the same time as the old winch.
B. The new winch takes twice as much time to do the same work as the old winch.
C. The new winch can raise objects with twice as much mass at the same speed as the old winch.
D. The new winch can raise objects with the same mass at twice the speed of the old winch.

Lecture 4

Momentum, Machines, and Radioactive Decay

A baseball, when thrown by a major league pitcher, has approximately the same energy as a bowling ball thrown by a professional bowler. Why, then, can the baseball be knocked out of the park with a swing of a bat, when the same swing would only deflect the motion of the bowling ball? The answer is **momentum (p)**. The momentum of the bowling ball is much greater. Momentum is a measure of a moving object's tendency to continue along its present path. By increasing either an object's velocity or its mass, and thus its momentum, it becomes more difficult to change its path. Momentum is given by the equation:

$$p = mv$$

The units of momentum are kg m/s. Momentum is closely related to inertia (Physics Lecture 2).

There are two important points to know about momentum for the MCAT. The first is that in an isolated system **momentum is always conserved**. This law is as inviolable as the law of conservation of energy. The second important point is that **momentum is a vector**. When we put these two points together, we find that the initial momentum of the center of mass of an isolated system is always equal to its final momentum in both magnitude and direction. In other words, the momentum of the center of mass of an isolated system is constant in direction and magnitude.

A collision occurs in the following manner: Two bodies come into contact and are momentarily deformed while doing so. From Hooke's law we know that the force generated by the deformed bodies is proportional to the degree of the deformity. If the bodies follow Hooke's law perfectly, the force is conservative and the all energy is transferred (via $W = Fd\cos\theta$) back to the motion of the bodies. If the bodies do not follow Hooke's law perfectly, some or all of the energy is dissipated as internal energy. The two types of collisions just described are called elastic collisions and inelastic collisions, respectively.

Elastic collisions are collisions where the mechanical energy is conserved. In an elastic collision, no energy is dissipated to internal energy. When very small hard objects with no internal parts collide, the energy has no place to dissipate. This is an elastic collision. Atomic collisions approximately follow this model. Two magnets may slide into each other's magnetic field and repulse each other without ever touching. Their kinetic energies would be conserved momentarily in their magnetic fields. This represents a perfectly elastic collision. A rubber ball dropped from 1

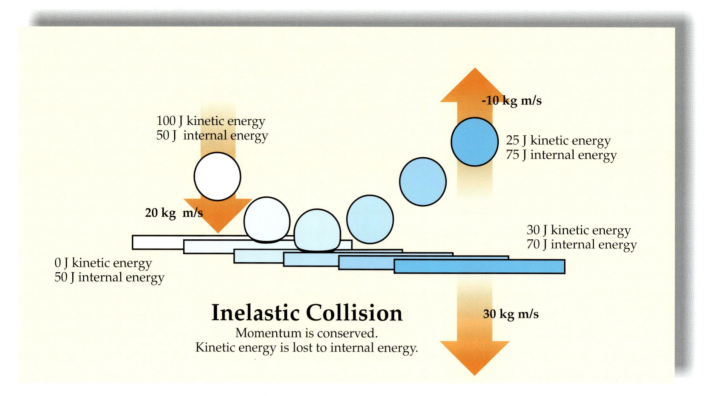

100 J kinetic energy
50 J internal energy

-10 kg m/s

25 J kinetic energy
75 J internal energy

20 kg m/s

0 J kinetic energy
50 J internal energy

30 J kinetic energy
70 J internal energy

Inelastic Collision
Momentum is conserved.
Kinetic energy is lost to internal energy.

30 kg m/s

meter bounces off a hard surface and returns to the same height. This is another elastic collision. In all these collisions, only conservative forces are at work resulting in conservation of mechanical energy.

Elastic collision problems are easy to solve because the sum of the mechanical energies before the collision is equal to the sum of the mechanical energies after the collision.

$$U_{\text{intitial}} + K_{\text{intitial}} = U_{\text{final}} + K_{\text{final}}$$

Since energy is a scalar, even the directions of the colliding objects are irrelevant.

Inelastic collisions occur when the colliding objects lose some of their mechanical energy to internal energy. Any collision that is not elastic is inelastic. Stated another way, if any mechanical energy is lost, the collision is inelastic. A *completely* inelastic collision occurs when the colliding objects stick together upon collision. Since mechanical energy is not completely conserved in any inelastic collision, we must use conservation of momentum to solve inelastic collision problems. The formula for solving inelastic collision problems is simple enough:

$$p_{\text{initial}} = p_{\text{final}}$$

The initial momentum of an isolated system equals the final momentum of an isolated system. However, because momentum is a vector, we must pay close attention to its direction. For instance in the inelastic collision diagram on the previous page, we see that by adding the momentum vectors of the final system, we arrive at a 20 kg m/s vector pointing downward, the same as the initial momentum. In multidimensional systems, the vector nature of momentum may require several equations. For instance, in a 2 dimensional system, if we have momentum in both the *x* and *y* directions, one equation is required for each direction. Thus a 2 dimensional collision may require the following equations:

$$p_{(x)\text{initial}} = p_{(x)\text{final}}$$
$$p_{(y)\text{initial}} = p_{(y)\text{final}}$$

When solving a collision problem on the MCAT, be sure that your chosen system in step 3 is an isolated system. Repeat step 2, drawing two diagrams of your system. The first should be a diagram of the system immediately before the collision and the second a diagram immediately after the collision. Then, for elastic collisions, set the total mechanical energy in the first diagram equal to the total mechanical energy in the second diagram. For inelastic collisions, set the initial and final momentums equal.

The x and y components are found by using the cosine and sine of the angles as shown in the example below. Since this involves lengthy calculations, the MCAT probably will not test it in this manner. Instead, the MCAT is likely to ask only about the momentum in the x direction or only about the momentum in the y direction.

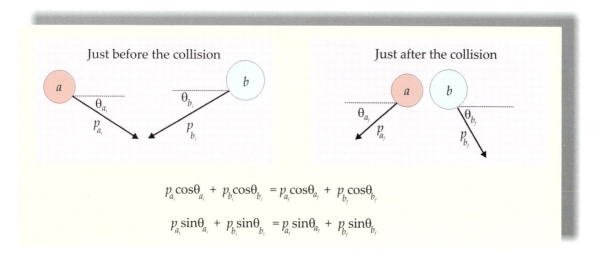

Just before the collision   Just after the collision

$$p_{a_i}\cos\theta_{a_i} + p_{b_i}\cos\theta_{b_i} = p_{a_f}\cos\theta_{a_f} + p_{b_f}\cos\theta_{b_f}$$

$$p_{a_i}\sin\theta_{a_i} + p_{b_i}\sin\theta_{b_i} = p_{a_f}\sin\theta_{a_f} + p_{b_f}\sin\theta_{b_f}$$

4-3
Reverse Collisions

Imagine watching a short film of two objects colliding and sticking together. This is a completely inelastic collision. The final momentum equals the initial momentum. If the objects stop when they collide, the final momentum is zero, so the initial momentum must have been zero as well. Now play the film again, only this time run it backwards. The two objects start together and suddenly burst apart. This is a reverse collision. Of course, just running the film backwards didn't change the momentums. The final and the initial momentums must still be zero. This is true of any explosion or radioactive decay where the pieces start from rest. Notice that the vector nature of momentum dictates that, in a two-piece explosion, the two pieces must separate in exactly opposite directions.

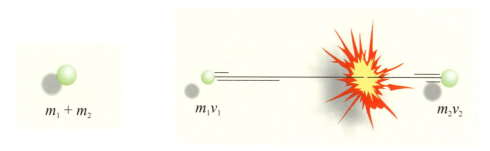

$m_1 + m_2$ m_1v_1 m_2v_2

Now imagine a cat standing on a board on top of a frozen, frictionless lake. The momentum of the cat and the board together is zero. If the cat tries to jump to the right, the board must be pushed to the left in order to conserve momentum.

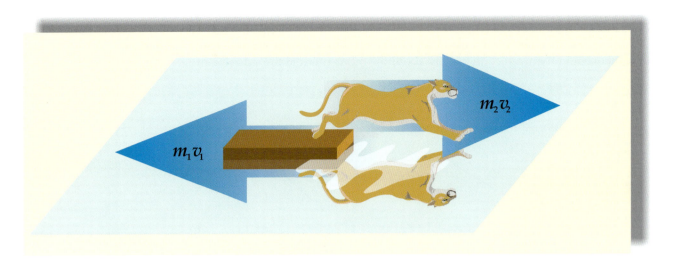

4-4

Intuition about Collisions

Collisions will be fully elastic, partially elastic, or fully inelastic. If you study the table and the graph below, you will be able to make simple predictions concerning such collisions. Knowing this table and graph is by no means crucial for the MCAT, but it will provide you with a deeper understanding concerning collisions. Don't try to memorize the table!

	Elastic		Partially Elastic		Inelastic
	v_1	v_2	v_1	v_2	$v_{combined}$
Equations	$\dfrac{v_1}{v_o} = \dfrac{m_1 - m_2}{m_1 + m_2}$	$\dfrac{v_2}{v_o} = \dfrac{2m_1}{m_1 + m_2}$	$\dfrac{v_1}{v_o - v_2} = -\dfrac{m_2}{m_1}$	$\dfrac{v_2}{v_o - v_1} = \dfrac{m_1}{m_2}$	$\dfrac{v_c}{v_o} = \dfrac{m_1}{m_1 + m_2}$
$m_1 < m_2$	$-v_o < v_1 < 0$	$0 < v_2 < v_o$	$-v_o < v_1 < \dfrac{v_o}{2}$	$0 < v_2 < v_o$	$0 < v_c < \dfrac{v_o}{2}$
$m_1 = m_2$	$v_1 = 0$	$v_2 = v_o$	$0 < v_1 < \dfrac{v_o}{2}$	$\dfrac{v_o}{2} < v_2 < v_o$	$v_c = \dfrac{v_o}{2}$
$m_1 > m_2$	$0 < v_1 < v_o$	$v_o < v_2 < 2v_o$	$0 < v_1 < v_o$	$\dfrac{v_o}{2} < v_2 < 2v_o$	$\dfrac{v_o}{2} < v_c < v_o$

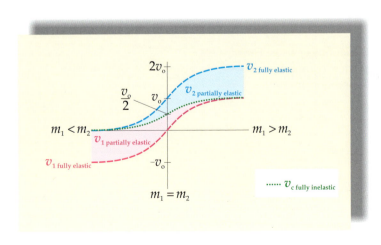

The table above is based upon a collision between a mass m_1 moving at v_o and a stationary mass m_2. The velocities v_1 and v_2 represent the respective velocities of the masses after the collision. The velocity v_c represents the velocity of the combined mass after a fully inelastic collision.

The graph to the left represents the information in the table. If you understand the graph, it is an excellent guide to answering collision questions qualitatively. If you don't understand the graph, don't sweat it. It won't be on the MCAT.

An example using the graph above: A partially inelastic collision occurs when an object moving with velocity v_o collides with a stationary object of equal mass. We examine the y axis of the graph because the masses are equal along the y axis. We see that the stationary object must have a velocity in the darkly shaded region along the y axis, so it must have a final velocity less than v_o but greater than $v_o/2$. The first object must have a velocity in its original direction, greater than zero but less than $v_o/2$.

The graph also shows that in order for the first object to bounce backwards, it must have a mass less than the object it strikes.

Impulse (*J*) is equal to the change in momentum.

$$J = \Delta p$$

If you examine any collision, you will notice that, if the materials approximately follow Hooke's law, the force during the time of contact is not constant. The average force on either colliding body can be found from the equation:

$$J = F_{avg} \Delta t$$

To find the average force from the change in momentum simply put the two impulse equations together to make:

$$\Delta mv = F_{avg} \Delta t$$

Impulse shows us that if the time over which the force acts is increased, the same change in velocity can be achieved with a lower force. For instance, air bags on an automobile don't change the momentum, but they increase the time over which the collision occurs, and thus decrease the force on the driver. The graphs below show three separate ways that the same particle might change its velocity.

The area under the curve represents impulse or change in momentum. Since the particle is the same each time, the mass remains constant, and the initial and final velocities are the same for each graph. However, the way that the final velocity is achieved is very different in each graph. If the particle were an egg, which graph represents the conditions under which the egg would be least likely to break?

4-5

Impulse

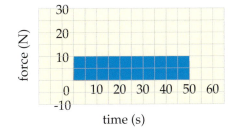

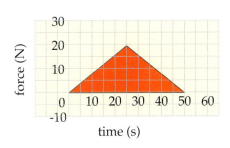

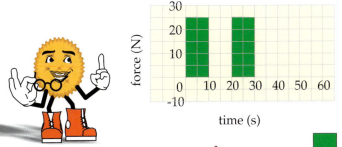

73. A rocket with a mass of 7.2×10^4 kg starts from rest in outer space and fires its thrusters until it is moving with a velocity of 100 m/s. What was the average force on the rocket due to the thrusters?

  A. 7.2×10^3 N
  B. 7.2×10^4 N
  C. 7.2×10^6 N
  D. The average force cannot be determined with the information given.

74. A boy is sliding down a long icy hill on his sled. In order to decrease his mass and increase his velocity, he drops his heavy winter coat and heavy boots from the sled while he is moving. Will his strategy work?

  A. No, because he loses the potential energy of the objects that he leaves behind.
  B. No, because although his kinetic energy increases, his momentum decreases.
  C. Yes, because although his kinetic energy decreases, his momentum increases.
  D. Yes, because although his momentum decreases, his kinetic energy decreases.

75. Ball A moving at 12 m/s collides elastically with ball B as shown. If both balls have the same mass, what is the final velocity of ball A? (Note: $\sin 60° = 0.87$; $\cos 60° = 0.5$)

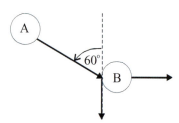

  A. 3 m/s
  B. 6 m/s
  C. 9 m/s
  D. 12 m/s

76. The chemical potential energy in gasoline is converted to kinetic energy in cars. If a car accelerates from zero to 60 km/h, compared to the energy necessary to increase the velocity of the car from zero to 30 km/h, the energy necessary to increase the velocity of the car from 30 to 60 km/h is:

  A. half as great.
  B. the same.
  C. twice as great.
  D. three times as great.

77. A 3 kg cat sitting on a 1.5 kg piece of cardboard on a frozen lake wants to jump to shore without touching the ice. If there is no friction between the cardboard and the ice, when the cat jumps, the cardboard will move in the opposite direction with a velocity:

  A. half as great as the cat's velocity.
  B. equal to the cat's velocity.
  C. twice as great as the cat's velocity.
  D. four times as great as the cat's velocity.

78. A block of mass m_1 slides across a frictionless surface with speed v_1 and collides with a stationary block of mass m_2. The blocks stick together after the collision and move away with a speed v_2. Which of the following statements is (are) true about the blocks?

  I. $m_1 v_1 = (m_1 + m_2)v_2$
  II. $\frac{1}{2}m_1 v_1^2 = \frac{1}{2}(m_1 + m_2)v_2^2$
  III. $v_1 = v_2$

  A. I only
  B. II only
  C. I and II only
  D. I, II and III

GO ON TO THE NEXT PAGE.

79. Two 1 kg carts with spring bumpers undergo a collision on a frictionless track as shown in the before and after pictures below.

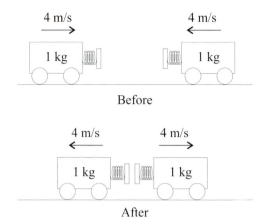

Before

After

The total momentum of the system is equal to:

A.   0 kg-m/sec before the collision and 0 kg-m/sec after the collision.
B.   −4 kg-m/sec before the collision and 4 kg-m/sec after the collision.
C.   −8 kg-m/sec before the collision and 8 kg-m/sec after the collision.
D.   8 kg-m/sec before the collision and 0 kg-m/sec after the collision.

80. A trapeze artist who accidentally falls builds up a great deal of momentum before he is brought safely to rest by a safety net. The safety net serves to:

A.   increase the force of the collision by decreasing the collision time.
B.   decrease the force of the collision by decreasing the collision time.
C.   increase the force of the collision by increasing the collision time.
D.   decrease the force of the collision by increasing the collision time.

STOP.

4-6 Machines

Now that we've covered the more simple topics in classical mechanics, let's examine one of the ways these topics may appear on the MCAT; let's examine machines. **Machines** are mechanical devices that reduce force when doing work. Every time that you see a machine on the MCAT, remind yourself that ideal machines reduce force but don't change work. (Nonideal machines increase work because they increase internal energy through friction.) Remembering that ideal machines don't change work can make some otherwise difficult MCAT problems fast and simple. In this lecture we will examine the **ramp, lever, and pulley**. In Physics Lecture 5 we will examine one more simple machine called a hydraulic lift.

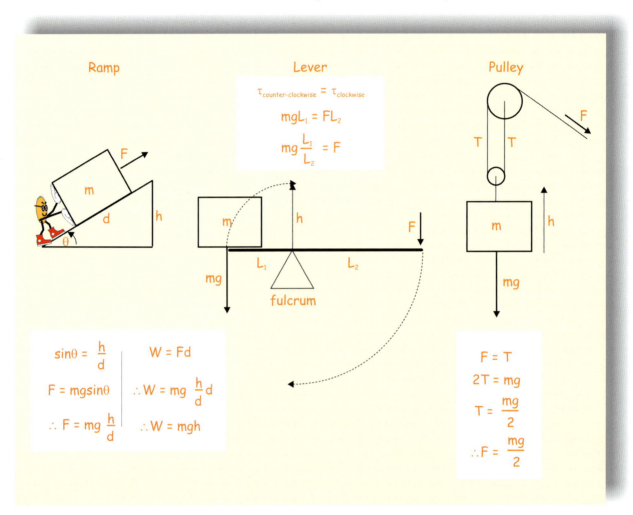

Ramp

$$\sin\theta = \frac{h}{d}$$

$$F = mg\sin\theta$$

$$\therefore F = mg\frac{h}{d}$$

$$W = Fd$$

$$\therefore W = mg\frac{h}{d}d$$

$$\therefore W = mgh$$

Lever

$$\tau_{counter-clockwise} = \tau_{clockwise}$$

$$mgL_1 = FL_2$$

$$mg\frac{L_1}{L_2} = F$$

Pulley

$$F = T$$

$$2T = mg$$

$$T = \frac{mg}{2}$$

$$\therefore F = \frac{mg}{2}$$

4-7 The Ramp

A **ramp** is simply an inclined plane (see Physics Lecture 3). If we examine the work necessary to lift a mass m to a tabletop of height h, we find that it is the force mg times the distance h, or mgh. By building a frictionless ramp, we can achieve the same result with a reduced force. To push the mass up the incline plane, we must only overcome the force that is pushing the mass down the plane, which is $mg\sin\theta$. Since the sine of any angle is a fraction, we know that this force is only a fraction of mg and thus reduced by the machine. To prove that the work is still the same we can multiply the force times the distance. From SOH CAH TOA, we know that the distance along the ramp is the opposite, or h, divided by $\sin\theta$. Thus, $W = mg\sin\theta \times h/\sin\theta$. This reduces to $W = mgh$, the same work as without the machine. From this it becomes clear that the fraction by which we want to *reduce* the force must be the same as the fraction by which we *increase* the length of the ramp. In other words, if we want to reduce the force to $\frac{1}{2} mg$, we must make a ramp with length $2h$. This is the same as saying that, when work is held constant in $W = Fd$, force and distance are inversely proportional to each other.

4-8
The Lever

The **lever** is based on the principle of torque. Again, let's examine lifting a mass m to a height h. Like the ramp, the lever simply allows us to increase the distance through which our force acts. Since we want to move the mass at a constant velocity, we want to establish a dynamic equilibrium. This means that the clockwise torques must be equal to the counter-clockwise torques. Torque is force times lever arm. So, by doubling the length of the lever arm, we reduce the force necessary by a factor of two. We can do this by placing our fulcrum twice as far from our force as from our mass. By the diagram below, we can see that the curve traveled by the mass to reach height h_1 is only half as long as the curve traveled by the force-bearing end of the lever. Once again, the force is inversely proportional to the distance, and the work is the same with or without the machine. (Notice that as soon as the lever begins to move, the lever arm shortens. However, as long as both gravity and the force point downward, the lever arms remain in the same proportions.)

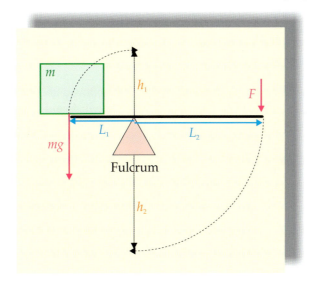

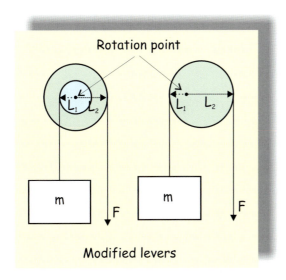

Modified levers

Although the machines in the diagram to the right appear to be pulleys, they are actually modified levers. They work on the principle of torque. In each, the force F is acting on a greater lever arm than mg. Thus the force necessary to lift mg is reduced. Of course, the work remains the same. Notice that the tension is not the same throughout these ropes as it is throughout the ropes of a true pulley.

4-9
The Pulley

A **pulley** acts on the same principle as the ramp and lever; it allows force to act over a greater distance and thus do the same amount of work with less force. The key to understanding a pulley is remembering that tension throughout a massless rope attached to a frictionless, massless pulley is constant. In other words, in the diagram below, the tension T is the same at every point in the rope. Now, in our 5-step-system, let's choose our system to be pulley number 1. We choose pulley number one, because pulley number 1 will move exactly as the mass moves. (If you have trouble visualizing this, imagine that the rope attaching pulley number 1 to the mass is a solid, inflexible bar. It won't change the problem.) If you first chose the mass as your system, you would not get the problem wrong, you would simply arrive at the conclusion that the rope connecting the mass to pulley number 1 has a tension of mg. Then you would be forced to choose a new system. Eventually, you would have to find a system on which your unknown, T, was acting directly. This system is pulley number 1. Like the lever, we wish to create a dynamic equilibrium where our mass has a constant velocity upward. To do this, we want the upward forces to equal the downward forces. The downward force is mg. The upward forces are the two tensions in the rope attached to the pulley. The tension throughout a rope in an ideal pulley is the same at every point, so the two tensions here must be equal. Setting upward forces equal to downward forces gives us $mg = 2T$, or $T = \frac{1}{2} mg$. Of course the work necessary to lift the mass to the table has not changed. So, since the force is halved, how is the force applied over twice the distance? If we look closely at the pulley system and imagine that the mass is raised one meter, we see that in order for the rope to lift evenly, one meter must come off of both sides of the pulley rope. Since it is all one rope, this amounts to pulling the rope a distance of two meters where the force F is applied. Thus we have reduced the force by two and increased the distance over which it acts by two as well. Again, when work is held constant, force and distance are inversely proportional.

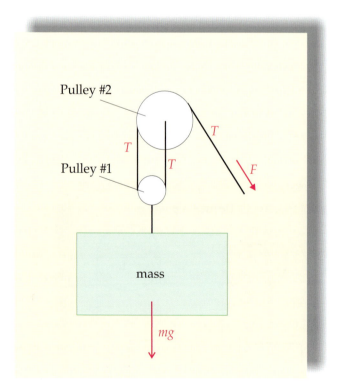

81. The frictionless pulley system below reduces the force necessary to lift any mass by a factor of 3. How much power is required to lift a 30 kg object 2 meters in 60 seconds using this pulley system?

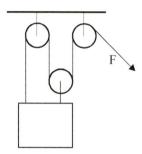

    A.   4 W
    B.   10 W
    C.   24 W
    D.   120 W

82. An eccentric pulley can be used on a compound bow to increase the velocity of an arrow. The pulleys pivot around the dots as shown. Below is a compound bow in two positions. The tension at point A compared to point B is most likely:

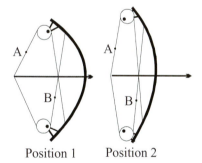

Position 1   Position 2

    A.   less in both position 1 and position 2.
    B.   less in position 1 and greater in position 2.
    C.   greater in both position 1 and position 2.
    D.   greater in position 1 and less in position 2.

83. A crate is to be lifted to a height of 3 meters with the assistance of an inclined plane. If the inclined plane is a non-ideal machine, which of the following statements is most likely true?

    A.   The non-ideal inclined plane increases the force required and decreases the work.
    B.   The non-ideal inclined plane decreases the force required and increases the work.
    C.   The non-ideal inclined plane increases the force and the work required.
    D.   The non-ideal inclined plane decreases the force and the work required.

84. A girl riding her bicycle up a steep hill decides to save energy by zigzagging rather than riding straight up. Ignoring friction, her strategy will:

    A.   require the same amount of energy but less force on the pedals.
    B.   require the same amount of energy and the same amount of force on the pedals.
    C.   require less energy and less force on the pedals.
    D.   require less energy and more force on the pedals.

85. An inventor designs a machine that he claims will lift a 30 kg object with the application of only a 25 N force. If the inventor is correct, what is the shortest possible distance through which the force must be applied for each meter that the object is raised?

    A.   5 m
    B.   8 m
    C.   12 m
    D.   15 m

GO ON TO THE NEXT PAGE.

86. The pulley system shown below operates as a modified lever. Pulley A and pulley B turn together so when a person pulls on rope A the mass attached to rope B will be lifted. Which of the following changes to the system will reduce the force needed to lift the mass?

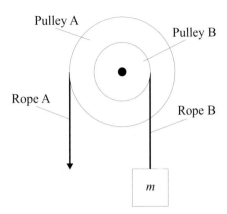

A. Increase the length of rope A.
B. Increase the length of rope B.
C. Increase the diameter of pulley A.
D. Increase the diameter of pulley B.

87. The mechanical advantage for a machine is defined as the output force divided by the input force. Since the output force is typically greater than the input force, this value is normally greater than one. For an ideal machine, what would be another way of representing the mechanical advantage?

A. (output distance)/(input distance)
B. (input distance)/(output distance)
C. (output distance) (input distance)
D. (input distance) + (output distance)

88. A wheelchair access ramp is to be designed so that 1000 N can be lifted to a height of 1 meter through the application of 50 N of force. The length of the ramp must be at least:

A. 5 m
B. 10 m
C. 20 m
D. 100 m

STOP.

Radioactive decay concerns atoms that spontaneously break apart. All atoms other than hydrogen are subject to some type of spontaneous decay. However, the rate at which decay occurs varies dramatically. Atoms with a high decay rate are said to be radioactive. Of the 2000 known nuclides (atoms and their isotopes), only 266 are stable. Atomic stability can be reasonably predicted by an atom's neutron to proton ratio. No atoms with more than 83 protons are considered stable. In smaller atoms, a stable neutron to proton ratio is 1:1. As atoms get heavier, they require a larger number of neutrons for stability and the ratio increases to as much as 1.5:1.

4-10

Radioactive Decay

Particle	Symbol
alpha	α_2^4
beta	$^-\beta$ or $_{-1}\beta$ or $_{-1}^0 e$
positron	$^+\beta$ or $_{+1}^0 e$
gamma	γ_0^0

There is no way to predict how long a single atom will take to spontaneously decay. However, since atoms are small, we are usually concerned with millions of them at a time. Thus we can apply the rules of probability and make predictions concerning large groups of atoms. Any substance (a large group of identical atoms) has a predictable rate of decay. This predictable rate of decay is usually given in terms of a half-life. A **half-life** is the length of time necessary for one half of a given amount of a substance to decay.

4-11

Half-Life

In any half-life problem, there are 4, and only 4, possible variables. They are the initial amount of substance, the final amount of substance, the number of half-lives (often given as a time period, in which case you simply divide by the length of a half-life), and the length of the half-life. Any MCAT half-life question will provide you with some form of three of these, and ask you to find the fourth. Any half-life question on the MCAT should be a fast, free point. To answer a half-life question on the MCAT, count the number of half-lives on your fingers. For instance, if after 5 years, 12.5% of a substance remains, what is the half-life? The initial amount is, of course, 100%. The final amount is 12.5%. The number of half-lives is found by dividing the initial amount by 2 until you arrive at the final amount. Keep track on your fingers of the number of times that you divide by 2. 50% is once, 25% is twice, 12.5% is thrice. That's three half-lives. In another example: how long will it take for 500 grams of a substance with a half-life of 2 years to decay to 62 grams? The initial amount equals 500, the final amount equals 62, the half-life is 2 years. Divide the initial amount by 2 until you arrive at the final amount. Keep track of the number of half-lives on your fingers. 250 is one, 125 is two, 62.5 is three. Rounding off numbers is the rule on the MCAT, so the answer is 3 half-lives or 6 years. Whatever the combination, look for the 3 variables and solve for the fourth by counting half-lives on your fingers.

4-12
Types of Radioactive Decay

There are five types of radioactive decay on the MCAT: alpha decay, beta decay, positron emission, electron capture, and gamma ray production. (Positron emission and electron capture are actually types of beta decay.) If you remember how each particle is written and on which side of the equation it belongs, solving a decay problem on the MCAT becomes a very simple math problem. Simply be sure that the sum of the atomic numbers and the sum of the mass numbers on the left side of the equation equal the sum of the atomic numbers and the sum of the mass numbers on the right side, and look up the proper elements in the periodic table.

Alpha decay (or α-decay) is probably the easiest to remember. An alpha particle is a helium nucleus. Thus, it contains 2 protons and 2 neutrons. In alpha decay, an alpha particle is lost. An example of alpha decay is:

$$^{238}_{92}U = ^{4}_{2}\alpha + ^{234}_{90}Th$$

Beta decay (β-decay) is the expulsion of an electron. (Some books include positron emission as a type of beta decay.) A beta particle is an electron or positron. (A positron is like an electron with a positive charge.) Notice that beta decay is not the destruction of an electron; instead, it is the creation of an electron and a proton from a neutron, and the expulsion of the newly created electron. An example of beta decay is:

$$^{234}_{90}Th \rightarrow ^{234}_{91}Pa + ^{0}_{-1}e$$

A *neutrino* (not shown) is also emitted during beta decay. A neutrino is a virtually massless particle. A neutrino is typically represented with the Greek letter nu (ν).

Positron emission is the emission of a positron when a proton becomes a neutron. In positron emission, a proton is transformed into a neutron and a positron is emitted. An example of positron emission is:

$$^{22}_{11}Na \rightarrow ^{0}_{1}e + ^{22}_{10}Ne$$

Electron capture is the capture of an electron along with the merging of that electron with a proton to create a neutron. In electron capture, a proton is destroyed and a neutron is created. An example of electron capture is:

$$^{201}_{80}Hg + ^{0}_{-1}e \rightarrow ^{201}_{79}Au + ^{0}_{0}\gamma$$

A **gamma ray** is a high frequency photon. It has no charge and does not change the identity of the atom from which it is given off. Gamma ray emission often accompanies the other decay types. An example of gamma ray emission is when an electron and positron collide:

$$^{0}_{-1}e + ^{0}_{1}e \rightarrow ^{0}_{0}\gamma + ^{0}_{0}\gamma$$

This is a matter-antimatter collision called *annihilation*. Mass is destroyed releasing energy in the form of gamma rays.

The matter-antimatter collision between an electron and positron brings up an interesting question. Did the energy exist before the collision occurred? Is this a violation of the conservation of energy? Einstein had the answer with:

4-13
Mass Defect

$$E = mc^2$$

This equation gives the *rest mass energy* of an object. For the MCAT just think of rest mass energy as latent energy within the mass of an object. It will only appear on the MCAT if mass is created or destroyed. Otherwise, never even think about rest mass energy. If mass is created or destroyed, always use $E = mc^2$ to find the answer, where m represents the amount of mass created or destroyed and c is the speed of light (3×10^8 m/s). The forces holding the nucleons (protons and neutrons) together are the result of a change in the rest mass energy of the individual nucleons. In other words, if we measured the mass of the nucleons before forming the nucleus of an atom, and then measured the mass of the nucleus, there would be a discrepancy; the nucleus would have less mass than the sum of the masses of its individual parts. The difference in the masses is called the **mass defect**. To find the binding energy holding the nucleons together, plug the mass defect into $E = mc^2$.

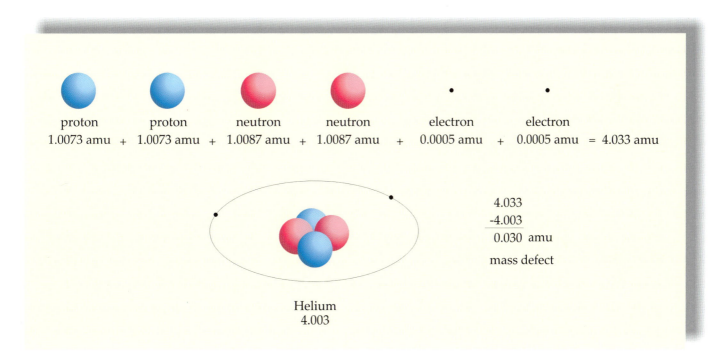

4-14
Fission and Fusion

Fusion is the combining of two nuclei to form a single heavier nucleus. **Fission** is the splitting of a single nucleus to form two lighter nuclei. How can large amounts of energy be released in both processes? The energy comes from the mass defect. If we think of the binding energy as a bond, we know that energy must be added in order to break a bond (including ATP bonds). Thus, when we make a bond in fusion, we can see from where the energy can come; energy is always released when a bond is formed. The energy comes from the bonds between the nucleons in the new nucleus. These new bonds are stronger and more stable than those of the nucleus that was just divided. Thus more energy was released in the formation of the stronger bonds than was absorbed in the breaking of the weaker bonds.

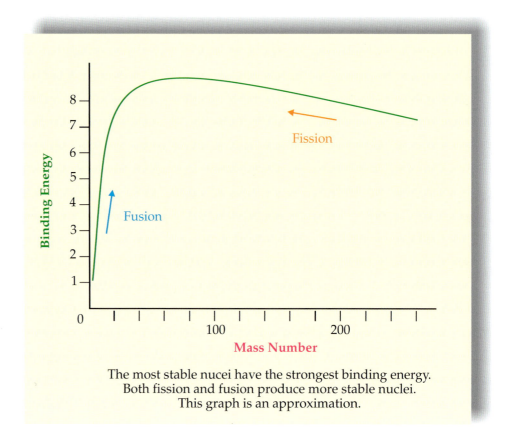

The most stable nucei have the strongest binding energy.
Both fission and fusion produce more stable nuclei.
This graph is an approximation.

Momentum

$$p = mv$$

Elastic collisions

$$p_{initial} = p_{final}$$

$$K_{initial} = K_{final}$$

Inelastic collisions

$$p_{initial} = p_{final}$$

Impulse

$$F_{avg.}\Delta t = \Delta mv$$

Rest mass energy

$$E = mc^2$$

89. The half-life of substance X is 45 years, and it decomposes to substance Y. A sample from a meteorite was taken which contained 1.5% of X and 13.5% of Y by mass. If substance Y is not normally found on a meteorite, what is the approximate age of the meteorite?

    A.   45 years
    B.   100 years
    C.   140 years
    D.   270 years

90. When ^{224}Ra undergoes alpha decay an alpha particle is emitted at 1.0×10^7 m/s. What is the velocity of the other particle?

    A. 1.6×10^4
    B. 1.8×10^5
    C. 1.8×10^6
    D. 5.4×10^6

91. In nuclear fission, a uranium nucleus combines with a neutron, becomes unstable, and splits into Ce and Zr plus two neutrons. The change in the mass of the interacting parts is 0.211 amu. How much energy is released in this reaction? (Note: $c^2 = 931.5$ MeV/amu)

    A.   98 MeV
    B.   130 MeV
    C.   157 MeV
    D.   197 MeV

92. ^{216}Po undergoes two alpha decays and two beta decays to form:

    A. ^{208}Tl
    B. ^{224}Ra
    C. ^{212}Pb
    D. ^{208}Pb

93. Which of the following graphs best represents the radioactive decay of ^{238}U?

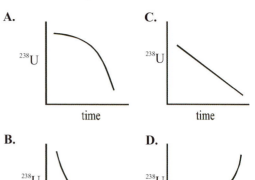

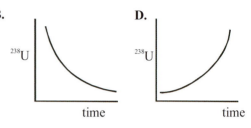

94. A diagram showing the changing mass of an unstable isotope undergoing radioactive decay over time is shown below. What is the half-life of the isotope?

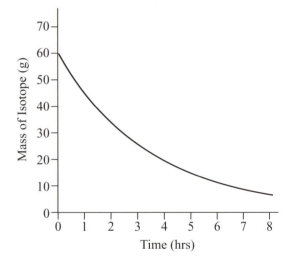

    A.   1.5 hours
    B.   2.5 hours
    C.   4.0 hours
    D.   6.0 hours

70

GO ON TO THE NEXT PAGE.

95. Which of the sequences below could describe the decay process from Bi-210 to Pb-206?

    A.   alpha, beta

    B.   beta, beta

    C.   alpha, alpha

    D.   beta, beta, beta

96. The mass number of an atom undergoing radioactive decay will remain unchanged in all of the processes below EXCEPT:

    A.   alpha decay.

    B.   beta decay.

    C.   electron capture.

    D.   gamma emission.

STOP.

Lecture 5

Fluids and Solids

Most substances can be classified as either a solid or a fluid. The molecules of a solid are held in place by molecular bonds that can permanently resist a force from any direction. A **fluid** is a liquid or gas. Unlike a solid, any existing molecular bonds in a fluid are constantly breaking and reforming due to the high kinetic energy of the molecules. Since the molecules of a fluid are not arranged with any order or structure, but move about in random directions relative to each other, a fluid has only temporal (impermanent) resistance to forces that are not perpendicular to its surface. However, since fluid molecules require room to move, collectively they can create a permanent force outward from within the fluid. This outward force allows a fluid to permanently withstand forces perpendicular to its surface. In other words, the only permanent force that a resting fluid can exert is one normal to its surface. Thus, a fluid is pushed and molded until its surface matches the shape of its container exactly. When the fluid comes to rest, it experiences only the normal force from the surface of its container and the force of gravity. (A liquid takes on a flat upper surface so that the gravitational force is also perpendicular. In a gas, gravity has an insignificant effect on the path of an individual molecule due to the high average velocity of the molecules, and a gas will fill an enclosed container.)

5-1
Fluids

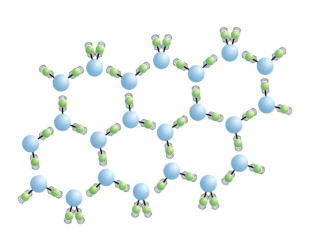

**Molecules of a solid
bond strongly and
vibrate in a fixed position.**

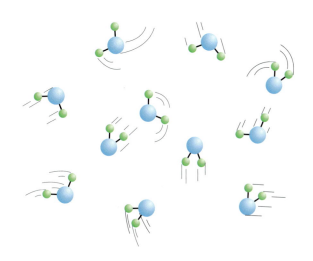

**Molecules of a fluid
bond weakly and
rotate, spin, and move past each other.**

In other words, a fluid conforms to the shape of its container. The ocean, a fluid, will withstand the weight of a motionless battleship forever by conforming its surface to that of the battleship's so that all forces are normal to its surface. However, the ship can move through the water propelled by a much smaller force than its own weight. This is because the net force from the moving ship is not perpendicular to the surface of the water and thus the water provides only temporal resistance. (The forces shown in the diagram are the forces on the water due to the ship, and not meant to represent the forces on the ship.)

In particle mechanics we discussed mass and energy. These properties were useful because we knew exactly how much substance with which we were dealing. Externally, we could view the entire object and measure these properties. Properties such as these, which are concerned with quantity, are called *extensive properties*. Extensive properties change with the quantity of a substance. In fluid mechanics, we often don't know how much of a fluid with which we are dealing, thus we cannot measure its mass or energy. In order to analyze such fluids we use *intensive properties* or properties that are concerned with the intrinsic nature of a substance. Intensive properties do not change with the quantity of a substance. The two intensive properties that are analogous to mass and energy are, respectively, density and pressure.

5-2 Density

Density (ρ) is the 'heaviness' of a fluid; it is how much mass it contains in a specified volume (V). The formula for density is:

$$\rho = m/V$$

The S.I. units of density are kg/m^3. Notice that changing the amount of a given substance will not change the density of that substance. Compression of a fluid changes its volume without changing its mass, and therefore will change density. Since gases compress more easily than liquids, the density of a gas is easily changed while that of a liquid is not. Unless otherwise indicated, for the MCAT, assume that all liquids and solids are totally incompressible, and thus have constant density. In reality, gases are far more compressible than liquids, and liquids are far more compressible than solids. Gases on the MCAT change their volume (and thus their density) as per the ideal gas law: $PV = nRT$.

We have a strong intuition about the concept of mass because we use it everyday; however, few of us have a strong sense of density. For instance, you can appreciate how it feels to lift a 13 kg mass (about 29 pounds), but can you lift a bucket full of mercury, which has a density of about 13,600 kg/m^3? Most of us have no idea. We just don't know density well enough. In order to make density a more intuitive concept, specific gravity was created. The **specific gravity (S.G.)** of a substance is the density of that substance ($\rho_{substance}$) compared to the density of water (ρ_{water}).

$$\text{S.G.} = \rho_{substance}/\rho_{water}$$

Notice that a specific gravity of less than one indicates a substance lighter than water; a specific gravity of one indicates a substance equally as heavy as water; a specific gravity greater than one indicates a substance heavier than water. Since we all have an intuitive feel for the heaviness of water, we can relate this to a substance, if we know its specific gravity. The specific gravity of mercury is 13.6, so lifting one bucket of mercury would be equivalent to lifting 13.6 buckets of water.

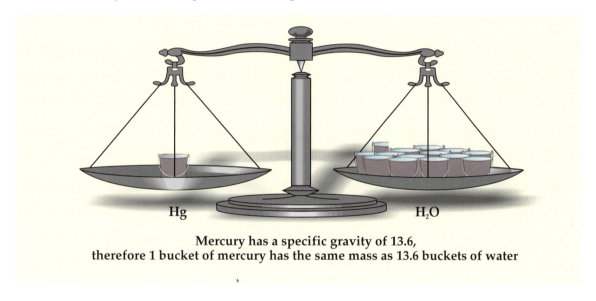

Hg   H$_2$O

**Mercury has a specific gravity of 13.6,
therefore 1 bucket of mercury has the same mass as 13.6 buckets of water**

For the MCAT you should memorize the density of water in the following two forms:

$$\rho_{water} = 1000 \text{ kg/m}^3$$

$$\rho_{water} = 1 \text{ gm/cm}^3$$

5-3 Pressure

Recall from Lecture 4 our discussion about impulse. Impulse is the change in momentum or the force of a collision multiplied by the duration of the collision ($F\Delta t$). Since the millions of molecules in a fluid are moving rapidly in random directions, some will collide with an object submerged in that fluid. In any given time t, such a submerged object will experience millions of collisions. If we measure the magnitude of the impulse of each collision and divide it by the time over which the collisions occur, we arrive at the average magnitude of force created by the collisions.

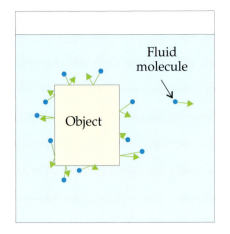

Since the molecules are moving in random directions and at random speeds, no single direction or speed will be more likely than any other, and the force on one side of the object will be exactly countered by the force on its other side. (We will ignore gravity for the moment and we will also assume that, if the fluid is moving, the object is moving at the same velocity as the fluid.) If we take the average magnitude of the force, and divide it by the area over which the collisions are taking place (the surface area of the object), we have the pressure experienced by the object. This is the **fluid pressure**. Fluid pressure results from the impulse of molecular collisions. It is the average of the magnitudes of the change in momentum of these collisions divided by the time duration of the collisions and the area over which these collisions occur. Pressure (P) is defined as force per unit area (A).

$$P \quad F/A$$

The S.I. unit of pressure is the **Pascal (Pa)**. Pressure is a scalar; it has no direction. Pressure exists in a fluid whether or not an object is immersed in that fluid.

Another way to think of fluid pressure is as a measure of the kinetic energy due to the random velocities of molecules within a fluid distributed over the fluid volume. The units of pressure are equivalent to energy per unit volume. So pressure can be thought of as a type of 'stored' energy per unit volume.

5-4
Fluids at Rest

A fluid at rest is one that is experiencing forces only perpendicular to its surface. At any given depth, the pressure is equal to the weight of the fluid above a disk with area A divided by the area of the disk. Notice from the diagram that the pressure is independent of the area chosen.

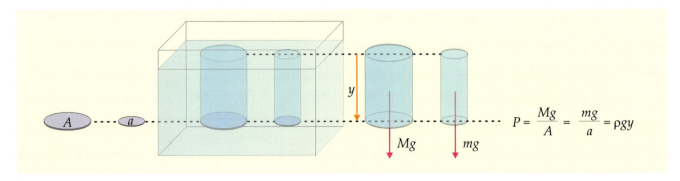

$$P = \frac{Mg}{A} = \frac{mg}{a} = \rho g y$$

For a fluid at rest with uniform density in a sealed container, pressure P is given by:

$$P = \rho g y$$

where ρ is the density of the fluid, g the gravitational constant, and y is the depth of the fluid.

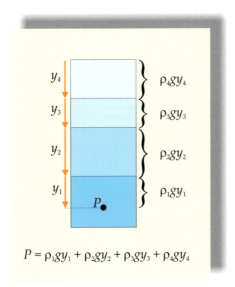

$$P = \rho_1 g y_1 + \rho_2 g y_2 + \rho_3 g y_3 + \rho_4 g y_4$$

Since fluid pressure is simply weight divided by area, additional fluids on top of the first fluid simply add their weight toward the total pressure. The total pressure can be found by summing the pressures due to each fluid as shown in the diagram on the right.

Air is a fluid. If we open our sealed container and expose it to the atmosphere, we must add atmospheric pressure to any point in our fluid. In any fluid open to the atmosphere, the pressure can be found from $P = \rho g y + P_{atmos.}$. (Note: If you are using meters and kilograms, you must measure the atmospheric pressure in pascals (Pa). $P_{atmospheric} = 101,000\ Pa$)

You can think of the atmosphere as a sea of air. As you move closer to the top of this sea, its depth (y) decreases. Near the top, you have fewer molecules above you, which means less weight and lower pressure.

Biologists often talk about negative pressure created in your chest when you suck in air. If you think of the molecular collision model of pressure (Chemistry Lecture 2), you will realize that negative pressure is impossible. It would indicate less than zero collisions; an absurdity. The negative pressure that biologists refer to in the chest cavity is **gauge pressure**. Gauge pressure is a measure of the pressure compared to local atmospheric pressure. In other words, local atmospheric pressure is arbitrarily given a value of zero. So when a biologist says there is negative pressure inside your chest, there is still pressure in your chest; it is just less pressure than atmospheric pressure. The higher pressure of the atmosphere pushes air into your lungs. The same thing happens when you 'suck' fluid through a straw. You create a partial vacuum inside the straw. But a vacuum doesn't really 'suck' anything into it. The atmospheric pressure pushes down on the fluid outside the straw pushing up the fluid inside the straw. Without atmospheric pressure, a straw would not work. Just remember, in real life, **physics never sucks.**

By the way, pressure measured relative to a vacuum as zero is called **absolute pressure**. To find absolute pressure from gauge pressure, just add atmospheric pressure.

$$P_{abs} = P_{gauge} + P_{atm}$$

Since fluid pressure is a function of depth, the shape of the container does not affect it. The pressure everywhere at a given depth in the same resting fluid will be constant.

Just as each block in a stack of blocks must bear the weight of all the blocks above it, each point in an enclosed fluid must bear any increase in pressure. This is called **Pascal's principle**. Pascal's principle states that pressure applied anywhere to an enclosed incompressible fluid will be distributed undiminished throughout that fluid. Notice that Pascal's principle does not apply to a gas because a gas is compressible.

5-5 Hydraulic Lift

The **hydraulic lift** is a simple machine that works via Pascal's principle. A force on piston 1 acts to apply a pressure on the incompressible fluid. This pressure is transferred undiminished to piston 2. Since piston 2 has a greater area than piston 1, the force on piston 2 is proportionally greater. However, recall that an ideal machine does not change work. Thus, the distance through which the force is applied is proportionally less. $F_1 d_1 = F_2 d_2$; $F_1/A_1 = F_2/A_2$.

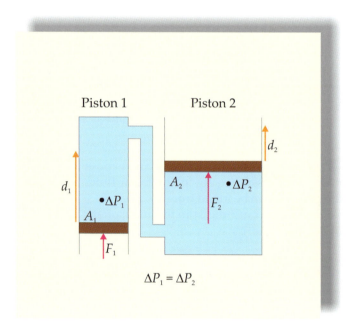

5-6 Archimedes' Principle

In the 3rd century B.C., the king of Syracuse was given a crown and told that it was solid gold. Archimedes was given the task of proving or disproving that the crown was solid gold. Archimedes knew the density of gold and decided to find the density of the crown. To find the volume of the crown, he submerged it into a bucket of water and measured the amount of water displaced. He then weighed the crown and divided its mass by its volume. The density of the crown was not the density of gold; Archimedes had proven that the crown was a fake.

This story reminds us that an object submerged in a fluid displaces a volume of fluid equal to its own volume. Before the object is submerged, the upward force on the fluid that it will displace must equal the weight of that fluid ($F_{buoyant} = mg_{water}$). Once the object is submerged, the net upward force remains, but the fluid is gone, replaced by the object. Thus the upward force acts on the submerged object. This force is called the buoyant force. Archimedes' principle says that the **buoyant force** **(F_b)** is an upward force acting on a submerged object, and is equal to the weight of the fluid displaced by the submerged object. The buoyant force is given by:

$$F_b = \rho_{fluid} V g$$

where V is the volume of the fluid displaced. The buoyant force is always equal to the weight of the fluid displaced. In the diagram below the buoyant force is $F_{buoyant}$.

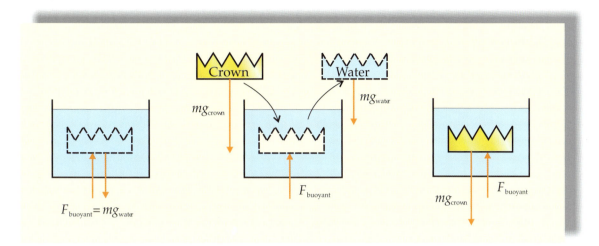

A *floating* object displaces an amount of fluid equal to its own weight. The *floating equation* says that the submerged fraction of a floating object is equal to the ratio of the density of the object to the density of the fluid in which it is floating. If the object is floating in water, this ratio is the specific gravity of the floating object.

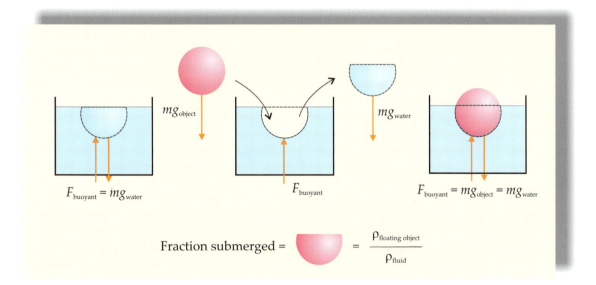

Another way to understand the buoyant force is as a result of the pressure difference between the upper and lower surfaces of a submerged object. Since pressure increases with depth, the lower surface of an object experiences greater pressure than the upper surface. This pressure difference multiplied by the upper or lower surface area is equal to the buoyant force.

Make sure that you understand that, since the buoyant force is due to the 'difference' in pressure, the buoyant force does not change with depth.

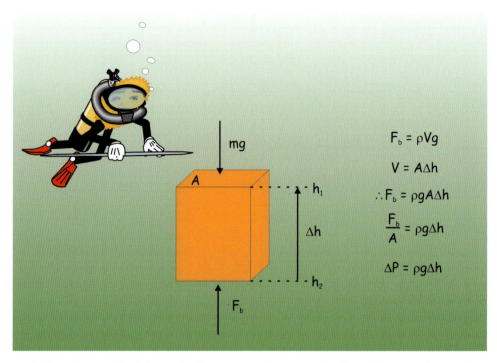

$$F_b = \rho V g$$
$$V = A\Delta h$$
$$\therefore F_b = \rho g A \Delta h$$
$$\frac{F_b}{A} = \rho g \Delta h$$
$$\Delta P = \rho g \Delta h$$

A fully submerged object displaces its volume in fluid; a floating object displaces its weight in fluid.

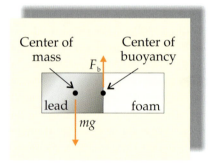

If we consider an object to be a single particle, the buoyant force acts at the *center of buoyancy*. The center of buoyancy is the point where the center of mass would be, if the object had a uniform density. If the object is not uniformly dense, the center of mass and the center of buoyancy will not coincide. This could create a torque on the object and cause it to spin as shown in the diagram below. Center of buoyancy explains why a fishing bobber always floats upright.

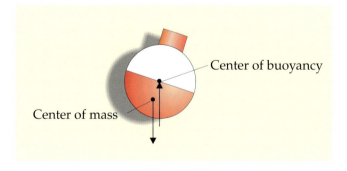

97. Mercury has specific gravity of 13.6. The column of mercury in the barometer below has a height $h = 76$ cm. If a similar barometer were made with water, what would be the approximate height h of the column of water?

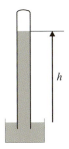

A. 5.6 cm
B. 76 cm
C. 154 cm
D. 1034 cm

98. Two identical discs sit at the bottom of a 3 m pool of water whose surface is exposed to atmospheric pressure. The first disc acts as a plug to seal the drain as shown. The second disc covers a container containing nearly a perfect vacuum. If each disc has an area of 1 m², what is the approximate difference in the force necessary to open the containers? (Note: 1 atm = 101,300 Pa)

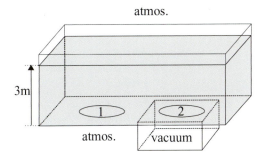

A. There is no difference.
B. 3000 N
C. 101,300 N
D. 104,300 N

99. A brick with a density of 1.4×10^3 kg/m³ is placed on top of a piece of Styrofoam floating on water. If one half the volume of the Styrofoam sinks below the water, what is the ratio of the volume of the Styrofoam compared to the volume of the brick? (Assume the Styrofoam is massless.)

A. 0.7
B. 1.4
C. 2.8
D. 5.6

100. A helium balloon will rise into the atmosphere until:

A. The temperature of the helium inside the balloon is equal to the temperature of the air outside the balloon.
B. The mass of the helium inside the balloon is equal to the mass of the air outside the balloon.
C. The weight of the balloon is equal to the force of the upward air current.
D. The density of the helium in the balloon is equal to the density of the air surrounding the balloon.

101. A child's bathtub toy has a density of 0.45 g/cm³. What fraction of the toy floats above the water?

A. 5%
B. 45%
C. 55%
D. 95%

102. The diagram below shows a hydraulic lift. A force is applied at side 1 and an output force is generated at side 2. Which of the following is true?

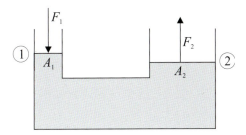

A. The force at side 1 is greater than the force at side 2.
B. The force at side 1 is less than the force at side 2.
C. The pressure at side 1 is greater than the force at side 2.
D. The pressure at side 1 is less than the pressure at side 2.

GO ON TO THE NEXT PAGE.

103. The pressure at the bottom of a cylindrical tube filled with water was measured to be 5000 Pa. If the water in the tube were replaced with ethyl alcohol, what would be the new pressure at the bottom of the tube? (The density of ethyl alcohol is 0.8 g/cm3.)

A. 4000 Pa
B. 4800 Pa
C. 5000 Pa
D. 6250 Pa

104. Three containers are filled with water to a depth of 1 meter. At the bottom of which container is the pressure the greatest?

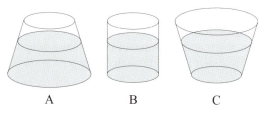

A   B   C

A. Container A
B. Container B
C. Container C
D. The pressure is the same at the bottom of all the containers.

STOP.

The molecules of a moving fluid can be thought of as having two types of motion:

1. the **random translational motion** that contributes to fluid pressure as in a fluid at rest and;

2. a **uniform translational motion** shared equally by all the molecules at a given location in a fluid.

The uniform translational motion is the motion of the fluid as a whole. This motion does not contribute to fluid pressure. If we recall our molecular model of fluid pressure, an object moving along with the fluid will not experience additional collisions due to this uniform translational motion. Thus, it will not experience any additional pressure. In fact, the energy from the two types of motion can be converted back and forth; some of the random translational motion can be converted to uniform translational motion and vice versa. For instance, if we remove a portion of the wall of a container holding a fluid at rest, the fluid will move through the opening. This happens because the molecules moving in the direction of the opening do not collide with anything, but instead continue in their present direction. Some of the random motion has changed to uniform motion. Since there are fewer collisions in the fluid moving through the opening, there is less pressure. We will come back to this point later in this lecture.

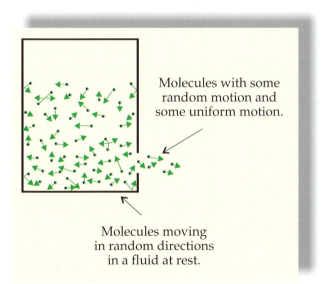

Molecules with some random motion and some uniform motion.

Molecules moving in random directions in a fluid at rest.

Because moving fluids are very complicated, it is useful to create a hypothetical fluid which lacks certain characteristics of real fluids. This hypothetical fluid is called **ideal fluid**. Ideal fluid differs from real fluids in the following four ways:

1. Ideal fluid has **no viscosity**. Viscosity is a measure of a fluid's temporal resistance to forces not perpendicular to its surface. (More precisely, viscosity is the rate of shear stress divided by the rate of strain.) For the MCAT think of a fluid's viscosity as its tendency to resist flow. For example, syrup has greater viscosity than water. A closely related concept to viscosity is drag. *Drag* is force, similar to friction, created by viscosity and pressure due to motion. Drag always opposes the motion of an object through a fluid.

2. Ideal fluid is **incompressible**; it has uniform density. This is the same assumption that we make for any liquid on the MCAT unless otherwise indicated, but not for gasses.

3. Ideal fluid lacks *turbulence*; it experiences steady (or *laminar*) flow. Steady flow means that all fluid flowing through any fixed point will have the same velocity. Remember, velocity specifies magnitude and direction. Turbulence means that, at any fixed point in the fluid, the velocity may vary with time.

4. Ideal fluids experience *irrotational flow*. This means that any object moving with the ideal fluid will not rotate about its axis as it flows, but will continue to point in one direction regardless of the direction of flow. The MCAT is not likely to touch this one.

No ideal fluid actually exists. However, we can use ideal fluid to make crude predictions about real fluids. We do this by imagining how ideal fluid would behave in a given situation, and then considering how the above characteristics would affect this behavior. On the MCAT, all liquids are ideal, unless otherwise indicated.

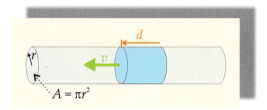

Since ideal fluids are incompressible, their volume remains constant. The volume of a fluid moving through a section of pipe is given by the cross-sectional area (A) of the pipe times the distance (d) of the pipe section. If this same volume of fluid moves completely through this pipe section in a given time (t), the rate (Q) at which volume passes through the pipe is Ad/t. Since the fluid moves a distance d in time t, its velocity is $v = d/t$. Putting these two equations together we get the **continuity equation**:

$$Q = Av$$

where Q is called the '**volume flow rate**'. Flow can be given in terms of mass as well. For the mass flow rate (I) multiply the volume flow rate by density:

$$I = \rho Q = \rho Av$$

In an ideal fluid, flow rate is constant. Notice from these equations that area is inversely proportional to velocity; the narrower the pipe, the greater the velocity.

A second important equation that you must memorize for the MCAT is **Bernoulli's equation**:

$$P + \rho gh + \frac{1}{2}\rho v^2 = K$$

Where K is a constant specific to a fluid in a given situation of flow, and P, h, and v refer to the pressure, height, and velocity of the fluid at any given point. (**Warning:** h is not the same as y in $P = \rho gy$. h is the distance *above* some arbitrary point; y is the distance beneath the surface.) Bernoulli's equation states that, given one continuous ideal flow, the sum of its three terms is a constant at any point in the fluid. If we look closely at Bernoulli's equation, we see that it is actually a restatement of conservation of energy. Notice that if we multiply any of the terms by volume, we get units of energy. In fact, the second term gives the gravitational potential energy per unit volume (mgh/V). The third term gives the kinetic energy from the uniform translational motion of the molecules per unit volume (($\frac{1}{2}mv^2$)$/V$). The first term, pressure, is the energy per volume from the random motion of the molecules. Because energy is conserved in ideal fluid flow, the total energy must remain constant; thus, the sum of the three terms is constant throughout the fluid. This is an easy method for remembering Bernoulli's equation. This also aids our understanding of the terms. For instance, the h in the second term is similar to the h in gravitational potential energy; the zero value for h can be chosen arbitrarily. Like the h term in gravitational potential energy, it is measured from bottom to top. Notice this is the opposite direction of measurement for the y term in hydrostatic pressure: $P = \rho g y$. Also, recall the equation that predicts the velocity of a body in free fall when all of its potential energy is converted to kinetic energy. You may see that Bernoulli's equation predicts the same result for a fluid. If a spigot attached to a tank of fluid is opened, and we choose $h = 0$ to be the point of the spigot, the velocity of the fluid coming from the spigot can be derived from Bernoulli's equation as:

$$v = \sqrt{2gh}$$

$P_1 = $ atmos.

$v_1 = 0$

h_1

$$P_1 + \rho g h_1 + \tfrac{1}{2}\rho v_1^2 = P_2 + \rho g h_2 + \tfrac{1}{2}\rho v_2^2$$

$$\rho g h_1 = \tfrac{1}{2}\rho v_2^2$$

v_2 $h_2 = 0$

$$2 g h_1 = v_2^2$$

$P_2 = $ atmos.

$$\sqrt{2 g h_1} = v_2$$

From Bernoulli's equation we can derive an important (and possibly counter-intuitive) notion about the relationship between pressure and velocity in ideal fluid flow. As velocity increases, pressure decreases.

The concept of *streamlines* was created to assist in the visualization of an ideal fluid. A streamline is a path followed by a hypothetical fluid particle. This particle follows only the uniform translational motion of the moving fluid. The magnitude and direction can change from one point to the next, but its velocity at any fixed point will remain the same. The velocity of the particle at any point along a streamline is tangent to the curve made by the streamline. The magnitude of the velocity is inversely related to the distance between streamlines; the closer the streamlines, the greater the velocity. Streamlines can never intersect, since this would indicate two possible velocities for the same fixed point. A group of streamlines three-dimensionally encompass a *tube of flow*.

A helpful analogy might be to think about a swarm of bees. Imagine that the swarm represents a fluid with each bee as a fluid molecule. Bee stings represent pressure-causing collisions. Now if I stand still in the swarm, its gonna hurt. The bees can swarm around and sting me at their leisure. I'm gonna get stung a lot; this is analogous to lots of molecular collisions and high pressure. But if I run, each bee must use some of its swarming energy to keep up with me. Therefore, they can't swarm as much, and I won't get stung as often. Less stings means less pressure. The same is true with molecules in a fluid; uniform translational kinetic energy is achieved by borrowing energy from the random translational kinetic energy, thus pressure goes down.

"Ouch!"
"Ouch!"

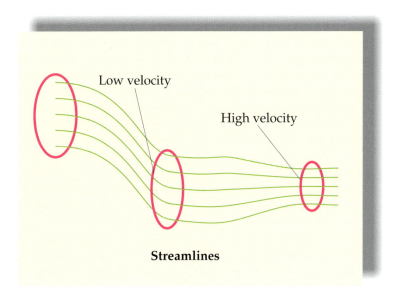

Streamlines

Low velocity

High velocity

5-9
Non-ideal Fluids
(Real Fluids)

All real fluids are **non-ideal**. The MCAT only requires that you understand non-ideal fluids qualitatively. This means that you must predict the general deviation to ideal fluid when we add the first three of the four lacking characteristics. (Irrotational flow will not be on the MCAT.)

Drag and viscosity are like friction and always act to impede flow. Increasing viscosity increases drag. Drag occurs at the fluid-object interface and is a force working against flow. As we move away from the fluid-object interface the effect of drag lessens. In a real fluid flowing through a pipe, the greatest velocity would be at the center of the pipe, the spot furthest from the fluid-object interface. You can remember this general rule about drag by recalling the dusty blades of a well-used fan. The dust on the fan blade remains despite the high speed of the fan. This is because the air immediately adjacent to the fan moves extremely slowly or not at all due to drag. Because the sides of the pipe create the greatest drag, the longer the pipe, the greater the amount of fluid-object interface, and the greater is the resistance to flow. Also notice that if the radius of a pipe is reduced by a factor of 2, the fluid volume ($V = \pi r^2 d$) is reduced by a factor of 4, but the surface area is only cut in half ($A = 2\pi r d$). Thus, the more narrow the pipe, the greater the effect of drag.

Notice from the tube of flow that fluid does not necessarily move from high pressure to low pressure. Pressure has no direction. The driving force behind the direction of fluid flow is the fluid's tendency to find its greatest entropy. For the MCAT, just use common sense. Ask yourself in which direction you would expect the fluid to flow. If all other things are equal, fluid will move from high pressure to low pressure. In a horizontal pipe of constant cross-sectional area, fluid will flow from high pressure to low pressure according to the following equation:

$$\Delta P = QR$$

where R is the resistance to flow. In Physics Lecture 7, we will discuss the similarity of this equation with Ohm's law for voltage and the analogy of pressure to voltage. The volume flow rate for real fluid in a horizontal pipe with constant cross-sectional area can also be given in terms of pressure, viscosity (η), pipe length (L), and pipe radius (r):

$$Q = \Delta P \frac{\pi r^4}{8\eta L}$$

This equation is known as *Poiseuille's Law*. It is given here because it is a common equation and you should recognize that it is concerned with real fluids, not ideal fluids.

Warning: a non-ideal fluid does not behave in an opposite manner to an ideal fluid. Narrowing a pipe increases the velocity of an ideal fluid. It will probably increase the velocity of a non-ideal fluid as well. However, with a non-ideal fluid you must also consider drag, which impedes flow. Thus, if you narrow the pipe in a non-ideal fluid, velocity will probably increase, but not as much as if there were no drag.

As stated earlier, Bernoulli's equation describes conservation of energy within an ideal fluid. If each term in Bernoulli's equation is divided by the specific weight ρg of the fluid, the units of each new term become meters. Each new term is referred to as a 'head'. ρgh becomes h, and is called the *elevation head*. $\frac{1}{2}\rho v^2$ becomes $\frac{1}{2}v^2/g$, and is called the *velocity head*. P becomes $P/(\rho g)$, and is called the *pressure head*. We shall refer to the original terms by the heads, but, for simplicity, we shall not divide by the specific weight.

If we examine the figure below, a hypothetical fluid particle at the top of the tank is stationary. Its energy is completely contained as gravitational potential energy. The height of the fluid at this point <u>is</u> its elevation head. The zero point is arbitrary, so we will choose the floor. The velocity and pressure heads are zero because the particle is at zero velocity and zero gauge pressure. Since energy is conserved in ideal fluid flow, the sum of the three heads (the *piezometric head*) always measures to this same value. An *energy line (EL)* can be drawn horizontally at this level. The *piezometer tube* measures the piezometric head. A *static pressure tap* measures the pressure head and the elevation head, but not the velocity head. The *hydraulic gradient line (HGL)* can be drawn along the top of the static pressure taps.

With this knowledge, you can use the continuity equation ($Q = Av$) to better understand fluid flow. The difference between the piezometric tube and the static pressure tap is the velocity head. The top of the elevation head is at the center of mass of the moving fluid. In the diagram below, the displacement from where the elevation head ends to where the velocity head begins is the pressure head. If that displacement is downward, there is negative guage pressure. Notice if a static pressure tap were placed at a position where there is negative guage pressure, atmospheric pressure would push air into the fluid.

5-10
A Method for Greater Understanding of Fluid Flow

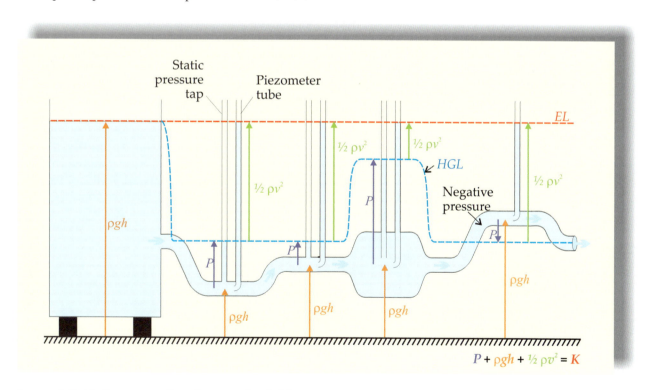

In a real fluid, the energy line drops as the fluid progresses.

5-11
Surface Tension

You should understand surface tension qualitatively for the MCAT. Any formula will be provided with a passage.

Although more dense than water, a tiny needle can be made to float on the surface of water. The force supporting the needle is not the buoyant force; no water is displaced. The force supporting the needle is created by surface tension. **Surface tension** is the intensity of the intermolecular forces per unit length. Much like a spring, when the molecules at the surface of the water are pushed downward by the weight of the needle, the intermolecular bonds of the water are stretched, and pull upward. Surface tension is also responsible for the formation of water droplets. The **intermolecular forces** pull inward tending to minimize the surface area by creating a more spherical shape. (A sphere has the least surface area per volume of any shape.) Since surface tension is a function of the intermolecular forces, it is dependent upon the temperature of the fluid (the higher the temperature, the weaker the surface tension) and upon the fluid with which it is interfacing.

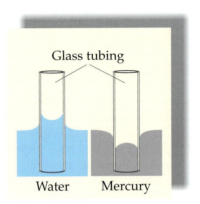

Glass tubing

Water   Mercury

Related to surface tension is the phenomenon of *capillary action*, where a fluid may be pulled up a thin tube. For capillary action, recognize that there are two types of forces acting: the intermolecular forces responsible for surface tension (*cohesive forces*); and the forces between the molecules of the tube and the fluid molecules (*adhesive forces*). If the cohesive forces are stronger, a convex meniscus is formed and the fluid is pulled downward by the vertical component of the surface tension. If the adhesive forces are stronger, a concave meniscus is formed and the fluid is pulled upward by the vertical component of the surface tension. In the diagram above, the adhesive forces between water and glass are stronger than the cohesive forces between water molecules, so the water is pulled upward. In the other tube, the adhesive forces between mercury and glass are weaker than the cohesive forces between mercury molecules, so the mercury is pulled downward.

Questions 105 through 112 are **NOT** based on a descriptive passage.

105. An ideal fluid with pressure P flows through a horizontal pipe with radius r. If the radius of the pipe is increased by a factor of 2, which of the following most likely gives the new pressure?

A. P
B. $4P$
C. $16P$
D. The new pressure cannot be determined without more information.

106. If the container pictured below is filled with an ideal fluid, which point in the fluid most likely has the greatest pressure?

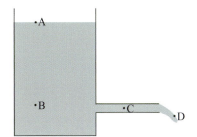

A. A
B. B
C. C
D. D

107. Water in moist soil rises through capillary action. The intermolecular forces between water molecules are:

A. weaker than the intermolecular forces between water and soil molecules.
B. equal to the intermolecular forces between water and soil molecules.
C. stronger than the intermolecular forces between water and soil molecules.
D. The comparative strength between the intermolecular forces cannot be determined with the information given.

108. All of the following would increase the volume flow rate of a fluid being pumped through a pipe EXCEPT:

A. increasing the pressure difference between the ends of the pipe.
B. decreasing the fluid viscosity.
C. increasing the pipe radius.
D. increasing the length of the pipe.

109. A spigot is to be placed on a water tank below the surface of the water. Which of the following gives the distance of the spigot below the surface h compared to the velocity with which the water will run through the spigot?

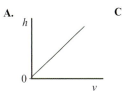
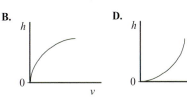

110. Two drops of equal volume of different substances were placed on the same flat surface. A side view of drop A and drop B is shown below.

Drop A   Drop B

Compared to drop B, drop A has:

A. stronger intermolecular forces and lesser surface tension.
B. stronger intermolecular forces and greater surface tension.
C. weaker intermolecular forces and lesser surface tension.
D. weaker intermolecular forces and greater surface tension.

GO ON TO THE NEXT PAGE.

111. The diagram below shows a cross-sectional view of a cylindrical pipe of varying diameter.

If an ideal fluid is flowing through the pipe, all of the following statements are true EXCEPT:

A. The cross-sectional area is greater at point A than at point B.

B. The pressure is lower at point B than at point A.

C. The volume flow rate is greater at point A than at point B.

D. The flow speed is greater at point B than at point A.

112. A spigot was opened at the bottom of a barrel full of water and the water was allowed to run through the spigot until the barrel was empty. Which of the following describes the speed of the water flowing through the spigot as the barrel emptied?

A. Always decreasing

B. Always increasing

C. Constant

D. Decreasing, then increasing.

In Chemistry Lecture 4, we discussed the different structures of a solid. In general, atoms or molecules tend to be held together rigidly. However, all solids are, to some extent, elastic. In other words, they can change their dimensions by stretching or compressing, but not breaking, these rigid bonds. To discuss the elasticity of solids we must understand two concepts: stress and strain.

5-12
Solids

Stress is the force applied to an object divided by the area over which the force is applied. It has the same units as pressure but by convention we use N/m^2 and not Pa in order to distinguish it from pressure.

$$\text{Stress} = F/A$$

Strain is the fractional change in an object's shape. Strain is a ratio of change in dimension compared to original dimension, and has no units.

$$\text{Strain} = \frac{\Delta \text{dimension}}{\text{original dimension}}$$

Stress is what is done to an object, and strain is how the object responds.

Like force and displacement in Hooke's law, stress and strain are proportional to each other. This proportionality can be given as a ratio known as the **modulus of elasticity**.

$$\text{Modulus of elasticity} = \frac{\text{stress}}{\text{strain}}$$

Up to some maximum stress, the modulus of elasticity is a constant for a specific substance. This constant is arrived at through experiment. Like Hooke's law, the maximum stress point is called the *yield point*. An object strained to its yield point will regain its shape once the stress is removed. Up to this point, the ratio of stress to strain is described accurately by the modulus of elasticity. Beyond the yield point an object will remain intact, but will not regain its original shape. The stress-strain ratio is not described accurately by the modulus when the stress exceeds the yield point. When a stress is applied that is significantly greater than the yield point, the object will break. This is called the *fracture point*.

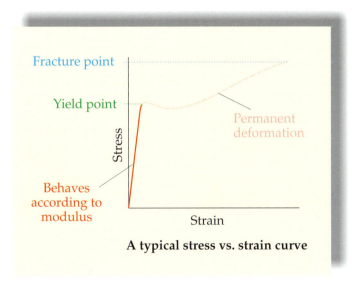

A typical stress vs. strain curve

There are three separate moduli that you should know for the MCAT:

1. **Young's modulus** (E) for tensile stress;

2. the **shear modulus** (G) for shear stress; and

3. the **bulk modulus** (B) for compression and expansion.

All moduli work in both directions. For instance, Young's modulus works for tensile compressive forces and tensile stretching forces. Also, in each case, the force used in the equation is not the sum of the forces, which would be zero, but the magnitude of one of the forces.

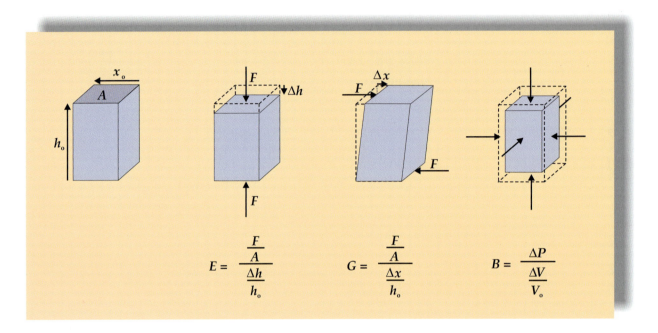

$$E = \frac{\frac{F}{A}}{\frac{\Delta h}{h_o}} \qquad G = \frac{\frac{F}{A}}{\frac{\Delta x}{h_o}} \qquad B = \frac{\Delta P}{\frac{\Delta V}{V_o}}$$

The trickiest thing about moduli on the MCAT is proportionality problems. For instance, if the area of an object is increased by a factor of 2, how will this affect the fractional change in length? If you can't answer this quickly, review proportions from the Introductory Lecture of this course.

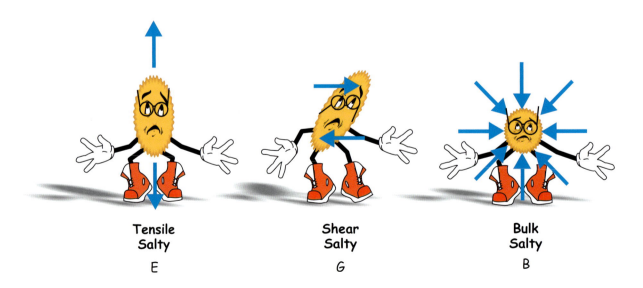

Tensile Salty

E

Shear Salty

G

Bulk Salty

B

Solids typically expand when heated. As their molecules absorb energy, their vibrations require more room. Expansion is typically considered in one dimension (linear expansion) or three dimensions (volume expansion). The formula for linear expansion is:

$$\Delta L = L\alpha\Delta T$$

where L is the original length of the object, ΔT is the change in temperature, and α is a constant unique to the particular substance. Notice that the change in temperature is proportional to the change in length.

The formula for volume expansion is:

$$\Delta V = V\beta\Delta T$$

Don't memorize the thermal expansion equations unless you just have absolutely nothing to do and you plan to be on Jeopardy someday.

where V is the original volume and β is a constant unique to the particular substance. It is a simple exercise to show that $\beta = 3\alpha$.

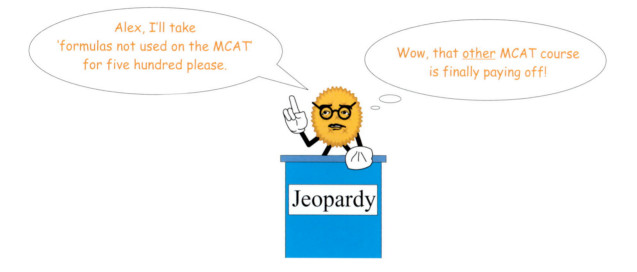

5-14
Equation Summary

Fluids at rest

$$\rho = \frac{m}{V} \qquad\qquad P \equiv \frac{F}{A}$$

$$\text{S.G.} = \frac{\rho_{\text{substance}}}{\rho_{\text{water}}} \qquad\qquad P = \rho g y$$

$$F_{\text{buoyant}} = \rho V g$$

Fluids in motion

$$Q = A v$$

$$K = P + \frac{1}{2}\rho v^2 + \rho g h$$

$$v = \sqrt{2gh}$$

Solids

$$\text{modulus of elasticity} = \frac{\text{stress}}{\text{strain}}$$

113. If a solid will buckle under pressure greater than 12 atm, and that solid has a specific gravity of 4, what is the maximum height of a circular column made from the solid that can be built at the earth's surface? (Note: 1 atm = 101,000 Pa.)

    A.   4 m
    B.   12 m
    C.   24 m
    D.   30 m

114. Which of the following gives the percent change to the Young's Modulus for a substance, when its cross-sectional area is increased by a factor of 3?

    A.   0%
    B.   33%
    C.   300%
    D.   900%

115. The Young's modulus for bone is 9×10^9 N/m^2. What is the percent change in length of a tibia with a cross-sectional area of 6 cm^2, if it experiences a compressive force of 5.4×10^3 N?

    A.   0.001%
    B.   0.1%
    C.   1%
    D.   10%

116. A single steel column is to support a mass of 1.5×10^8 kg. If the yield strength for steel is 2.5×10^8 N/m^2 and safety regulations require the column to withstand five times the weight it presently holds, what should be the approximate cross-sectional area of the base of the column?

    A.   0.6 m^2
    B.   3 m^2
    C.   6 m^2
    D.   30 m^2

117. The sole of a certain tennis shoe has a shear modulus of 4×10^7. If the height of the sole is doubled, the strain will:

    A.   decrease by a factor of two.
    B.   remain the same.
    C.   increase by a factor of two.
    D.   increase by a factor of four.

Questions 118 through 119 are based on the table of Young's moduli shown below.

Substance	Young's modulus (N/m^2)
Copper	1.0×10^{11}
Aluminum	7.0×10^{10}
Magnesium	4.1×10^{10}
Lead	1.5×10^{10}
Glass	6.0×10^{10}

118. If all of the substances listed are subjected to the same stress, which one will undergo the smallest fractional change in length?

    A.   Copper
    B.   Aluminum
    C.   Lead
    D.   Glass

119. A glass rod is subjected to a stress and undergoes a fractional change in length of 1.0%. If a lead rod is subjected to the same stress, it will undergo a fractional change in length of:

    A.   0.25%
    B.   0.50%
    C.   1.0%
    D.   4.0%

120. The bulk modulus for a substance would be most important to a researcher who is testing material that will be:

    A.   used in high tension cables.
    B.   submerged deep in the ocean.
    C.   subjected to high temperatures.
    D.   transported at great speeds.

STOP.

Waves

A **wave** is the transfer of momentum and energy from one point to another. There are three types of waves: mechanical; electromagnetic; and matter. Although many of the concepts discussed early in this lecture are applicable to electromagnetic and *matter* waves, these waves have some special features that will be discussed toward the end of this lecture and in Physics Lecture 8. **Mechanical waves** obey the laws of classical physics and **require some medium** through which to travel. The medium, if it is perfectly elastic, is momentarily displaced by a wave and then returned to its original position. Such a medium is called *nondispersive* because a wave maintains its shape and does not disperse as it travels. Nondispersive waves can be considered *ideal waves*. On the MCAT assume all media to be nondispersive unless otherwise indicated.

Mechanical waves can be further separated into transverse and longitudinal waves. A **transverse wave** is one in which the medium is displaced perpendicularly to the direction of wave propagation, such as waves on a string. A **longitudinal wave** (also called a sound wave) is one in which the medium is displaced parallel to the direction of wave propagation, such as a sound wave in air.

6-1
Wave Characteristics

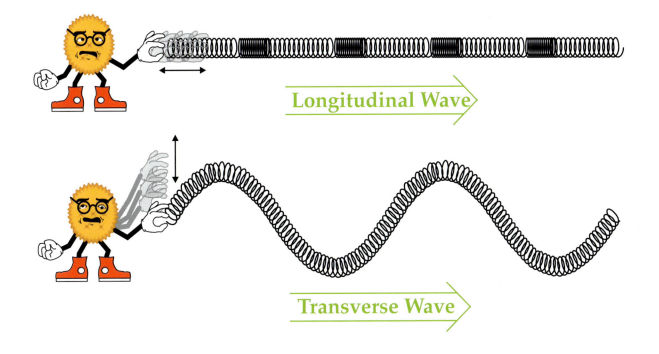

Simple transverse and simple longitudinal waves can be represented mathematically by the sine function. For a transverse wave, the sine function represents vertical displacement of the medium with respect to time or displacement of the wave. For a longitudinal wave, a phase-shifted sine function represents either the change in pressure or the horizontal displacement of the medium with respect to the time or displacement of the wave.

If we examine this mathematical representation of a wave, when the *x*-axis is displacement of the wave, the **wavelength (λ)** is measured from any point in the wave to the point where the wave begins to repeat itself. For a simple sine function, the wavelength can be measured from trough to trough, or peak to peak. For any other function, a wavelength is measured from any point, to the next point where the function begins to repeat itself. Wavelength has units of meters.

The **frequency (*f*)** of a wave is the number of wavelengths that pass a fixed point in one second. Frequency is measured in **hertz (Hz)**, or cycles per second. It is often written simply as 1/s.

The product of wavelength and frequency is velocity.

$$v = f\lambda$$

The reciprocal of frequency is called the **period (*T*)**. The period is the number of seconds required for one wavelength to pass a fixed point. When the *x*-axis is time, the period is from any point on the wave function, to the next point where the function begins to repeat itself.

$$T = \frac{1}{f}$$

The **amplitude *A*** of a wave is its maximum displacement from zero. Amplitude is always positive.

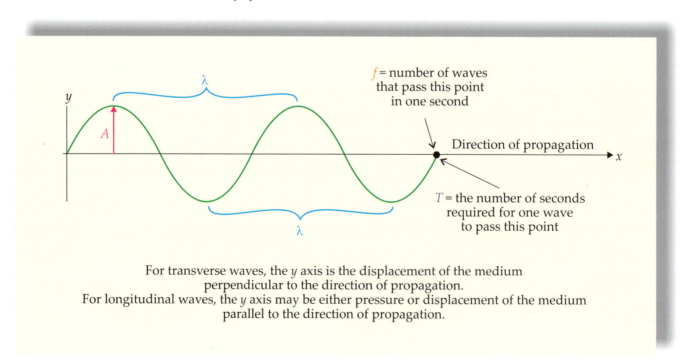

f = number of waves that pass this point in one second

Direction of propagation

T = the number of seconds required for one wave to pass this point

For transverse waves, the *y* axis is the displacement of the medium perpendicular to the direction of propagation.
For longitudinal waves, the *y* axis may be either pressure or displacement of the medium parallel to the direction of propagation.

Be aware that the wave function can be plotted against either displacement or time. For a sinusoidal wave moving along a string in the *x* direction, the transverse displacement *y* is given by:

$$y(x, t) = A \sin(kx - \omega t)$$

where *k* is the *angular wave number*, and ω is the angular frequency (see Physics Lecture 2). This equation will not be useful on the MCAT, but understanding it helps to understand waves.

Although the velocity of a wave is always given by the product of the wavelength and frequency, the **velocity is dictated by the medium** through which the wave travels. A change in frequency or wavelength does not change the velocity of a wave in a given *nondispersive* medium. Nor does the velocity of the wave source affect the velocity of the wave itself. In other words, the sound waves made by a speeding jet travel at the same speed as the sound waves made by a crawling turtle. Only the medium affects the velocity.

Two aspects of the medium affect the velocity:

   1.   the medium's resistance to change in shape (or elasticity); and

   2.   the medium's resistance to change in motion (or inertia).

For instance, the velocity of a wave traveling along a perfectly elastic string is:

$$v = \sqrt{\frac{T}{\mu}} \quad \text{(Here, } T \text{ is tension not period.)}$$

where *T* is the tension in the string (not the period), and μ is the mass per unit length of the string. From this equation, we see that we change the medium without changing the string, but by increasing the tension on the same string.

The velocity of a sound wave is given by:

$$v = \sqrt{\frac{B}{\rho}}_{\text{(small pressure variations only)}} = \sqrt{\frac{P}{\rho}}_{\text{(isothermal gases only)}}$$

where *B* is the bulk modulus of the medium and *P* is the pressure of the gas. It is not important to memorize these equations, but it is important to be able to predict how a change in medium might change the wave velocity. For instance, if the tension is equal, a wave will travel faster on a lighter string than a heavier one. However, notice that, when comparing sound waves in water and air, we cannot predict the relative velocities without actual values. Since water is heavier than air, it should slow the sound waves. But actually, water more than makes up for its higher density with a much greater bulk modulus, and sound waves travel significantly faster in water.

You should also be aware that **for a gas, the velocity increases with temperature** according to the equation:

$$v = \sqrt{\frac{\gamma R T}{M}}_{\text{(Here, } T \text{ is temperature.)}}$$

where γ is a constant for a specific gas (about 1.4 for air) which compensates for temperature changes during contractions, *R* is the universal gas constant, and *M* is the molecular mass. This indicates that the random velocity of the gas molecules is a limiting factor for the velocity of a sound wave. The greater the temperature, the greater the random velocity, the greater the sound wave velocity. In fact, the velocity of a sound wave through a gas is on the order of magnitude of (but slightly less than) the random velocity of its molecules.

Hold on! Too many formulas! Don't memorize all of these formulas; just the ones given in the equation summary at the end of each Lecture. Instead of memorizing, look at the relationships each formula implies.

For instance, notice that heavier mediums tend to slow waves down, while stiffer mediums tend to speed waves up. Since a wave must move the medium in order to pass through it, the inertia of the medium (its resistance to motion) tends to slow it down. On the other hand, the greater the elasticity of the medium, the faster it snaps back to position moving the wave along. The elastic component stores potential energy; the inertial component stores kinetic energy. Wave velocity is a constant in a nondispersive medium; it is independent of frequency, wavelength, and amplitude.

Surface waves, such as waves on the surface of water, have some special properties. They are neither completely transverse nor completely longitudinal. If the MCAT were to test your knowledge of surface waves, it would probably give you a formula in a passage. Surface waves are also called *gravity waves*, because gravity acts as the elastic component. Because gravity acts as the elastic component, just like a projectile, the mass (or density) of the liquid does not change the rate at which a surface wave rises and falls. Thus, the velocity of wave propagation is not changed by the density of the liquid. In shallow liquid, where the depth y is much smaller than the wavelength λ, the velocity of a surface wave is given approximately by:

$$v = \sqrt{gy} \qquad (y \ll \lambda)$$

Notice that the velocity increases as the depth increases. Although not shown by this approximation, the velocity also increases slightly with amplitude.

In deep liquid, a *dispersive* medium, the velocity increases with the wavelength as follows:

$$v = \sqrt{\frac{g\lambda}{2\pi}} \qquad (y \gg \lambda)$$

Power is the rate at which a wave transfers energy. Power in waves is typically discussed in terms of **intensity (I)**. It has units of W/m^2. Intensity of a sound wave is given by:

$$I = \tfrac{1}{2}\rho\omega^2 A^2 v$$

where ρ is the density of the medium, ω is the angular frequency, A is the amplitude, and v is the wave velocity. For a wave on a string, simply replace ρ with μ. Recall from Physics Lecture 2 that $\omega = 2\pi f$, so intensity is proportional to the square of the frequency. Dependence of intensity (or power) on the square of frequency and square of amplitude is true for all types of waves. Notice that frequency and amplitude depend upon the wave source, while density and velocity are factors of the medium.

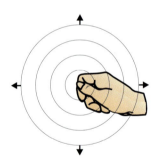

Intensity is a useful way to discuss the rate of energy transfer of waves because a wave may travel in several directions at once. For instance, if you snap your fingers in the air, some of the energy is transferred away from your fingers in the form of a sound wave moving in all directions. Although this energy remains constant, it is moving away from your fingers and spreading out over the surface area of an ever enlarging sphere. The increase in area means that the intensity of the sound is decreasing. Here, the intensity at any given radius r is the power divided by the surface area of a sphere and given by:

$$I = \frac{P}{4\pi r^2}$$

This is not a useful equation to memorize because it is applicable only under very limited circumstances.

Although intensity for sound waves is a measure of energy rate transfer per area, humans do not perceive intensity on a linear scale. For instance, the sound waves created by the rustling of leaves are about 10 times more intense than those created by normal breathing; yet, we don't perceive them as 10 times louder. In order to compensate for this and to make intensity more intuitive, an artificial scale for **intensity level (β)** has been created, based upon a logarithmic scale of intensities. The units of this scale are **decibels (dB)**. The relationship between β and I is given by:

$$\beta = 10 \log \frac{I}{I_o}$$

where I_o is the threshold intensity of human hearing (the lowest intensity audible by the typical human).

All you need to understand about decibels on the MCAT is that, if the intensity increases by a factor of 10, the decibels increase by the addition of 10 decibels. In other words, an increase in intensity from 30 W/m² to 3000 W/m² is equivalent to an increase of 20 decibels; I added 2 zeros to intensity, so I add 20 decibels to the decibel level. If I had added 3 zeros to the intensity, I would have added 30 decibels to the decibel level, and so on.

ΔI	$\Delta \beta$
x10	+10
x10^2	+20
x10^3	+30
x10^4	+40

121. If an ocean wave hits a particular beach once every four seconds, and the wave peaks are 12 meters apart, with what velocity are the waves coming into shore?

    A. 3 m/s
    B. 4 m/s
    C. 12 m/s
    D. 48 m/s

122. Waves generally travel faster in solids than in gases because:

    A. The density of solids is generally greater than the density of gases.
    B. The density of gases is generally greater than the density of solids.
    C. Solids are less compressible than gases.
    D. Gases are less compressible than solids.

123. One end of a string is shaken each second sending a wave with an amplitude of 10 cm toward the other end. The string is 5 meters long, and the wavelength of each wave is 50 cm. How many waves reach the other end of the string in each 10 second interval?

    A. 2
    B. 5
    C. 10
    D. 50

124. The sound level of the chirping made by a bird at a distance of 5 meters is measured at 30 dB. When the same bird is 50 meters away the sound level is measured at 10 dB. How many times greater is the amplitude of the sound wave at 5 meters away compared to 50 meters away?

    A. 3 times greater.
    B. 10 times greater.
    C. 20 times greater.
    D. 100 times greater.

125. Sound waves are an example of:

    A. longitudinal waves because the medium moves perpendicularly to the propagation of the wave.
    B. longitudinal waves because the medium moves parallel to the propagation of the wave.
    C. transverse waves because the medium moves perpendicularly to the propagation of the wave.
    D. transverse waves because the medium moves parallel to the propagation of the wave.

126. When the frequency of a sound wave is increased, which of the following will decrease?

    I. Wavelength
    II. Period
    III. Amplitude

    A. I only
    B. III only
    C. I and II only
    D. I and III only

127. A ship uses a depth finder to discover the depth of water beneath it at any time. The depth finder operates by sending a sound wave towards the bottom of the ocean and measuring the time it takes for the wave to be reflected off the bottom and return to the ship. At a certain point, it takes 1 second for the wave to return. What is the depth at that point? (The speed of sound in water is 1500 m/s)

    A. 750 m
    B. 1500 m
    C. 3000 m
    D. 4500 m

128. If the intensity of a sound is doubled, the decibel level will increase by:

    A. less than 10 dB.
    B. exactly 10 dB.
    C. more than 10 dB.
    D. exactly 20 dB.

STOP.

The **phase** of a wave relates to its wavelength, frequency, and place and time of origin. In a nondispersive medium, the phase is constant and given by:

$$kx - \omega t = \text{the wave phase}$$

The angular values in this equation are beyond the MCAT. Don't memorize this equation. It is sufficient for the MCAT to think of phase as a horizontal shift of a wave on a Cartesian graph as shown below. Each wavelength represents 360°. So half a wavelength represents 180°. Two waves that are the same wavelength, and begin at the same point, are said to be in phase with each other. Two waves that are the same wavelength but travel different distances to arrive at the same point, will be out of phase if that distance is not some multiple of the wavelength. The angle by which two waves differ is called their *phase constant*.

Two or more waves can occupy the same space. When this happens, if the waves are transverse, their displacements add at each point along the wave to form a new wave. This superposition of waves is called interference. Interference can be constructive or destructive. **Constructive interference** occurs when the sum of the displacements results in a greater displacement. **Destructive interference** occurs when the sum of the displacements results in a smaller displacement. After passing through each other, waves that interfere will revert to their original shape, unaffected by the interference.

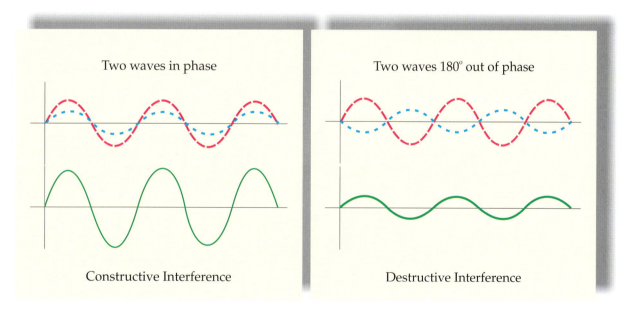

Two waves in phase — Constructive Interference

Two waves 180° out of phase — Destructive Interference

Any waveform, no matter how irregular, can be created by superposition of a sufficient number of sine waves with the correct amplitudes and wavelengths.

A special case of superposition of waves is the phenomenon known as beats. **Beats** occur when two waves with slightly different frequencies are superimposed. At some points they will be nearly in phase and experience constructive interference. At other points they will be out of phase and experience destructive interference. These points will alternate with a frequency equal to the difference between the frequencies of the original two waves. This difference is called the beat frequency.

$$f_{\text{Beat}} = |f_1 - f_2|$$

6-2
Superposition, Phase, and Interference

Notice the lines below. They occur at slightly different frequencies. Your eye perceives equally spaced light and dark spots, which correspond to the beat frequency.

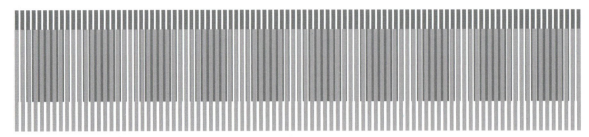

A good way to remember the beat frequency is to think about tuning a piano. It is impossible to tune a piano perfectly. The piano tuner listens to the beat frequency of the tuning fork and the piano note. In order to bring the piano into perfect tune, the beat frequency must be zero. The tuner would have to wait forever while the beats get farther and farther apart until they are infinitely separated. By the way, the beat frequency is an alternating increase and decrease in the intensity of the noise. What the tuner actually hears is called the **pitch**. The frequency creating the pitch would be an average of the frequencies from the piano and the tuning fork. Pitch correlates with frequency; a high note has high pitch and high frequency.

When a wave reaches an interface between two media, some or all of the energy and momentum will reflect back into the first medium. Any energy and momentum not reflected will *refract* into the second medium. Any refracting wave will continue in the same orientation with the same frequency but with a smaller amplitude and a different wavelength. The orientation of the reflected wave will depend upon the relative density of the two media. When the wave reflects off a denser medium, the wave is inverted (Its phase is shifted 180°). When the wave reflects off a less dense medium, it is reflected upright (No phase shift occurs).

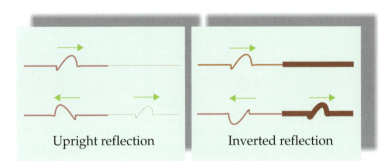

Upright reflection   Inverted reflection

Important: When a wave transfers from one medium to the next, the wavelength changes and the frequency remains the same.

The reflection of a wave is most easily visualized by examining a wave pulse. A *wave pulse* is a single wavelength. If you imagine a string attached to a thread, and then imagine sending a wave pulse down the string, some of the energy would continue into the thread (the light medium) as an upright wave pulse, and the rest of the energy would reflect back as an upright wave pulse. Now imagine the same string attached to a heavy rope. The reflected wave is inverted.

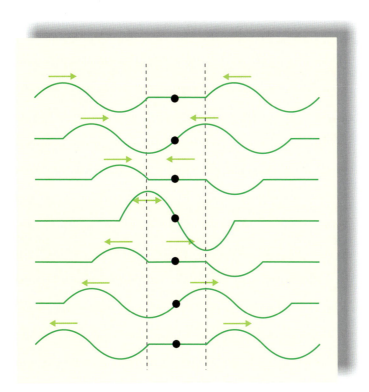

Now let's look at two sine waves with the same wavelength traveling in opposite directions on the same perfectly elastic string. As shown by the diagram, when they pass through each other something interesting happens. The point where they collide is never displaced. It doesn't move at all. This point is represented by the black dot in the diagram and is called a **node**. Notice also that only the points intersected by the two vertical lines experience maximum constructive interference. These points are called **antinodes**. Now imagine two endless rows of sine waves traveling in opposite directions on the same string. The string would hold perfectly still at the nodes and move violently up and down at the antinodes. This condition is known as a **standing wave**.

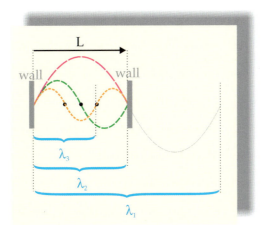

What would happen if we locked both ends of the string at zero displacement by tying them to a wall and then generated a row of sine waves on the string? Let's assume that, at the string-wall interface, the entire wave is reflected back to the string and no energy is refracted into the wall. In this situation, since two nodes, one at each wall, are already specified, only certain wavelengths would create a standing wave. All other wavelengths would create very small, irregular oscillations of the string. A list of the wavelengths from largest to smallest of the possible standing waves for a given situation is called a **harmonic series**. The harmonics are numbered from longest to shortest wavelength. The longest wavelength, called the **first harmonic (λ₁)** or **fundamental wavelength**, is created with the fewest number of nodes, two. This means that the distance from one wall to the other is half a wavelength. The **second harmonic (λ₂)** is created by adding another node. This makes the wavelength of the second harmonic equal to the distance between the walls. Each successive harmonic is created by adding a node. The equation for the harmonic series where each end is tied down as a node or where each end is loose creating an antinode is:

$$L = \frac{n\lambda_n}{2} \quad (n = 1, 2, 3, \ldots)$$

where L is the distance between the two ends of the string and n is the number of the harmonic. This equation is the same for longitudinal waves such as sound. A pipe closed or open at both ends with sound waves inside will follow this equation. If only one end of the string is tied down, or only one end of a pipe is open, the untied or open end is an antinode. For a string tied at only one end, or a pipe open at only one end, the equation changes to:

$$L = \frac{n\lambda_n}{4} \quad (n = 1, 3, 5, \ldots)$$

Notice when one end is an antinode, the even numbered harmonics are missing.

The standing waves described above cause the string to **resonate** or vibrate at its **natural frequency** or **resonant frequency**. Since velocity is constant for a given medium, the resonant frequency can be found for any given harmonic from the equation $v = f\lambda$.

All mechanical structures have natural frequencies at which they resonate. If an outside driving force is applied to a structure at the resonant frequency, the structure will experience maximum vibration velocities and maximum displacement amplitudes. The condition where the natural frequency and the driving frequency are equal is also called **resonance**. An examination of the resonating string discussed above will reveal the driving force to be the reflected wave. This demonstrates that both definitions of resonance are the same. In a non-ideal situation, energy is lost to some *damping effect* at the resonant frequency, and must be replaced by some outside driving force at the same frequency. A maximum displacement is produced resulting in a standing wave.

129. How many wavelengths are shown between the dotted lines in the wave form below?

    A.   1
    B.   2
    C.   3
    D.   4

130. When two waves are superimposed, the resulting wave can be found by summing their:

    A.   frequencies
    B.   periods
    C.   wavelengths
    D.   displacements

131. In order for two sound waves to have an audible beat frequency, the two waves must be:

    A.   in phase.
    B.   out of phase.
    C.   close in frequency.
    D.   of the same wavelength.

132. All of the following statements are true about a resonating string EXCEPT:

    A.   A resonating string forms a standing wave.
    B.   The wavelength of a resonating string must coincide with one of its harmonics.
    C.   Some spots on a resonating string will not move at all.
    D.   If left alone, the amplitude of a wave on a resonating string will grow infinitely large.

133. If a guitar string is 0.5 m long, what is the wavelength of its third harmonic?

    A.   0.25 m
    B.   0.33 m
    C.   0.5 m
    D.   1 m

134. Two violinists are playing together, slightly out of tune. If one violinist produces a frequency of 883 Hz and the other produces a frequency of 879 Hz, beats would be heard with a frequency of:

    A.   2 Hz.
    B.   4 Hz.
    C.   881 Hz.
    D.   1762 Hz.

135. A vibrating string has consecutive harmonics at wavelengths of 2.0 m and 4.0 m. What is the length of the string?

    A.   1.0 m
    B.   2.0 m
    C.   4.0 m
    D.   8.0 m

136. Waves A and B, pictured below, may or may not be in phase. If wave A and wave B are superimposed, the range of possible amplitudes for the resulting wave will be:

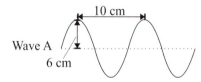

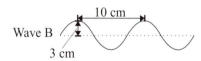

    A.   from 0 cm to 3 cm.
    B.   from 0 cm to 9 cm.
    C.   from 3 cm to 6 cm.
    D.   from 3 cm to 9 cm.

STOP.

6-3
Simple Harmonic Motion

Any motion that repeats itself is called *periodic* or *harmonic motion*. If we stand directly in front of someone who is steadily peddling a stationary bicycle, and we watch the peddles, they appear to move straight up and down. They move faster in the middle of the motion and slow down at the top and bottom. If we recorded this up and down motion on paper as the paper was pulled to our right, we would draw a perfect sine wave. This type of motion is a specific type of harmonic motion. It is called **simple harmonic motion**, which means that it **is a sinusoidal function** in time. Objects in simple harmonic motion exhibit similar properties of which you must be aware for the MCAT.

The function that gives the displacement *x* of an object in simple harmonic motion with respect to time is a simplified form of the equation for a wave moving along a string. It is:

$$x(t) = A \cos(\omega t + \phi)$$

where *A* is the maximum displacement, ω is the angular frequency ($\omega = 2\pi f$), and ϕ is the phase constant that depends on what displacement *x* we call $t = 0$. (When $x = A$ at $t = 0$, then $\phi = 0$.) You will never need this equation on the MCAT. By taking the first and second derivatives of this equation we get the velocity and acceleration of the object in simple harmonic motion. Although these equations are not required for the MCAT, by combining the displacement and the acceleration equations we arrive at:

$$a(t) = -\omega^2 x(t)$$

This simple relationship identifies two important properties of simple harmonic motion; the acceleration is directly proportional to the displacement, but opposite in sign, and the acceleration and displacement are related by the square of the frequency.

If we multiply both sides of $[a(t) = -\omega^2 x(t)]$ by mass *m*, we get Hooke's law! $F = -m\omega^2 x$, and we can see that the spring constant *k* is $m\omega^2$. Therefore, since a spring follows Hooke's law, a mass bouncing on the end of a massless spring exhibits simple harmonic motion. If we lay the mass and spring on a frictionless horizontal table, stretch the spring, and release it, we get the same motion, and we can examine it without the complication of gravity. When the spring is fully stretched or fully compressed, the restoring force is at a maximum. Since the force is at a maximum, the acceleration is also at a maximum. Since displacement is at a maximum, the elastic potential energy, $\frac{1}{2} kx^2$, is also at a maximum. At this point the velocity is zero because the mass is reversing directions. Since the velocity is zero, the kinetic energy, $\frac{1}{2} mv^2$, is also zero. When the mass is crossing the equilibrium point of the spring (the length of the spring at rest), the net force on the mass is zero because Δx is zero ($F = -k\Delta x$). The potential energy is zero for the same reason. The velocity, however, is at a maximum, which means that kinetic energy is also at a maximum. Of course, no force means that acceleration is zero. So we see that another characteristic of most systems in simple harmonic motion is an oscillation between kinetic energy and potential energy. No energy is lost to the surroundings.

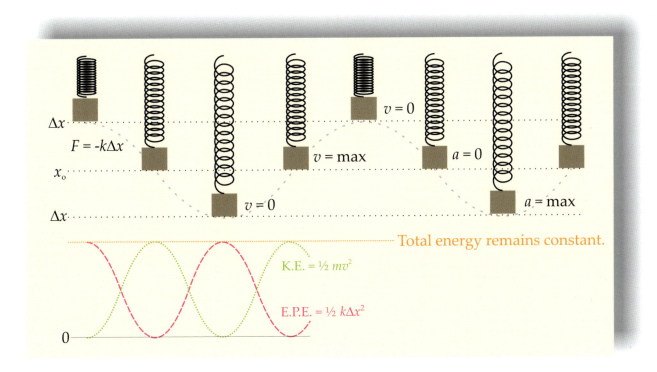

Total energy remains constant.

K.E. $= \frac{1}{2} mv^2$

E.P.E. $= \frac{1}{2} k\Delta x^2$

Since $k = m\omega^2$, and $\omega = 2\pi f$, the period of the motion for the mass on a spring is given by:

$$T = 2\pi\sqrt{\frac{m}{k}}$$

Notice that the inertial factor is on top and the elastic factor is on the bottom. Since period is inversely proportional to velocity, this is what we would expect from a wave phenomenon.

Another apparatus that simulates simple harmonic motion is a **pendulum** swinging at a small angle. (A 5 degree angle equals approximately 0.1% deviation from simple harmonic motion. For the MCAT, assume simple harmonic motion on all pendulums unless otherwise indicated.) Just like the mass on a spring, the pendulum exchanges energy forms between potential and kinetic. A pendulum has total gravitational potential at the top of its swing and total kinetic at the bottom.

$$T = 2\pi\sqrt{\frac{L}{g}}$$

Simple harmonic motion can take many forms and is easily disguised on the MCAT. For example: the orbit of a planet viewed from the side; a tetherball spinning around a pole viewed from the side; and electrons oscillating back and forth in AC current are all forms of simple harmonic motion.

Use Hooke's law to help you remember that the acceleration of any system in simple harmonic motion is proportional to the displacement of that system. Also, remember that it is proportional to the square of the frequency.

Recognize that for most systems in simple harmonic motion, energy oscillates between kinetic and one or more forms of potential.

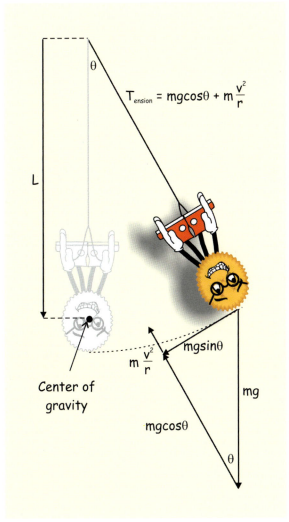

$T_{ension} = mg\cos\theta + m\frac{v^2}{r}$

Center of gravity

$m\frac{v^2}{r}$ $mg\sin\theta$ mg $mg\cos\theta$

Finally, I can't resist giving this mnemonic. To remember the angular frequencies for a mass on a spring and for a pendulum, just remember WACK'EM and WIGGLE:

$$\omega = \sqrt{\frac{k}{m}} \qquad \omega = \sqrt{\frac{g}{L}}$$

wack'em   &   wiggle

Even though these formulas will not be on the MCAT, they can help you remember things like the period of a pendulum is independent of the mass.

6-4
The Doppler Effect

<u>**The Doppler effect**</u> results because waves are unaffected by the speed of the source which produces them. If the source moves relative to the receiver of the waves (here called 'the observer'), each wave will travel a different distance in order to reach the observer, and therefore the observer will not receive them at the same frequency as they were emitted. For instance, if the source were to move toward the observer as fast as the waves, all the waves would arrive at the observer at the same time; obviously this would not be the frequency with which they were emitted. If we are talking about sound waves, where pitch changes with frequency, the observer would not hear the same pitch that the source emitted. With light, the observer would not observe the same color that was emitted.

If needed, the formula for the Doppler Effect for mechanical waves will be given to you on the MCAT as:

$$f_s = f_o \left(\frac{v \pm v_s}{v \pm v_o} \right)$$

This formula is unlikely to be useful on the MCAT. The difficult aspect of this formula is to understand when to use the plus sign and when to use the minus sign. The easy way to solve this problem is to follow these steps: 1) assume that the observer is not moving; 2) if the source is moving toward the object, label that direction negative and use the minus sign for v_s; 3) now check the direction that the observer is moving. If the direction is the same, use the same sign for v_o; if not, use the opposite sign for v_o. This system is possible because velocity is a vector and once you label a direction positive for one vector it must be so for all vectors.

For all waves, the Doppler Effect can be approximated by:

$$\frac{\Delta f}{f_s} = \frac{v}{c} \qquad \text{and} \qquad \frac{\Delta \lambda}{\lambda_s} = \frac{v}{c}$$

(c is not neccessarily the speed of light)

You should always use these formule for any Doppler MCAT problem, and not the more complicated formula above. These formulae approximate the Doppler Effect when the relative velocity v of the source and the observer are much smaller than the wave velocity c. Δf and $\Delta \lambda$ are the change to the source frequency f and the source wavelength λ.

$$\left| \Delta f \right| = \left| f_o - f_s \right| \qquad \left| \Delta \lambda \right| = \left| \lambda_o - \lambda_s \right|$$

Notice that you must make a qualitative judgement as to the direction of the change in frequency and wavelength. This is simple: when the relative velocity brings the source and observer closer, observed frequency goes up and observed wavelength goes down; in the opposite case, the opposite is true. If the objects are getting farther apart as time passes, subtract Δf from f_s or add $\Delta\lambda$ from λ_s; if they are approaching each other as time passes, add Δf to f_s or subtract $\Delta\lambda$ from λ_s.

The relative velocity v is sometimes difficult to grasp. It is simply the net speed at which the source and object are approaching each other. For objects moving in the same direction, subtract their individual speeds; for objects moving in opposite directions, add their individual speeds.

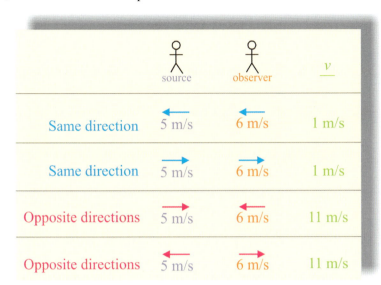

	source	observer	$\dfrac{v}{}$
Same direction	← 5 m/s	← 6 m/s	1 m/s
Same direction	→ 5 m/s	→ 6 m/s	1 m/s
Opposite directions	→ 5 m/s	← 6 m/s	11 m/s
Opposite directions	← 5 m/s	→ 6 m/s	11 m/s

In the diagram below, the train's velocity tends to make me hear the whistle with a higher pitch. Notice that the wave peaks to the right of the train are closer than those to the left. The movement of the train pushes the peaks closer together. By running to the right, I tend to spread the wave peaks back out again as they strike me. I'm not as fast as the train, so the net result is that I hear the whistle at a higher frequency.

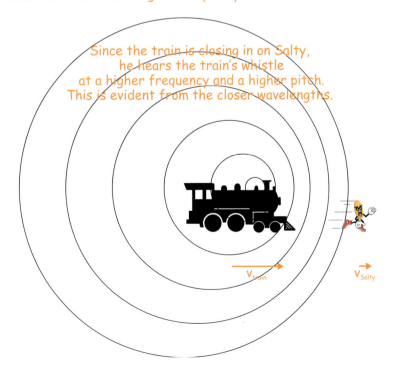

Since the train is closing in on Salty, he hears the train's whistle at a higher frequency and a higher pitch. This is evident from the closer wavelengths.

V_{train} V_{Salty}

Be sure to remember that, for light, when the source and observer are approaching each other, the wavelength shortens creating a blue shift. When they separate, a red shift is created.

Also remember that for objects moving in the same direction at the same speed, there is no Doppler Effect; the relative velocity is zero, so the change in frequency is zero.

6-5
Equation Summary

Waves

$$v = f\lambda$$

$$T = \frac{1}{f}$$

Sound

$$\beta = 10 \log\frac{I}{I_o}$$

$$L = \frac{n\lambda_n}{4} \quad (n = 1, 3, 5,...)$$

$$f_{Beat} = |f_1 - f_2|$$

$$L = \frac{n\lambda_n}{2} \quad (n = 1, 2, 3,...)$$

The Doppler Effect

$$\frac{\Delta f}{f_s} = \frac{v}{c}$$

$$\frac{\Delta\lambda}{\lambda_s} = \frac{v}{c}$$

137. If the mass on the bob of a pendulum is increased by a factor of 3, the period of the pendulum's motion will:

   A. be increased by a factor of 2.
   B. remain the same.
   C. be decreased by a factor of 2.
   D. be decreased by a factor of 4.

138. Which of the following would most accurately demonstrate the kinetic energy of a pendulum?

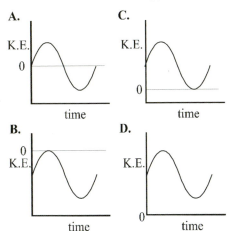

139. If the amplitude of a sine wave is doubled, the intensity:

   A. remains the same.
   B. increases by a factor of 2.
   C. increases by a factor of 4.
   D. increases by a factor of 16.

140. Which of the following factors by itself will increase the frequency at which an observer hears a sound emanating from a source?

   A. A wind blows from the source to the observer.
   B. The source and the observer move away from each other at the same speed.
   C. The source and the observer move in the same direction at the same speed.
   D. The source moves away from the observer more slowly than the observer moves toward the source.

141. A piano creates a musical note when a metal wire stretched between two fixed ends is struck by a hammer, creating a standing wave. As the force with which the hammer strikes the string is increased, the amplitude of the string's motion is increased. Which of the following properties of the wave on the string will remain the same as the force of the hammer is increased?

   I. frequency
  II. wavelength
 III. velocity

   A. I only
   B. I and II only
   C. II and III only
   D. I, II, and III

142. As a pendulum pictured below swings through point A, which of the following is at a maximum?

   A. tangential acceleration
   B. displacement from rest
   C. kinetic energy
   D. gravitational potential energy

143. A clock uses the motion of a pendulum to keep time. If the clock were placed at a height several thousand kilometers above the earth's surface, it would run:

   A. faster than it would on the surface of the earth.
   B. slower than it would on the surface of the earth.
   C. at the same speed that it would at the surface of the earth.
   D. at a speed that can't be determined from its speed at the surface of the earth.

144. All of the following are examples of harmonic motion EXCEPT:

   A. a pendulum moving back and forth
   B. a skydiver falling through the atmosphere.
   C. a car moving around a circular track.
   D. a string vibrating on a musical instrument.

STOP.

Lecture 7

Electricity and Magnetism

Like energy, **charge** is an entity that defies definition. Yet, all of us have an intuitive idea about what it is; we've all experienced a shock from static electricity, for instance. Charge is intrinsic to the nature of some subatomic particles; it is part of their identity. Most of us are aware that there is positive charge and negative charge. The 'positive' and 'negative' signify nothing more than that these charges are opposite to each other. Instead of positive and negative, they could have been called up and down, black and white, or even had their names reversed to 'negative' and 'positive'. It is an accident of science that electrons were labeled negative and not positive, and, as a result of this accident, current runs in the opposite direction of electrons. Charge (q) is given in units of **coulombs (C)**.

Just as there is a universal law of conservation of energy, there is a **Universal Law of Conservation of Charge**. The universe has no net charge. In the majority of situations (and for the MCAT), net charge is created by separating electrons from protons. If we were to put all the positive and negative charges in the universe together, they would cancel each other out, right down to the last electron and proton. Thus, anytime a negative charge is created, a positive charge is created, and vice versa.

Charge is quantized. This means that any charge must be at least as large as a certain smallest possible unit. The smallest possible unit of charge is one electron unit ($e = 1.6 \times 10^{-19}$ C), the charge on one electron or one proton.

Opposite charges attract each other; like charges repel each other. The formula describing the magnitude of the force of the repulsion or attraction between two charged objects is called **Coulomb's law**, and is analogous to the formula for gravitational force:

$$F = k\frac{q_1 q_2}{r^2}$$

where k is the Coulomb constant ($k = 8.988 \times 10^9$ N m^2/C^2), q represents the respective charges, and r is the distance between the centers of charge.

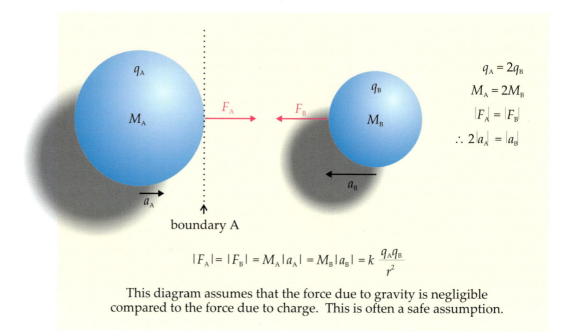

$$|F_A| = |F_B| = M_A|a_A| = M_B|a_B| = k\,\frac{q_A q_B}{r^2}$$

This diagram assumes that the force due to gravity is negligible compared to the force due to charge. This is often a safe assumption.

Notice that the diagram above is the same as that used for gravity in Lecture 2. We want to emphasize the similarity between these two forces. Both gravitational and electric forces change inversely with the square of the distance between the centers of mass or charge. One major difference is that gravitational forces are always attractive while electrical forces may be either attractive or repulsive.

Also notice that the force due to gravity in the diagram above is ignored. Coulomb's forces are usually of a far greater magnitude than gravitational forces, and, unless the masses are very large, gravitational forces are negligible.

In defining Coulomb's law, we used the phrase 'center of charge'. Similar to center of mass, the **center of charge** is a point from which the charge generated by an object or system of objects can be considered to originate. For example, the charges on a hollow, positively charged sphere made from conducting material will repel each other so that they move as far apart as possible. This results in the positive charge spreading uniformly along the outer surface of the sphere. Due to the symmetry, the center of charge exists at the center of the sphere, even though there is no actual charge at the center of the sphere. The electrostatic force on a charged object placed outside the sphere can be found using Coulomb's Law, where r is the distance between the object and the center of the sphere.

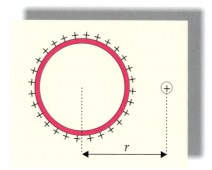

Notice the same is true for gravity.

The similarities between gravity and electricity stem from the fact that both mass and charge create fields. A **field** is a man-made concept designed to explain action at a distance. Recall that on the MCAT, any force that acts on your system must be physically contiguous to it, except for the forces of gravity, electricity, or magnetism. This is because these forces are created by fields and can act at a distance.

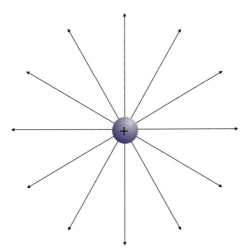

Any field can be represented by **lines of force**. Lines of force point in the direction of the field (**positive to negative** for electric fields, towards the mass creating the field for gravitational fields). The relative distance between lines indicates the strength of the field; the closer the lines, the stronger the field. Lines of force can never intersect, as this would indicate a field pointing in two different directions from the same location, an impossibility. The lines of force for a single positive point charge are shown in the diagram above.

Examine the lines of force for the field created by the positively charged, hollow sphere. Notice that the inside of the sphere has no electric field. A negatively charged sphere would produce the same result. This is because the lines of force must begin on a positive charge and end on a negative charge. This is an impossibility for lines entering the sphere. Thus there can be no lines of force inside a uniformly charged sphere. Again, the same is true for a gravitational field.

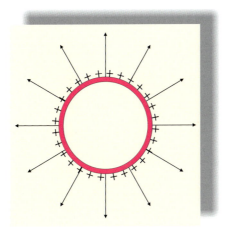

An electric field is defined as the electrostatic force per unit charge. The symbol for any **electric field** is *E*. *E* is a vector pointing in the direction of the field and has units of N/C or V/m. For a point charge, the electric field is found by dividing Coulomb's law by *q* giving:

$$E = k\frac{q_1}{r^2}$$

The electric field for a system of point charges is found by summing the fields due to each charge. Remember that E is a vector and you must use vector addition when summing fields.

The symbol for the gravitational field near the surface of the earth is the familiar g. When we wish to discuss the gravitational force on any object at the surface of the earth, we normally use 'mg' and not '$F = Gmm/r^2$'. This is because we are very familiar with the gravitational field near the surface of the earth, and thus we have created a shorthand method for describing the gravitational force for any mass; that method is the mass times the field, mg. Similarly, the force on a charge (q) in an electric field (E) is:

$$F = Eq$$

To find the potential energy of a mass in the earth's gravitational field relative to some other position, we multiply this force times the displacement in the direction opposite the field, mgh. Similarly, the **potential energy (U)** of a charge in an electric field is the force times the displacement (d):

$$U = Eqd$$

where d is measured from a zero point of our own choosing, similar to h in gravitational potential energy. Since this particular electric potential energy is dependent upon position, it is also a type of potential energy.

If the electric field is created by a point charge, we can derive the electric potential energy from Coulomb's law:

$$U = k\frac{q_1 q_2}{r}$$

Notice that according to this formula, electric potential is zero for particles separated by an infinite distance. Since energy is a state function, its value can be arbitrarily assigned, and it is given a zero value in this case by convention.

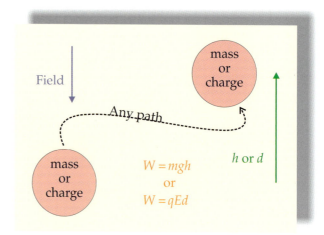

Recalling our study of gravity, if we wanted to create a function for the work required to move <u>any</u> given mass along any frictionless path near the surface of the earth, what would this function be? In other words, we are looking for a function intrinsic to the gravitational field, which is independent of any mass. What function would give us the 'potential' of the field in terms of work gained or lost per unit mass? The answer is gh, the field times the displacement in the direction opposite the field. If we multiplied any mass times gh, we would have the work done by the field in moving that mass. This is called the potential of the field. In electricity, potential has a special name, voltage. **Voltage (*V*)** is the potential for work by an electric field in moving any charge from one point to another.

$$V = Ed$$

Voltage is given in units of **volts (V)**, and is a scalar. You should also recognize voltage in units of J/C.

The voltage due to a point charge is:

$$V = k\frac{q_1}{r}$$

Since voltage is a scalar, when finding the voltage due to a group of point charges, the voltages due to each individual charge can be summed directly.

Notice from the diagram on the oppstie page that, like the work done by gravity, the work done by an electrostatic field is independent of the path. This is because both fields are conservative; they both conserve mechanical energy. As we will see when we discuss magnetism, this is not true of all electric fields.

	Units
$F = k\dfrac{q_1 q_2}{r^2}$	N
$E = k\dfrac{q_1}{r^2}$	N/C or V/m
$U = k\dfrac{q_1 q_2}{r}$	J
$V = k\dfrac{q_1}{r}$	V or J/C

Within an electric field, movement perpendicular to the field does not result in a change in potential, just as a mass moving along the surface of the earth does not experience a change in its gravitational potential. In any electric field we can define a surface normal to the field that describes a set of points all with the same potential. Examples of such surfaces are shown as dashed lines in the diagram below. They are called **equipotential surfaces**. All points on an equipotential surface are at the same voltage. An equipotential surface can be drawn at any point in the field.

When working electricity problems be sure to know what type of electric field you're working with. The formulas in the box above refer to an electric field created by a point charge. Point charges create electric fields that change with *r*. If your electric field is constant, like the field inside a capacitor, you should NOT use the formulas in the box above. If your field is created by a point, you should be careful about using formulas other than those in the box above.

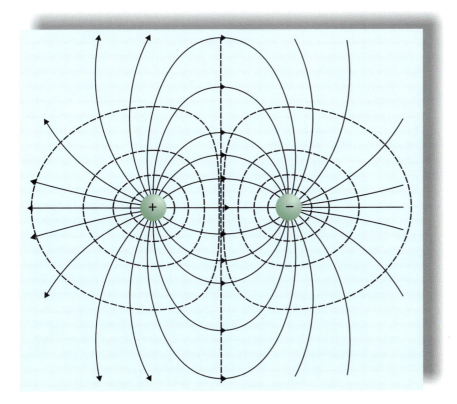

Also shown in the diagram are the field lines of an electric dipole. An **electric dipole** is created by two opposite charges with equal magnitude. An *electric dipole*

moment ($p = qd$) is a vector whose magnitude is the charge q on one of the charges times the distance d between the charges. In physics, this vector points in the opposite direction to the electric field, from the negative charge to the positive charge. In chemistry the vector points from positive to negative. At large distances the electric field of a dipole varies by $1/r^3$.

A dipole placed in an electric field will tend to align itself along the field in the opposite orientation to the field. Thus a dipole not perfectly aligned with an external electric field will have a potential energy of $U = -pE\cos\theta$ where θ is the angle between the dipole and the electric field.

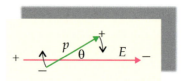

145. Two charged metal plates are placed one meter apart creating a constant electric field between them. A one coulomb charged particle is placed in the space between them. The particle experiences a force of 100 newtons due to the electric field. What is the potential difference between the plates?

- **A.** 1 V
- **B.** 10 V
- **C.** 100 V
- **D.** 1000 V

146. How much work is required to move a positively charged particle along the 15 cm path shown, if the electric field E is 10 N/C and the charge on the particle is 8 C? (Note: ignore gravity)

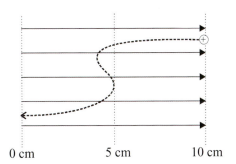

- **A.** 0.8 J
- **B.** 8 J
- **C.** 12 J
- **D.** 1200 J

147. If the distance between two point charges is increased by a factor of 3, the new force on either charge will be:

- **A.** decreased by a factor of 9.
- **B.** decreased by a factor of 3.
- **C.** remain the same.
- **D.** increased by a factor of 3.

148. If the distance between a point charge and an infinitely large charged plate is increased by a factor of 2, the new force on the point charge will:

- **A.** decrease by a factor of 4.
- **B.** decrease by a factor of 2.
- **C.** remain the same.
- **D.** increase by a factor of 2.

149. A positively charged particle starts at rest 25 cm from a second positively charged particle which is held stationary throughout the experiment. The first particle is released and accelerates directly away from the second particle. When the first particle has moved 25 cm, it has reached a velocity of 10 m/s. What is the maximum velocity that the first particle will reach?

- **A.** 10 m/s
- **B.** 14 m/s
- **C.** 20 m/s
- **D.** Since the first particle will never escape the electric field of the second particle, it will never stop accelerating, and will reach an infinite velocity.

150. The electric field for two point charges A and B is shown below. Which of the following is true?

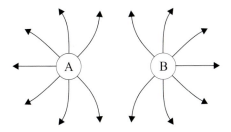

- **A.** Both charges are positive.
- **B.** Both charges are negative.
- **C.** The charges have opposite charges.
- **D.** The charges can not be determined.

151. Two particles are held in equilibrium by the gravitational and electrostatic forces between them. Particle A has mass m_a and charge q_a. Particle B has mass m_b and charge q_b. The distance between the charges is d. Which of the following changes will cause the charges to accelerate towards one another?

A. m_a is doubled and m_b is doubled.
B. m_a is doubled and m_b is halved.
C. q_a is doubled and q_b is doubled.
D. d is doubled.

152. When −10 C of charge are moved from point A to point B in the diagram below, 90 J of work is done.

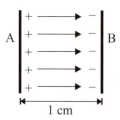

The voltage between point A and point B is:

A. 0.9 V
B. 9 V
C. 90 V
D. 900 V

STOP.

When charge moves along an object (usually in the form of electrons), that object is said to be conducting electricity. At the same time that it is conducting electricity, the object also resists the movement of charge. All substances conduct electricity to some extent, and all substances resist movement of charge to some extent (super-conductors excluded). Substances resist and conduct charge to different degrees. However, it turns out that the vast majority of substances either conduct charge very well or very poorly. Thus, we can safely classify most substances as conductors or resistors. Good **conductors**, such as metals, allow electrons to flow relatively freely. Poor conductors (good **resistors**) hold electrons tightly in place. Poor conductors are represented by, among other substances, network solids such as diamond and glass.

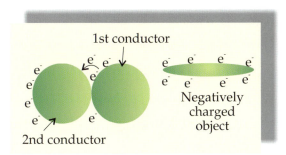

Since electrons flow easily along conductors, we can charge a conductor by **induction**. If we move a negatively charged object close to an electrically insulated conductor, the electrons on that conductor will be repelled to its opposite side. If we then touch a second conductor to the first, the electrons will move still further from the charged object by moving onto the second conductor. Once the second conductor is removed, the first conductor is left with fewer electrons than protons, and thus has an induced positive charge.

Moving charge is called **current**. Current is given in **amps (A),** or C/s. Current is a scalar, but we describe its flow to be in the direction of the movement of positive charge. Unfortunately, Ben Franklin designated electrons to be negative without realizing it. Because of this, current, which is usually created by flowing electrons, is in the opposite direction to the flow of electrons.

The flow of electrons resembles the flow of a fluid. Like molecules in a moving fluid, electrons move very fast in random directions, while there is a much slower uniform translational movement (called *drift speed*) opposite the direction of the current.

7-2
Movement of Charge

Notice that, since charge moves easily through a conductor, if an object is made of a conducting material, it can only hold excess charge on its surface. The excess charges try to move away from each other, and they end up only on the surface. To visualize this, imagine 10 people with terrible body odor in a round room. Obviously they want to get as far away from each other as possible. They move to the walls to maximize their distance from everyone else. Like the uniformly charged sphere, the electric field inside a uniformly charged conductor is zero.

A **circuit** is a cyclical pathway for moving charge.

As we learned earlier, all substances resist the flow of charge. The quantitative measure of this property is called **resistivity (ρ)**. The quantitative measure of an object of a particular shape and size to resist the flow of charge is called its **resistance (R)** and is measured in **ohms (Ω)**. If an object is made from a homogeneous conductor, the resistance of the object when a voltage is applied uniformly to its ends is related to the resistivity of the material that it is made from by:

$$R = \rho \frac{L}{A}$$

This formula demonstrates that if the length of a wire is doubled or its cross-sectional area is cut in half, its resistance is also doubled. This is similar to what we

7-3
Circuits

would expect for fluid flowing through a pipe. Many useful analogies can be made between fluid flow and electron flow.

The product of the resistance (R) and the current (i) gives the voltage.

$$V = iR$$

This is known as **Ohm's law**. Ohm's law is a very useful formula for analyzing circuits. This law also reveals another useful analogy between fluids and electricity. Recall from Lecture 5 that the change in pressure in a real fluid moving through a horizontal pipe with constant diameter is given by the product of the volume flow rate and the resistance ($\Delta P = QR$). Because we are probably more intuitive about fluids, it is often helpful to think of current as flow through a constant diameter pipe, and voltage as the difference in height between points in the pipe. (More precisely, voltage is analogous to gh.)

If we grasp this analogy, it makes a useful aid in remembering Kirchoff's two rules. **Kirchoff's first rule** states that the amount of current flowing into any node must be the same amount that flows out. A **node** is any intersection of wires. If we imagine current as fluid, it becomes obvious that the rate at which fluid flows into an intersection must match the rate at which fluid flows out. Otherwise, a pipe would burst. **Kirchoff's second rule** states that the voltage around any path in a circuit must sum to zero. If we imagine voltage as the height difference between two points, this rule states the obvious that the height of the starting point does not change when we go around some path (regardless of the path) and end up back where we started.

A battery adds energy to a circuit by increasing the voltage from one point to another. In our analogy to fluids, a battery pumps the fluid to a greater height. Batteries are rated with an **electromotive force (EMF)**. EMF is not a force at all, but is simply a fancy word for voltage. In fact, it is a mistake. EMF was named before scientists really understood voltage.

Real batteries have internal resistance. Most of the time on the MCAT, there will be no internal resistance. Always assume that there is no internal resistance unless otherwise indicated. To account for internal resistance, simply redraw the battery and place behind it, or in front of it, a resistor the size of the internal resistance.

Here is an example of my analogous fluid circuit. Each spinning wheel represents resistance as it resists the movement of the fluid. Technically, voltage should only drop across resistance as per Ohm's law, so in my fluid circuit, the height of the fluid should only change when the fluid goes through a resistor.

A battery works to put energy back into the circuit. To analyze this circuit, we add the voltage drop across each resistor, and set it equal to the voltage of the battery. This would be analogous to the work done on each wheel set equal to the work done by me. (More precisely, we would divide the work by the mass to arrive at the potential; however, this unnecessarily complicates the analogy.)

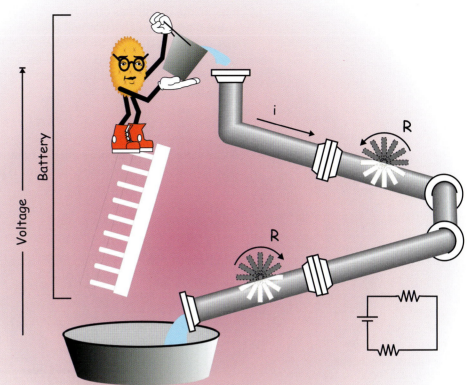

A **capacitor** is used to temporarily store energy in a circuit. It stores it in the form of separated charge. In a **parallel plate capacitor**, two plates made from conductive material are separated by a very small distance. On a charged capacitor, one plate holds positive charge, and the other plate holds the exact same amount of negative charge. This separation of charge creates an electric field that is constant everywhere between the plates. The electric field is given by:

$$E = \frac{1}{K}\frac{Q}{A\varepsilon_o}$$

Notice that this K is not the Coulomb's constant. This is the dielectric K, which we will discuss below. Q is the charge on either plate. The ε_o term is derived from Coulomb's constant k. It is related to k by:

$$k = \frac{1}{4\pi\varepsilon_o}$$

By definition, capacitance is the ability to store charge per unit voltage. In other words, something with a high capacity can store a lot of charge at low voltage.

$$C = \frac{Q}{V}$$

In a parallel plate capacitor, since the charge sits on the surface of the plates, the taller and wider the face of each plate, the more charge each plate will be able to store. Recall that charge sits on the surface of a charged conductor. In a charged capacitor, the charge sits on only the inside face of each plate. Therefore, the thickness of the plates of a capacitor will not increase their ability to store charge. Recall also that voltage is defined by distance ($V = Ed$). Thus, the farther the plates are separated, the greater the voltage, and the lower the capacitance. The physical makeup of a parallel plate capacitor in terms of plate area (A) and separation distance (d) is given by:

$$C = K\frac{A\varepsilon_\text{o}}{d}$$

It's easy to see where the formula for energy stored by a capacitor comes from. If we imagine a capacitor with no charge on it, the voltage across this capacitor must be zero. For each unit of charge that we add, the voltage increases proportionally ($Q = CV$). If we graph this, we get a straight line. The area under this line is the product of charge times voltage, or energy. The area is a triangle, which is ½ base times height or ½QV.

A capacitor's job is to store energy (generally for quick use in the future). The energy (U) stored in any shape capacitor is given by:

$$U = \frac{1}{2}QV \quad \text{or} \quad U = \frac{1}{2}CV^2 \quad \text{or} \quad U = \frac{1}{2}\frac{Q^2}{C}$$

If you know any one of these equations, the others can be derived from $Q = CV$.

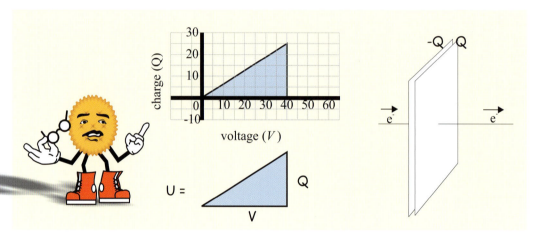

In our fluid circuit, a capacitor would look like this:

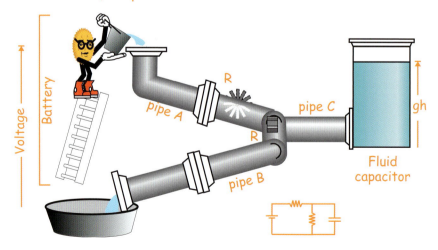

As the fluid comes to the fork at pipe B and C, some fluid would move in each direction. As the fluid capacitor fills, the fluid flow through pipe C would eventually come to a stop and all the fluid would move through pipe B. In order to maintain the fluid capacitor at height h, fluid flow through pipe A would have to have kinetic energy equal to the gravitational potential of the fluid capacitor. This results in the equation $v = \sqrt{2gh}$. The fluid capacitor now stores energy for the circuit. If flow through pipe A is suddenly blocked, the capacitor would empty with an initial velocity of $v = \sqrt{2gh}$. You should recognize the shape of the voltage vs. time graphs for charging and discharging a capacitor. Since gh is analogous to voltage, the gh vs. time graph is the same shape.

The **dielectric constant, _K_**, refers to the substance between the plates of a capacitor. The substance between the plates must be an insulator, otherwise it would conduct electrons from one plate to the other, not allowing any buildup of charge. A dielectric acts to resist the creation of an electric field, and thus allow the capacitor to store more charge (to have greater capacitance). Usually a dielectric contains dipoles oriented in random directions. Recall that a dipole in an external electric field has potential energy depending upon its orientation. When the electric field begins to build up between the plates of a capacitor, the dipoles are rotated to point in the direction of the electric field (from a physics not a chemistry sense). This rotation requires energy in the form of work done on the dielectric. The work is conserved in the field, thus the capacitor is able to store more energy. Another way to look at it is from the standpoint that each dielectric creates its own electric field that reduces the overall electric field within the capacitor. The more charge required to build an electric field, the more energy stored within a capacitor. The dielectric constant of a vacuum is defined to be unity (one). Air is very close to one, and all other dielectric constants increase from there.

One other effect of a dielectric is to limit the value of the possible voltage across the plates. At some maximum voltage, the dielectric will break down and conduct electricity. This value of a dielectric is called the _dielectric strength_. If dielectric strength appears on the MCAT, it will be explained in a passage.

In order to analyze a circuit you must recognize the symbols **for a battery, a capacitor, and a resistor**.

Work is done on the dielectric and energy is stored in the dielectric.

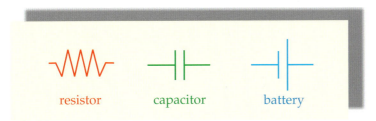

resistor   capacitor   battery

Lines connecting components should be considered completely non-resistive wires.

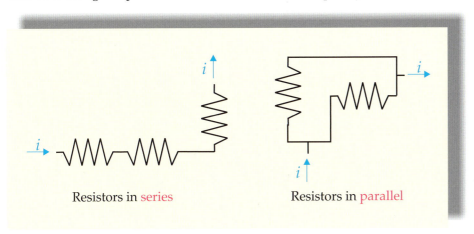

Resistors in series   Resistors in parallel

You also must be able to recognize when these components are in parallel and when they are in series. This has nothing to do with their orientation in space; parallel components are not always pointing in the same direction. Components lined up in a row, like train cars, are in **series**. More precisely, any two components not separated by a node are in series. Single components in alternate paths connecting the same nodes are in **parallel**.

When resistors are in series, their total resistance (effective resistance, R_{eff}) is the sum of their resistances.

$$R_{eff} = R_1 + R_2 + \dots \quad \text{(Resistors in series)}$$

When they are in parallel, their effective resistance can be arrived at through the following equation:

$$\frac{1}{R_{eff}} = \frac{1}{R_1} + \frac{1}{R_2} + \dots \quad \text{(Resistors in parallel)}$$

Capacitors are exactly opposite. In parallel their capacitance sums directly to give an effective capacitance:

$$C_{eff} = C_1 + C_2 + \dots \quad \text{(Capacitors in parallel)}$$

in series they follow the equation below:

$$\frac{1}{C_{eff}} = \frac{1}{C_1} + \frac{1}{C_2} + \dots \quad \text{(Capacitors in series)}$$

To solve any circuit on the MCAT, we must simplify it as shown below. We begin by replacing components in parallel and series with their corresponding effective components. We continue this process until we have our simplified circuit; one of each element. Next we use Ohm's law to find the missing quantity. For more complicated circuits we would have to use Kirchoff's rules. The solutions to more complicated circuits will not be required on the MCAT.

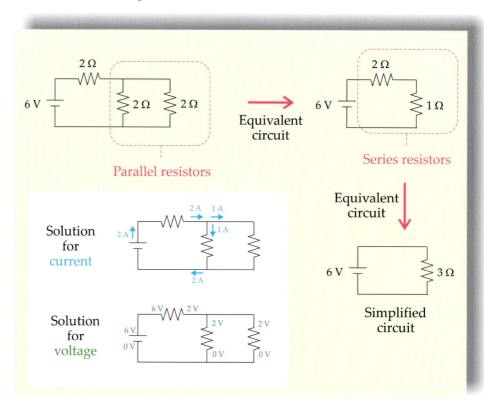

Electrical **power** is the same quality as mechanical power, just as electric energy is the same quality as mechanical energy. In other words, power is power regardless of what source produced it. Power is often used on the MCAT to integrate electricity and mechanics into the same question. For instance, you may be given the voltage and current of a machine and be asked how quickly it can lift a mass to a certain height. In such a problem you would set the electrical power equal to mechanical power. The equations for electric power are:

$$P = iV \quad \text{and} \quad P = i^2R \quad \text{and} \quad P = V^2/R$$

If you remember any one of these, the others can be derived from Ohm's law by plugging in for V, i, or R.

As current goes through a resistor, heat is generated. The rate at which heat is generated is the power dissipated. The second and third equation shown are applicable only to energy dissipated as heat by a resistor. This is unlikely to cause any confusion on the MCAT.

153. What is net force on the dipole inside the capacitor if the plates are separated by 1 cm?

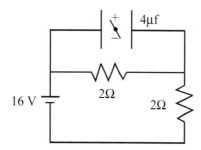

- **A.** 0 N
- **B.** 4 N
- **C.** 8 N
- **D.** 16 N

154. Each resistor in the circuit below has a resistance of 2 Ω. The battery is a 12 volt battery. What is the current across resistor B?

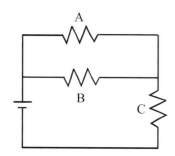

- **A.** 1 A
- **B.** 2 A
- **C.** 3 A
- **D.** 4 A

155. Which of the following changes to a parallel plate capacitor would not increase its capacitance?

- **A.** decreasing the distance between the plates
- **B.** increasing the area of the plates
- **C.** increasing the dielectric constant
- **D.** increasing the voltage across the plates

156. The resistors in the circuits below each represent a light bulb. If all three circuits use the same size battery, which circuit will produce the most light?

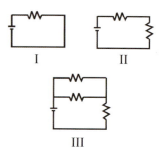

- **A.** I only
- **B.** II only
- **C.** III only
- **D.** I, II, and III will produce the same amount of light.

157. If all the resistors in the circuit pictured below have equal resistances, and the current flowing into resistor A is 4 amps, what is the current flowing into resistor F?

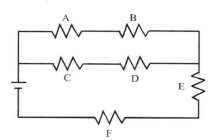

- **A.** 2 A
- **B.** A
- **C.** 8 A
- **D.** 16 A

158. What is the energy required to operate a 60 W light bulb for 1 minute?

- **A.** 1 J
- **B.** 60 J
- **C.** 360 J
- **D.** 3600 J

GO ON TO THE NEXT PAGE.

159. The circuit shown below has three resistors connected in parallel to a battery.

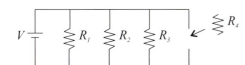

When an additional resistor, R_4 is added to the circuit:

A.   The voltage produced by the battery will be increased.
B.   The voltage produced by the battery will be decreased.
C.   The current produced by the battery will be decreased.
D.   The power produced by the batter will be increased.

160. All of the following expressions are equal to an Ohm EXCEPT:

A. $\dfrac{V\,\text{sec}}{C}$

B. $\dfrac{W}{A^2}$

C. $\dfrac{A}{V}$

D. $\dfrac{V^2}{W}$

 STOP.

7-5 AC Current

Up to now, we have considered only **direct current (dc current)**, where the net movement of electrons is in one direction around the circuit. Since movement of the electrons creates power regardless of direction, electrons do not have to be driven in one direction. **Alternating current (ac current)** is created by oscillating electrons back and forth in simple harmonic motion. This is the current that is commonly used in home outlets in the U.S. Since it is simple harmonic motion, the voltage or the current can be described by a sine wave. Maximum current occurs when the electrons are at maximum velocity. The important thing to know about ac current on the MCAT is that the maximum voltage or current is given by:

$$V_{max} = \sqrt{2}V_{rms}$$

$$i_{max} = \sqrt{2}i_{rms}$$

The 'rms' stands for root mean square. In other words, it is the square *root* of the average (*mean*) of the *squares*. To find the 'rms' value of something, you square all the terms, take the average, and then take the square root. The reason that rms values are used for sine wave functions is that the average value of a sine wave is zero. The electric company wants to charge you for the electricity that you have used. The average ac current is zero. Since the current is only at a maximum periodically, they can't charge you for the maximum either. Thus they charge you for the rms value.

It doesn't hurt to know that the 'rms' voltage in the U.S. is typically 120 volts. This corresponds to a 170 volt maximum.

7-6 Magnetism

Magnetic fields have many similarities to electric fields. Magnetic field strength is measured in units of **tesla, *T***. Like the positive and the negative of electricity, a magnetic field comes with *north* and *south* poles, where **like poles repel and opposite poles attract**. Unlike electric charges, magnetic poles have never been found to exist separately; one pole always accompanies the other. Similar to the electric field, the magnetic field can be represented by lines of force. The lines of force in a magnetic field point from the north pole to the south pole. Interestingly, the Earth's magnetic field points from the geographic South Pole to the geographic North Pole. Thus, what is called the magnetic north pole is really the south pole of the Earth's magnetic dipole. (The actual magnetic poles are also 11.5° away from the geographic poles and constantly shifting very slowly.)

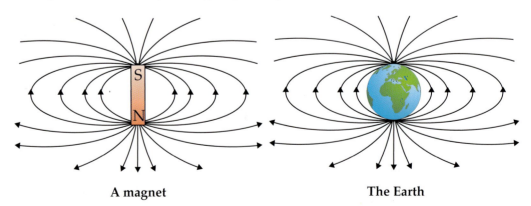

A magnet   **The Earth**

A changing electric field creates a magnetic field. A stationary charge does not create a magnetic field; a moving charge does. Current is moving charge. Thus, current creates a magnetic field. The magnetic field *B* created at a displacement *r* by a current *i* moving through a small section of wire with length *L* is given by:

$$B = \frac{\mu_o}{4\pi} \frac{iL\sin\theta}{r^2}$$

where μ_0 is a constant, called the permeability constant, and θ is the angle between the direction of the current and the displacement r. This equation (a form of the Biot-Savart Law) should not be memorized for the MCAT. It should be noted, however, that, like electric fields, magnetic field strength follows the inverse square law.

If we apply the Biot-Savart Law to a very long, straight wire the equation becomes:

$$B = \frac{\mu_o i}{2\pi r}$$

Notice that for a very long straight wire the magnetic field varies inversely with the displacement and not by its square. In other words, the magnetic field in this case varies with r, not r^2.

The direction of the magnetic field due to a current carrying wire is predicted by *right hand rule*. If, using the right hand, we place our thumb in the direction of the current and grab the wire, the direction in which our fingers wrap around the wire is the direction of the magnetic field.

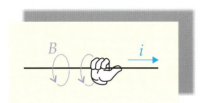

A charge moving through a magnetic field experiences a force. The force (F) on a charge (q) moving with velocity (v) through a magnetic field (B) is:

$$F = qvB\sin\theta$$

where θ is the angle between the magnetic field and the velocity of the charge. You must know that **the force is directed perpendicularly to both the velocity and the magnetic field**. This leaves only two possible directions for the force. Right hand rule also predicts which of these two directions is correct. The MCAT is unlikely to ask you to use the right hand rule, but it will require that you understand that the force is perpendicular to both the velocity and the magnetic field. To find the force with right hand rule, using your right hand, again point your thumb in the direction of the moving positive charge, and point your fingers in the direction of the magnetic field. Your palm will point in the direction of the force. For a negative charge moving in the same direction, the direction of the force is reversed. In the example to the right, a positive charge moves to the left through a magnetic field pointing downward. Right hand rule predicts that the force will be directed out of the page.

Since this force is always perpendicular to the velocity, it does no work ($W = Fd\cos\theta$). It changes the direction, but never the magnitude of the velocity. Thus, this force always acts as centripetal force and can be set equal to mv^2/r to find the radius of curvature of the path of the particle.

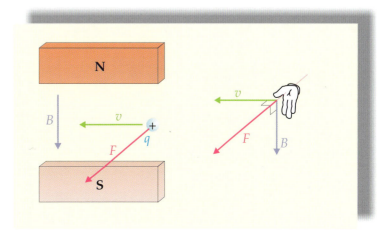

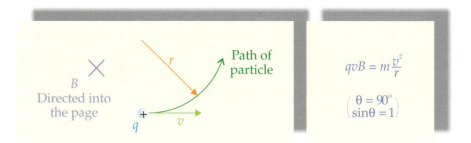

The force on a current carrying wire placed in a magnetic field is: $F = iLB\sin\theta$, where L is the length of the wire within the field and θ is the angle between the wire and the magnetic field. The direction of the force can be found using the right hand rule, and will be perpendicular to both the wire and the magnetic field.

A changing magnetic field creates an electric field. However, unlike the electric field created by a stationary charge, this field is <u>non</u>-conservative. The mechanical energy creating the electric field is not conserved, but is dissipated as heat in the charged object. Thus, electric potential has no meaning for electric fields induced by changing magnetic fields.

Imagine a loop of wire pulled out of a magnetic field. As the magnetic field around the wire changes, an electric field is created and a current develops in the wire. The current created in the wire as it moves out of the external magnetic field creates its own magnetic field. A force is required to remove the loop at a constant velocity. The work done by this force is not conserved, but, instead, creates thermal energy in the loop.

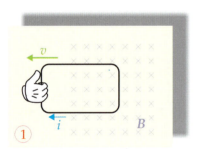

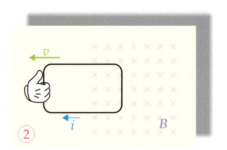

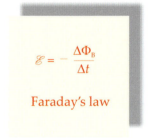

This effect is simply stated in *Faraday's law of induction*, which says that a changing *magnetic flux* ($\Delta\Phi_B/\Delta t$) induces an emf (E). The magnetic flux is the number of magnetic field lines running through the loop shown above. Since the number of these lines changes as the loop is removed from the magnetic field, an electric field and a current are produced inside the wire. By the way, the electric field is induced even if the loop is not there.

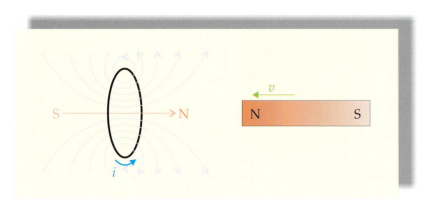

Lenz's law states that the induced current will create a magnetic field opposing the inducing magnetic field. Imagine a magnet moved toward a loop of wire. The magnetic flux through the loop changes, inducing a current in the wire. The current in the wire creates a magnetic field that opposes the magnetic field created by the magnet. The energy used to move the magnet becomes thermal energy in the ring.

Since an induced electric field is not dependent upon the presence of a loop, small eddies of current result when a conductor is moved through a magnetic field. Imagine a pendulum made from a conducting material swinging into and out of a magnetic field. *Current eddies* develop in the pendulum due to its electrons swinging through the magnetic field. The resistivity of the pendulum absorbs energy as internal energy (heat energy on the MCAT), thus changing the kinetic energy of the pendulum into internal energy. The swinging pendulum will stop swinging more quickly due to the magnetic field.

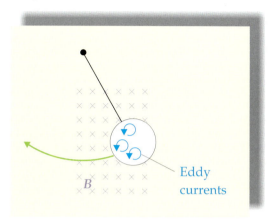

Eddy currents

Notice that in each example of an induced electric field, mechanical energy is transferred to internal energy. This is because the forces due to the induced electric fields are nonconservative.

Hold on! Don't get bent here. Most of this information on magnetism is background trivia that, if it shows up at all, is likely to be explained in a passage. Concentrate on the basics. Here's what you must know:

1. A magnetic field is generated by a moving charge, and

2. a moving charge experiences force when moving through a magnetic field.

From number 2 remember how to find the circular path of a charged particle moving through a magnetic field. Like poles repel; opposites attract. The only formula that you need to remember about magnetism for the MCAT is:

$$F = qvB$$

Don't forget that the direction of the force is perpendicular to both the velocity of the charge and the direction of the magnetic field.

7-7
Equation Summary

Electric fields due to a point charge

$$F = k\frac{q_1 q_2}{r^2} \qquad U = k\frac{q_1 q_2}{r}$$

$$E = k\frac{q_1}{r^2} \qquad V = k\frac{q_1}{r}$$

Constant electric fields

$$F = Eq \qquad U = qEd$$

$$V = Ed \qquad U = Vq$$

Resistors

$$V = iR$$

$$R_{eff} = R_1 + R_2 + \dots \quad \text{(Resistors in series)}$$

$$\frac{1}{R_{eff}} = \frac{1}{R_1} + \frac{1}{R_2} + \dots \quad \text{(Resistors in parallel)}$$

$$P = iV$$

$$P = i^2 R$$

$$P = \frac{V^2}{R}$$

Capacitors

$$C = \frac{Q}{V}$$

$$\frac{1}{C_{eff}} = \frac{1}{C_1} + \frac{1}{C_2} + \dots \quad \text{(Capacitors in series)}$$

$$C_{eff} = C_1 + C_2 + \dots \quad \text{(Capacitors in parallel)}$$

$$U = \tfrac{1}{2} QV$$

$$U = \tfrac{1}{2}\frac{Q^2}{C}$$

$$U = \tfrac{1}{2} CV^2$$

Alternating current

$$V_{max} = \sqrt{2}\, V_{rms}$$

$$i_{max} = \sqrt{2}\, i_{rms}$$

Magnetism

$$F = qvB\sin\theta$$

161. If the AC current delivered to a home by the electric company is delivered at 120 V_{rms}, what is the maximum voltage across an outlet?

   A.   86 V
   B.   120 V
   C.   170 V
   D.   220 V

162. The north pole of the earth's magnetic field is at the geographic south pole. A compass is a small magnet whose north pole end is drawn in the approximate direction of:

   A.   the geographic south pole along the lines of the magnetic field.
   B.   the geographic north pole along the lines of the magnetic field.
   C.   the geographic south pole against the lines of the magnetic field.
   D.   the geographic north pole against the lines of the magnetic field.

163. A charged particle moves horizontally through a magnetic field which points directly upward. The force on the particle due to the magnetic field is:

   A.   perpendicular to the magnetic field and parallel to the velocity of the particle.
   B.   parallel to the magnetic field and perpendicular to the velocity of the particle.
   C.   parallel to the magnetic field and parallel to the velocity of the particle.
   D.   perpendicular to the magnetic field and perpendicular to the velocity of the particle.

164. The magnetic field created by a long straight current carrying wire:

   A.   decreases in strength proportionally with the distance from the wire.
   B.   decreases in strength with the square of the distance from the wire.
   C.   increases in strength proportionally with the distance from the wire.
   D.   increases in strength with the square of the distance from the wire.

165. A charged oil drop is allowed to fall through the electric field created by the plates as shown. In order to give the oil drop a straight trajectory, a magnetic field should be established with field lines pointing:

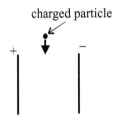

charged particle

   A.   left to right.
   B.   right to left.
   C.   out of the page.
   D.   into the page.

166. A positively charged particle is moving through a magnetic field of strength B as shown below.

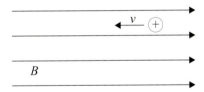

The force experience by the particle due to the magnetic field is:

   A.   to the right.
   B.   to the left.
   C.   into the page.
   D.   equal to zero.

167. A stationary loop of wire is placed in a magnetic field directed into the page as shown below.

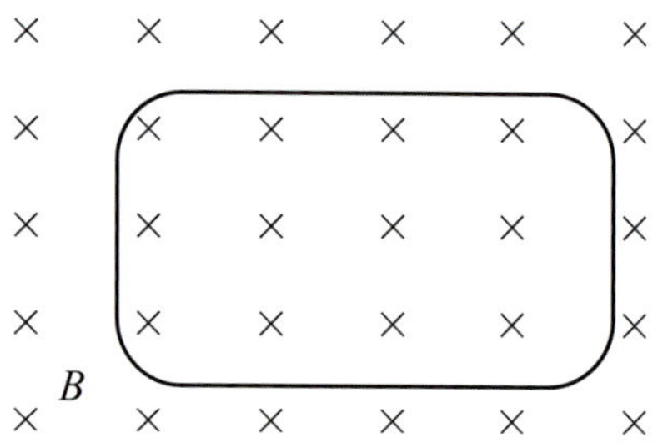

The current in the loop of wire is:

A. clockwise if the magnitude of the magnetic field is decreasing.

B. clockwise if the magnitude of the magnetic field is increasing.

C. clockwise if the magnitude of the magnetic field is increasing or decreasing.

D. No current will flow through the loop if the magnetic field is increasing or decreasing.

168. A particle of mass m is fired into a magnetic field of strength B at a speed v. The particle travels in a circular path inside the field with a radius r. Which of the following expressions gives the magnitude of the charge on the particle?

A. $\dfrac{vB}{mr}$

B. $\dfrac{mv}{Br}$

C. $\dfrac{mr}{v^2 B}$

D. $\dfrac{mv^2}{Br}$

STOP.

Lecture 8

Light and Optics

In Lecture 7 we learned that a changing electric field creates a magnetic field and vice versa. An **electromagnetic wave** is the traveling oscillation of an electric and a magnetic field. The fields are perpendicular to each other and the direction of propagation is perpendicular to both fields. An electromagnetic wave is a transverse wave.

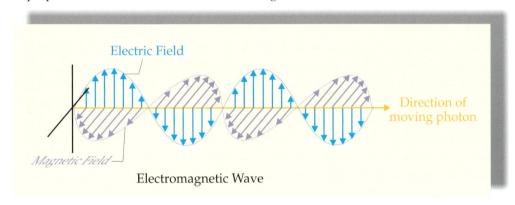

Electromagnetic Wave

The speed (c) at which an electromagnetic wave propagates through free space is constant and is always equal to the ratio of the magnitudes of the electric field and the magnetic field:

$$c = \frac{E}{B}$$

Although the electric field is much larger when compared in SI units, the energies of the two fields are exactly equal. The above equation is useless for the MCAT. It is given here to remind you of the nature of electromagnetic radiation.

It is interesting to note that all electromagnetic waves are generated by the acceleration of electric charge. If a charge oscillates with frequency f, it radiates energy in the form of electromagnetic radiation at the same frequency. The rate and the direction in which an electromagnetic wave is transporting energy per unit area is described by a vector S, called the *Poynting vector*. The Poynting vector is always perpendicular to both E and B, and has a magnitude of $EB\sin\theta$.

Electromagnetic radiation exists in all wavelengths. **Light** is a tiny sliver from the electromagnetic spectrum. For the MCAT you should memorize that visible light includes all wavelengths from 390×10^{-9} m to 700×10^{-9} m. You should also know that the shorter wavelengths correspond to violet light and the longer wavelengths to red light. Just beyond the visible spectrum is **ultraviolet** (beyond violet) light on the smaller wavelength side, and **infrared** (beyond red) on the longer wavelength side.

Notice that each wavelength has a corresponding frequency. This is because the speed of light in a vacuum is constant, which means that we can derive frequency f from wavelength λ. From our wave equation, $v = f\lambda$, we have:

$$c = f\lambda$$

Light is slower when propagating through a medium. The speed of light propagating through some medium is found using a constant for that medium, called the **index of refraction (n)**. The index of refraction compares the speed c of light in a vacuum to the speed v of light in a particular medium.

$$n = \frac{c}{v}$$

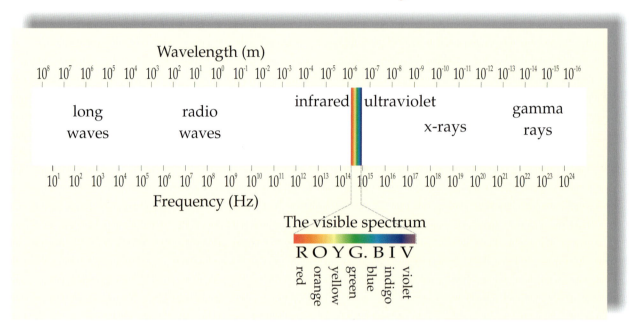

Since nothing exceeds the speed of light in a vacuum, all media have a refractive index greater than one. The greater the index of refraction for a medium, the slower light moves through that particular medium. Typically used on the MCAT are the indices of refraction for water and glass: 1.3 and 1.5 respectively. It helps to be familiar with these.

Light is made up of photons. Each photon represents an electromagnetic wave. If we examine only the electric fields of these electromagnetic waves, in typical visible light emanating from a point source (called *isotropic light*), the fields are oriented in random directions. If we use a device to screen out all photons not having an electric field in one particular direction, the resulting light with all electric fields oriented in the same direction is called **plane-polarized light**. When isotropic light is polarized, it loses one half of its intensity, since it loses from its electric field all components in one direction and keeps all components perpendicular to that direction.

Light has a **dual nature**. It acts like both a wave and a particle. The propagation properties of light can be described with wave theory, while the energy transformation properties of light are usually best described by particle theory. Neither wave nor particle theory alone explains the phenomenon of light.

We can approximate light as a ray moving in a straight line, and represent it as an arrow. This is called *geometrical optics*.

Like any other wave, when light meets an interface between two media, some of its energy reflects and some may also refract. The angles made by a light ray when it reflects or refracts are measured from a line normal to the interface. The angle at which the light ray strikes the interface is called the **angle of incidence**. The angle at which it reflects is called the **angle of reflection**. The angle at which it refracts is called the **angle of refraction**. The angle of incidence is equal to the angle of reflection. You can remember this because the collision of photons against the interface is completely elastic; the photons lose no kinetic energy.

$$\theta_{incidence} = \theta_{reflection}$$

The angle of refraction is given by **Snell's law**:

$$n_1\sin\theta_1 = n_2\sin\theta_2$$

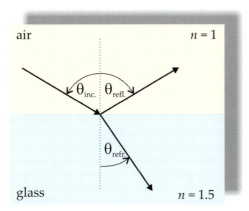

where the subscripts 1 and 2 specify the respective interfacing media. Notice that in Snell's law, the angle of incidence and refraction are not specified; it makes no difference if light is moving from medium 1 to medium 2 or from medium 2 to medium 1.

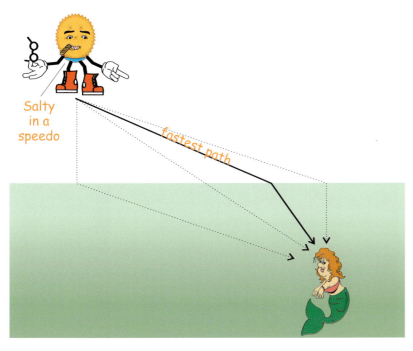

Salty in a speedo

fastest path

The path that light travels between any two points is the shortest possible path for light in terms of time. This should help you decide which way light will bend at any interface. Imagine that I must rescue a fair maiden in a swimming pool. She and I are both several yards from the edge of the pool. I must approximate at what point I should enter the pool in order to reach her the fastest. I could either find a pen and paper and calculate Snell's law based upon my velocity on land and in the pool, or I could just guess that since I am faster on land, I should travel farther on land. Just like light, I am looking for the shortest path in terms of time and I will bend my path in the same direction at the interface.

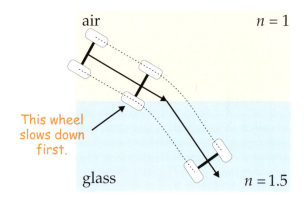

Another simple way to choose the direction that light will bend is to imagine a pair of wheels on an axle. The wheels move fastest where light moves fastest and they always straddle the light ray. When the wheels hit the interface, the first wheel to make contact will either speed up, if light would speed up ('n' decreases), or slow down if light would slow down ('n' increases). Since the wheels hit the interface at different times, the axle will turn as the wheels move at different speeds. The direction in which the axle turns is the direction in which light will bend.

When light crosses into a new medium, the frequency remains the same and the wavelength changes. If the medium's index of refraction is higher, the wavelengths become shorter; if the index is lower, then the wavelengths become longer.

The energy of a single photon is given by:

$$E = hf \text{ (E is energy not electric field.)}$$

where h is Planck's constant (discussed in Chemistry Lecture 6). This equation shows that higher frequencies, such as violet and blue light, have more energy than lower frequencies. (**Warning:** Do not be mislead by this equation: This equation gives the energy per photon. It turns out that if we double the frequency, we also double the number of photons increasing the intensity by a factor of four as expected.)

When light is coming from a medium with a higher index of refraction, the angle of incidence can be so great as to cause **total internal reflection**. In other words, if the angle of incidence is large enough, the entire amount of photons will be reflected at the angle of reflection, and none will refract. This angle is called the **critical angle**. The critical angle is derived from Snell's law by recognizing that the angle of refraction is 90° and that sin90° = 1:

$$\theta_{\text{critical}} = \sin^{-1}\left(\frac{n_2}{n_1}\right)$$

An interesting feature about Snell's law is that, at first glance, it seems to violate the conservation of energy. Since the frequency of the light wave does not change from one medium to the next, both the reflected light and the refracted light must have the same energy. This appears to be twice the energy with which the light started. The trick is that the light still has the same energy per photon. However, some of the photons have reflected and some have refracted. Thus, the sum of the intensities of the refracted and reflected beam equals the intensity of the incident beam. Energy is conserved.

The concept of the critical angle is used in fiber optics, where a beam of light is trapped inside a glass tube and signals are sent using the energy of the beam.

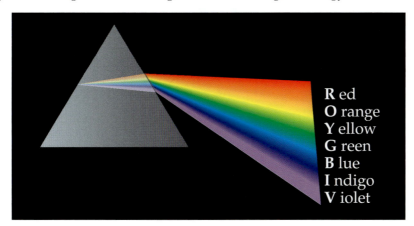

R ed
O range
Y ellow
G reen
B lue
I ndigo
V iolet

All types of waves refract. The index of refraction for any substance varies slightly with frequency. Longer wavelengths (lower frequencies) move faster through a medium than shorter wavelengths (higher frequencies), and therefore bend less dramatically at the media interface. As a result, white light, which is made up of all the frequencies in the visible spectrum, is split by a prism in a phenomenon known as **chromatic dispersion**.

Diffraction is another type of wave-bending phenomenon. All types of waves diffract. When a wave moves through a small opening, it bends around the corners of the opening. This is called diffraction. Significant diffraction occurs only when the size of the opening is on the order of the wavelength or smaller. The smaller the opening and the larger the wavelength, the greater the bending of the wave. Diffraction is a limiting factor for geometrical optics. If we attempt to create a ray of light by blocking out all the light from a single source except for a small hole, the light coming through the single hole experiences diffraction and spreads out, frustrating our efforts to create the ray. The smaller we make the hole, the greater the spreading of the light.

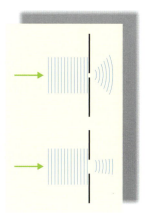

Diffraction of light can result in an image of light and dark bands or in dispersion and the creation of colors. Both phenomena depend upon destructive and constructive interference when waves with altered paths meet as shown below.

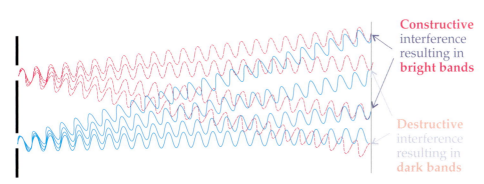

Constructive interference resulting in **bright bands**

Destructive interference resulting in **dark bands**

**Waves diffract as they move through the openings.
When the diffracted waves meet
interference forms bright and dark bands.**

169. A ray of light strikes a flat window as shown. Which ray most closely approximates the path of light as it exits the window?

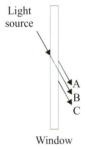

Window

A. A
B. B
C. C
D. Some light will follow all three paths.

170. Compared to humans, bees perceive a slightly higher frequency of electromagnetic waves. Based on only this information, to which of the following flower colors is a bee more likely to be attracted?

A. green
B. red
C. yellow
D. blue

171. The Coma Cluster is a galaxy approximately 2.7×10^{15} km away from earth. How many years does it take for light from the Coma Cluster to reach earth? (Note: light travels at approximately 3×10^8 m/s)

A. $\dfrac{2.7 \times 10^{15}}{1} \times \dfrac{1}{3 \times 10^8} \times \dfrac{1}{60} \times \dfrac{1}{60} \times \dfrac{1}{24} \times \dfrac{1}{365} \times \dfrac{1000}{1}$

B. $\dfrac{2.7 \times 10^{15}}{1} \times \dfrac{1}{3 \times 10^8} \times \dfrac{1}{60} \times \dfrac{1}{24} \times \dfrac{1}{365} \times \dfrac{1000}{1}$

C. $\dfrac{2.7 \times 10^{15}}{1} \times \dfrac{3 \times 10^8}{1} \times \dfrac{1}{60} \times \dfrac{1}{60} \times \dfrac{1}{24} \times \dfrac{1}{365} \times \dfrac{1000}{1}$

D. $\dfrac{1}{2.7 \times 10^{15}} \times \dfrac{3 \times 10^8}{1} \times \dfrac{60}{1} \times \dfrac{60}{1} \times \dfrac{24}{1} \times \dfrac{365}{1} \times \dfrac{1000}{1}$

172. All of the following are indicative of the wave nature and not the particle nature of light EXCEPT:

A. diffraction
B. interference
C. dispersion
D. reflection

173. A piece of glass shaped as shown, with a refractive index of 1.5 allows light to pass through it striking point B. In order to make the light strike point A, the piece of glass should be:

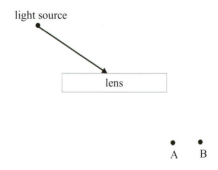

Note: diagram not drawn to scale

A. raised.
B. lowered.
C. made thicker from top to bottom.
D. made thinner from top to bottom.

174. If a light on a dimmer switch is gradually turned down, it will generally show a red glow at the moment before it is turned off. This is because red light:

A. moves more slowly through air than light of any other color.
B. moves more quickly through air than light of any other color.
C. has more energy than light of any other color.
D. has less energy than light of any other color.

175. The index of refraction of glass is 1.5. How long does it take for light to pass through a plate of glass that is 1 cm thick?

A. 5×10^{-8} sec
B. 5×10^{-11} sec
C. 2×10^{-8} sec
D. 2×10^{-11} sec

176. All of the following are examples of wave diffraction EXCEPT:

A. A light wave bends when passing from air to water.
B. Music is audible around a corner from the source.
C. The shadow cast by statue is blurred at the edges.
D. Ripples in water become semicircular after passing through a small space.

STOP.

Mirrors reflect light; lenses refract light. In both cases light rays are bent. The mind may use reason and visual cues such as size and *parallax* to compensate, but the eye by itself cannot detect whether or not light rays have been bent. Without other visual cues, the mind assumes that light travels in a straight line. As a result, the mind traces straight back along the path of the light rays entering the eye and perceives an image. To the person in the diagram below, the fish appears to be where the image is formed because the person's eyes cannot detect the bending of the light.

8-2
Images

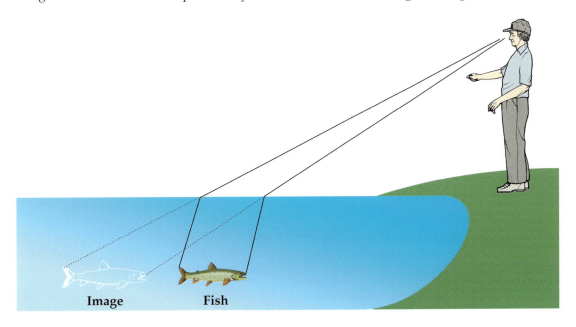

Image   Fish

An image may or may not exist. A **virtual image** does not actually exist outside the mind of the observer; no light rays emanate from a virtual image. If a sheet of white paper is placed at the position of a virtual image, no image will appear on the paper. A **real image** exists separately from the observer. Rays of light actually intersect and then emanate from the point of intersection to form a real image. If a sheet of white paper is placed at the position of a real image, the image will appear on the paper.

Your reflection in a flat mirror is an example of a virtual image. Your reflection appears to be behind the mirror, but if you go behind the mirror and look for it, you won't find it. On a warm day, light from the sky enters the hot air just above the pavement, refracts, and shines into a driver's eyes, forming an image that may appear like water. This image is called a mirage. If you went to the pavement at the position of the mirage, you would not find the image of the sky. The mirage is a virtual image. The image of the fish in the diagram above is also a virtual image.

8-3
Mirrors and Lenses

There are two types of mirrors: <u>**convex**</u> and <u>**concave**</u>. There are also two types of lenses: <u>**diverging**</u> (*concave*) and <u>**converging**</u> (*convex*). You should recognize both names for each lens type, but think of them as diverging and converging because a diverging lens acts like a convex mirror and a converging lens acts like a concave mirror.

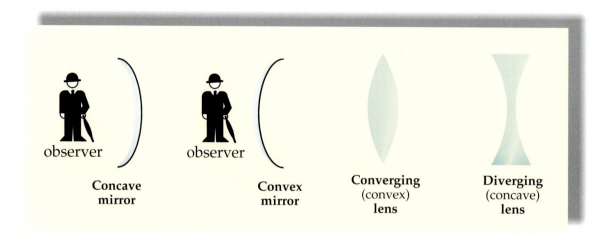

Concave mirror   Convex mirror   Converging (convex) lens   Diverging (concave) lens

Generally the light from the object originates from some other source and reflects off the object. However, to avoid confusion, when working with mirrors or lenses, always assume that light originates from the object.

Here's a little trick to help identify a converging lens. Just remember the three C's: A thick center converges light.

Thicker center converges

If the center of a lens is thicker than its ends, it will converge light, regardless of its shape or which direction light moves through the lens. If the center is thinner, it will diverge light.

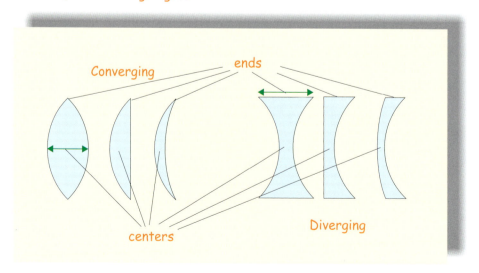

A small enough section of any curve can be extended to form a perfect circle. The **radius of curvature** for that small section of the curve is the radius of the extended circle. The diagram below shows the radii of curvature for two sections of a curved line. Notice that a smaller radius of curvature indicates a sharper curve. The straighter the line, the larger the radius of curvature. A straight line has an infinitely large radius of curvature.

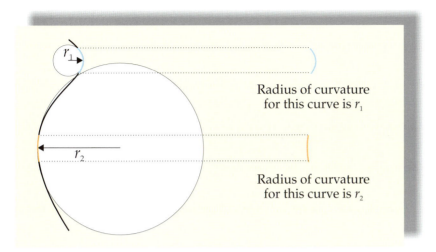

Although the mirrors in this lecture are called **spherical mirrors**, only a parabolically curved surface will focus all parallel lines to a single focal point. In other words, the equations for the rest of the chapter are only approximations for spherical mirrors, and they require that the rays of light are at small angles. For the same reasons, spherical lenses produce flawed images in a phenomenon called *spherical aberration*. This can lead to confusion if you are drawing ray-diagrams to find an image.

Light from horizontal rays is reflected by concave mirrors (or refracted by converging lenses) to focus on a single point called the **focal point**. For convex mirrors and diverging lenses, horizontal rays of light are reflected and refracted outward from a single point called the focal point. The focal point of convex mirrors and diverging lenses is found by tracing back along the reflected or refracted rays.

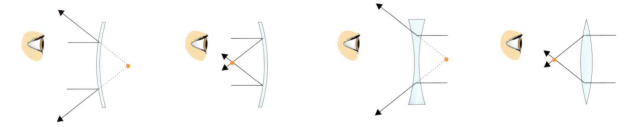

The focal point for any mirror or lens is separated from the mirror or lens by the **focal length**. The focal length (f_{mirror}) for a mirror is related to the radius of curvature (r) as follows:

$$f_{mirror} = \tfrac{1}{2}r$$

The focal length for a lens is affected by the refractive index of the lens (n_1) and the refractive index of the substance surrounding the lens (n_2). (Usually the substance surrounding the lens is air, $n = 1$.) The focal length of a lens (f_{lens}) is given by the *lens maker's equation*:

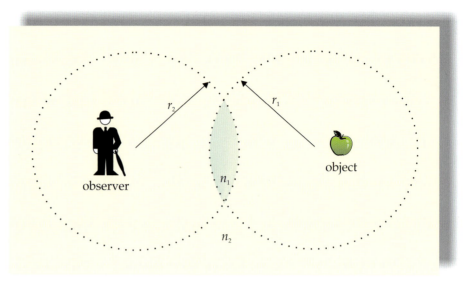

$$\frac{1}{f_{lens}} = \left(\frac{n_1}{n_2} - 1\right)\left(\frac{1}{r_1} - \frac{1}{r_2}\right)$$

In the example above, r_2 is negative. Notice that this equation indicates that a lens immersed in a fluid with an equal index of refraction will not bend light. In other words, when $n_1 = n_2$, a lens will not refract light.

You should be aware that since the index of refraction varies for different frequencies, the focal point of a lens also varies with frequency resulting in *chromatic aberration*. This is an entirely separate phenomenon from *spherical aberration* mentioned earlier in this lecture.

A lens has something called **power**. This power is not the same as the power in mechanics. The power of a lens is measured in **diopters**, which has equivalent units of m⁻¹. The power of a lens is simply the inverse of the focal length.

$$P = \frac{1}{f}$$

The rest of the equations in this lecture apply equally to both mirrors and lenses.

Ray-diagrams are a useful tool in understanding mirrors and lenses. They help locate the position of an image. However, they are not useful on the MCAT since they are time consuming and inaccurate. Later, Salty will offer a preferable alternative to ray-diagrams for solving optics problems on the MCAT, but for now, you should learn to draw them. When drawing a ray diagram for a mirror or lens, imagine the object emitting three photons from a single point. In the example below, this point is the tip of the candle flame. Each photon takes a different path. For simplicity, lenses will be considered infinitely thin, so refraction occurs at the center of the lens. The first photon (1°) moves parallel to the ground, strikes the mirror or lens and reflects or refracts so that its path can be traced back through the focal point. By definition, all rays of light parallel to the ground will reflect or refract through the focal point or so that their paths can be traced back through the focal point. The second photon (2°) moves through, directly away from, or directly toward, a focal point and reflects or refracts parallel to the ground. The third photon (3°) strikes the

This equation has several forms, and is quite complicated to apply. The MCAT would give this equation to you with an explanation if needed. Just remember that the focal point for a lens is affected by the refractive indices of the lens and the medium that the lens is in. It is also affected by the radii of curvature of both sides of the lens.

mirror or lens at the exact middle and reflects back and at an angle equal to the angle of incidence, or, in the case of a lens, moves straight through without being affected. (This is possible because the lens is considered to be infinitely thin and both sides of the lens are parallel at the middle). We follow the paths of the photons until they meet. Where the photons meet is where the image of the tip of the candle is formed. If the photons diverge, we trace their paths backwards from the mirror or lens to where they would meet.

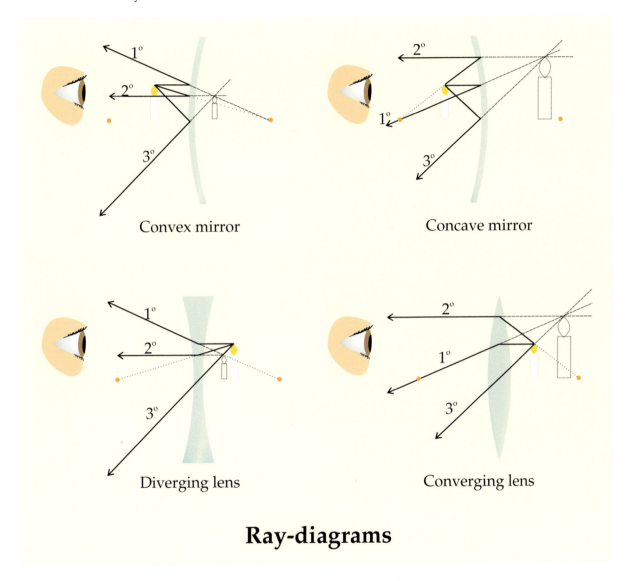

Ray-diagrams

Since light always travels the path that takes the least amount of time, although all our intersecting photons in the ray diagram travel different distances, all rays take the same amount of time for their trip. This can be explained as follows: Because light travels more slowly while in the lens, the ray that travels the farthest, travels the shortest distance through the lens. (In very strange cases where the lens has a lower index of refraction, the opposite is true.)

A mirror or a lens may magnify an image. The **lateral magnification m** is the ratio of the size of the image to the size of the object. For simplicity, we can compare only the height of the image h_i with the height of the object h_o. The magnification is also equal to the negative of the ratio of the distance of the image d_i and distance of the object d_o from the mirror or lens. The negative sign indicates that, if both distances are positive, the image is inverted.

$$m = -\frac{d_i}{d_o} = \frac{h_i}{h_o}$$

Another way to measure magnification is **angular magnification**. The closest an object can be to an individual while that individual can still focus clearly on the object is called that individual's *near point*. The angle occupied by the object θ_{np} when at the near point, compared to the angle occupied by an image θ_i of the object when in front of a lens is called the angular magnification m_θ:

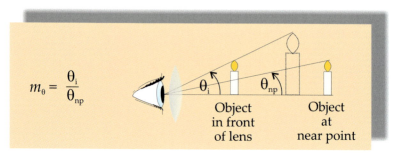

Do not confuse angular magnification with lateral magnification.

For any mirror or lens, distance of the image is related to the focal length and the distance of the object by the following equation:

$$\frac{1}{f} = \frac{1}{d_o} + \frac{1}{d_i}$$

This equation is called the **thin lens equation**; however, it applies to mirrors as well. It is called the thin lens equation because it assumes that the lens is so thin that the light bends only once when passing through the lens (instead of at both interfaces).

Objects, images, focal points, and radii of curvature are all given positive or negative values based upon their position relative to the mirror or lens. The difficult aspect of optics problems is identifying when a variable is positive or negative. The next section is devoted to a system for solving optics problems.

177. The focal distance on a mirror cut from a glass sphere with a radius of 10 cm is:

- **A.** 2.5 cm
- **B.** 5 cm
- **C.** 10 cm
- **D.** 20 cm

178. When an object is 10 cm from a certain converging lens, the image is magnified by a factor of 1.5. What is the distance of the image?

- **A.** 3.3 cm
- **B.** 6.6 cm
- **C.** 10 cm
- **D.** 15 cm

179. A glass magnifying-lens is submerged in water to view an underwater object. Compared to viewing the object with the magnifying-lens out of water, this will:

- **A.** increase the magnification.
- **B.** decrease the magnification.
- **C.** not change the magnification.
- **D.** The magnifying glass will not work at all under water.

180. Which of the following statements is (are) true?

- **I.** Virtual images can be projected onto a screen.
- **II.** Real images can never be seen.
- **III.** Real images can only be created by converging lenses and concave mirrors in a single lens or single mirror system.

- **A.** III only
- **B.** I and II only
- **C.** I and III only
- **D.** I, II, and III

181. Which of the following is not a possible path for a light ray through a glass lens?

A.   C.

B.   D.

182. The image seen in a flat bathroom mirror is a:

- **A.** real image that appears behind the mirror.
- **B.** real image that appear in front of the mirror.
- **C.** virtual image that appears behind the mirror.
- **D.** virtual image that appears in front of the mirror.

183. An increase in which of the following lens properties will increase the power of a lens?

- **I.** Index of refraction
- **II.** Focal length
- **III.** Radius of curvature on one side of the lens.

- **A.** I only
- **B.** I and II only
- **C.** II and III only
- **D.** I, II, and III

184. A concave mirror has a focal length of 4 cm. What is its radius of curvature?

- **A.** 2 cm
- **B.** 4 cm
- **C.** 8 cm
- **D.** 16 cm

STOP.

8-4
A System for Mirrors and Lenses

Mirrors and lenses may seem tricky, but, luckily, I have a system. The tough part of mirrors and lenses is deciding what's negative and what's positive. After that, it's just plug and chug with only three equations to memorize. My system with only three rules and one exception, finds the positives and negatives.

1. Begin by drawing your mirror or lens and an eye on the side on which the observer will stand. I will draw all four possibilities on the next page. Now comes the first of three rules: **"I (Eye) am positive that real is inverted."** You must memorize this sentence. On the side which the eye is drawn, write 'positive, real, inverted'. Images and focal points on this side will always be positive, real, and inverted. Images and focal points on the other side will be always be negative, virtual, and upright. No exceptions.

2. Of course, everyone knows that you must stand in front of a mirror to see anything, so the front is the side that I (eye) am on. Lenses are just the opposite, but you can also remember that a camera is a lens, and I (eye) stand behind a camera to view an object. Label the front and back of your mirror or lens. Now comes the second rule: **Objects are always positive when they are in front of a lens or a mirror and always negative when they are behind a lens or a mirror.** For single lens systems or single mirror systems, the object must be placed in front, so the object must be positive.

3. Rule number three states: As long as the object is in front, **convex mirrors and diverging lenses make negative, virtual, upright images.** As long as the object is in front, **concave mirrors and converging lenses make positive, real, inverted images _EXCEPT_ when the object is within the focal distance, in which case they make negative, virtual, upright images.**

In the case of a double lens or mirror system, simply find the image for the first lens or mirror, and use that image as the object of the second lens or mirror. _Caveat:_ For a two lens or two mirror system, you must be careful with rule number 3 because the image of the first lens or mirror may be behind the second lens or mirror. This results in a negative object distance for the second lens or mirror.

Now we can label f, d_o, and d_i positive or negative depending upon which side they are on. For a convex mirror and a diverging lens, f is always negative. For a concave mirror and a converging lens, f is always positive. Memorize the three formulas on the bottom of the next page. Any other formula for optics will be provided on the MCAT, including the lens maker's equation.

That's it. I have drawn one image for each mirror or lens to show you how the light rays are traced. However, if you are tracing light rays on the MCAT, you are wasting your time.

An image on this side is

+
real
inverted

An image on this side is

-
virtual
upright

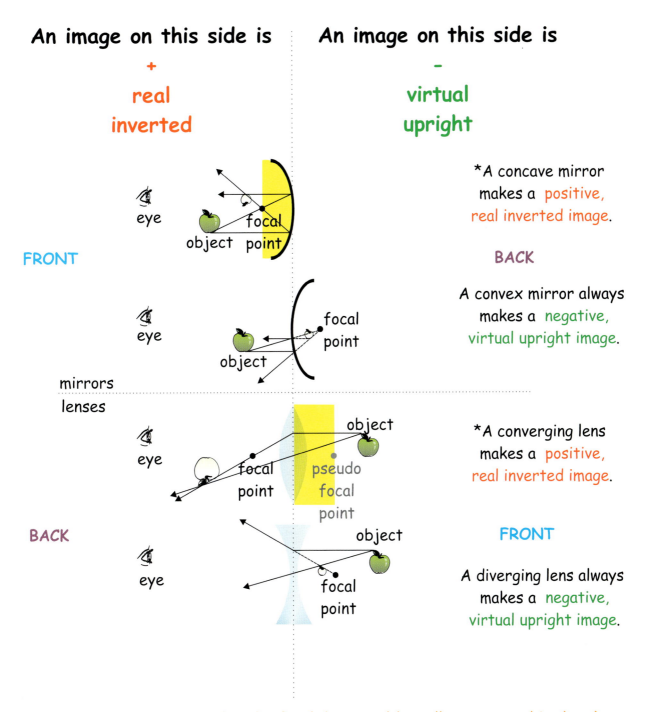

FRONT

mirrors

lenses

BACK

eye

object   focal point

eye

object   focal point

eye   focal point   pseudo focal point   object

eye   focal point   object

*A concave mirror makes a positive, real inverted image.

BACK

A convex mirror always makes a negative, virtual upright image.

*A converging lens makes a positive, real inverted image.

FRONT

A diverging lens always makes a negative, virtual upright image.

* If the object moves within the focal distance (the yellow area on this chart), a concave mirror and a converging lens will make a negative, virtual upright image.

$$P = \frac{1}{f} = \frac{1}{d_i} + \frac{1}{d_o}$$

$$M = -\frac{d_i}{d_o} = \frac{h_i}{h_o}$$

$$f_{mirrors} = \frac{1}{2}r$$

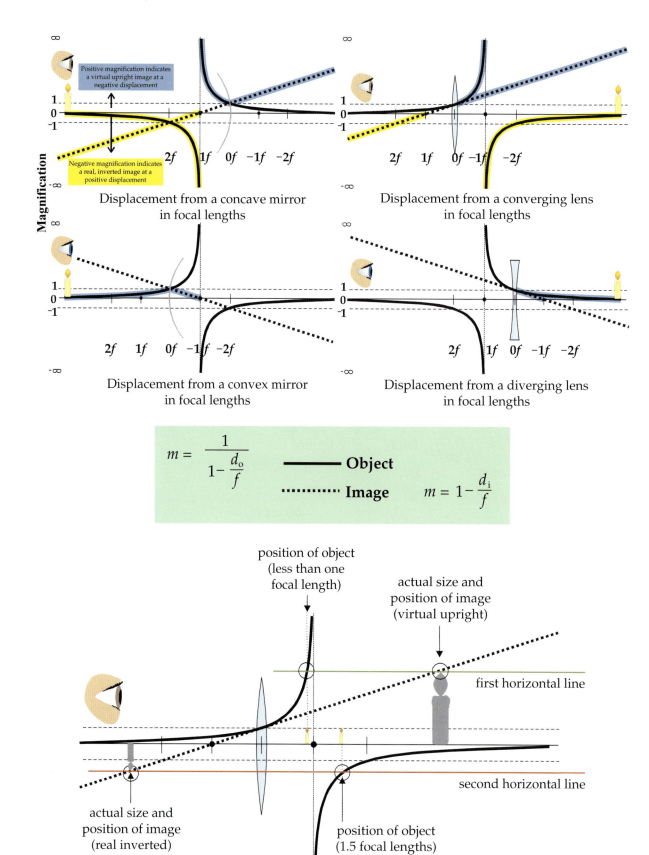

Displacement from a concave mirror in focal lengths

Displacement from a converging lens in focal lengths

Displacement from a convex mirror in focal lengths

Displacement from a diverging lens in focal lengths

Positive magnification indicates a virtual upright image at a negative displacement

Negative magnification indicates a real, inverted image at a positive displacement

Magnification

$$m = \frac{1}{1 - \dfrac{d_o}{f}}$$

—— **Object**

·········· **Image**

$$m = 1 - \frac{d_i}{f}$$

position of object (less than one focal length)

actual size and position of image (virtual upright)

first horizontal line

actual size and position of image (real inverted)

position of object (1.5 focal lengths)

second horizontal line

Handle a two lens system one lens at a time. Use the image of the first mirror or lens as the object of the second mirror or lens. Sometimes the image from the first mirror or lens is formed behind the second mirror or lens. The object distance for the second mirror or lens is negative in this case. In a single lens system, an object cannot be behind a mirror or lens, nor can it have a negative distance.

The lateral magnification of a two lens system is the product of the lateral magnification of each lens:

$$M = m_1 m_2.$$

Two lenses in contact with each other have an effective power equal to the sum of their individual powers:

$$P_{eff} = P_1 + P_2.$$

8-5
Two-lens Systems

Microscopes and telescopes can be built from two lens systems as well as from mirrors. The MCAT will give all necessary formulae concerning these apparatus.

The diagrams on the facing page are meant to increase your familiarity with lenses and mirrors. Understanding them is <u>not</u> a requirement in order to do well on the MCAT. The solid line in each diagram represents the magnification when the object is placed at a given distance. The dotted line represents the magnification when the image is formed at a given distance. Since the magnification for the image and object must match, you can find the corresponding positions of an image and an object as follows: draw a horizontal line anywhere on the graph and the object will be where your horizontal line crosses the solid line, while the image will be where your horizontal line crosses the dotted line. The magnification is the y-value of your horizontal line. The bottom diagram gives two examples.

Notice that a positive magnification indicates a virtual, upright image and a negative magnification indicates a real, inverted image. Notice that the diverging lens and convex mirror only produce smaller images for all object positions in front of the mirror or lens. In other words, in a single lens or single mirror system, a diverging lens and a convex mirror can only produce images smaller than the object. Notice that for all mirrors and lenses, the magnification of the image is directly proportional to the image distance from the focal point. For any lens or mirror, if the image is two focal lengths from the focal point, the image is magnified by two; if it is three focal lengths away, it is magnified by three; if it is half of a focal length away, it is magnified by one half (or reduced); and so on. Notice that converging lenses and concave mirrors produce smaller images while the object is outside 2 focal lengths, but larger images when the object is within 2 focal lengths.

8-6
Using the Diagrams on the Facing Page

8-7
Equation Summary

Electromagnetic radiation

$$c = f\lambda \qquad n = \frac{c}{v}$$

$$E = hf \qquad n_1\sin\theta_1 = n_2\sin\theta_2$$

Mirrors and lenses

$$f_{mirror} = \frac{1}{2}r \qquad \frac{1}{f} = \frac{1}{d_o} + \frac{1}{d_i}$$

$$P = \frac{1}{f} \qquad m = -\frac{d_i}{d_o} = \frac{h_i}{h_o}$$

185. An object stands 4 cm in front of a converging lens. If the lens has a focal distance of 1 cm, where is the image formed?

    A.   0.75 cm in front of the lens
    B.   0.75 cm behind the lens
    C.   1 cm behind the lens
    D.   1.33 cm behind of the lens

186. An inverted image is created 5 m in front of a mirror. Which of the following could be true about the mirror and the object?

    A.   The mirror is convex with less than a 5 m focal distance.
    B.   The mirror is concave with less than a 5 m focal distance.
    C.   The mirror is convex with more than a 5 m focal distance.
    D.   The mirror is concave with more than a 5 m focal distance.

187. A 1 cm candle stands 4 cm in front of a concave mirror with a 2 cm focal distance. The image is:

    A.   inverted and 1 cm tall.
    B.   inverted and 2 cm tall.
    C.   upright and 1 cm tall.
    D.   upright and 2 cm tall.

188. The focal distance of a lens is –3 m. The lens is a:

    A.   1/3 diopter converging lens.
    B.   –1/3 diopter converging lens.
    C.   1/3 diopter diverging lens.
    D.   –1/3 diopter diverging lens.

189. A lens is manufactured in such a way as to allow the object and the image to be at the same distance from the lens. If the lens is not flat, the only way this could be true is if the lens were:

    A.   a diverging lens with the object at the focal distance.
    B.   a diverging lens with the object at twice the focal distance.
    C.   a converging lens with the object at the focal distance.
    D.   a converging lens with the object at twice the focal distance.

190. An object is placed at the focal point of a converging lens. The image will appear:

    A.   on the surface of the lens.
    B.   at the focal point.
    C.   at a distance of twice the focal length.
    D.   not at all.

191. Light from the moon passes through a converging lens on the surface of the earth. If the lens has a focal length of 20 cm, at what distance from the lens will the image appear?

    A.   10 cm
    B.   20 cm
    C.   40 cm
    D.   at infinity

192. The diagram below shows an object placed in front of an unknown optical device and the image produced.

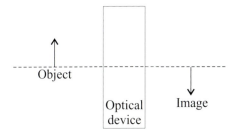

The optical device is a:

    A.   convex mirror.
    B.   concave mirror.
    C.   converging lens.
    D.   diverging lens.

STOP!

DO NOT LOOK AT THESE EXAMS UNTIL CLASS.

30-MINUTE
IN-CLASS EXAM
FOR LECTURE 1

Passage I (Questions 1-6)

In 1939 Emanuel Zacchini, a circus entertainer, had himself shot from a cannon over three 18 m tall Ferris wheels. He reached a velocity of 27 m/s and sailed to a height of nearly 24 m landing safely in a net on the other side of the Ferris wheels. The cannon muzzle and the net were 3 m above the ground. Zacchini's initial trajectory was at an angle of 53° above the horizontal.

Zacchini had two concerns about his flight. First, he could not be completely certain of the effects of air resistance and air currents. Second, the force on him while inside the cannon was so great that he would momentarily lose consciousness during the stunt. The second problem he solved by training himself to wake quickly.

Projectile motion near the surface of the earth can be approximated by the following three equations:

$$x = x_o + v_o t + \tfrac{1}{2} a t^2$$

$$v = v_o + at$$

$$v^2 = v_o^2 + 2a(x - x_o)$$

where x is displacement, v is either the horizontal or vertical velocity, t is time in flight, and a is either 0 or equal to the gravitational constant g which can be approximated at 10 m/s². The subscript denotes initial values. These equations do not take into account the effects of the medium through which the projectile moves. (Note: sin 53° = 0.8, cos 53° = 0.6)

1. Using the above equations and adjusting the net for the effects of air resistance, Zacchini should place the center of the net at a displacement:

   A.   exactly equal to x.
   B.   exactly equal to x_o.
   C.   greater than x.
   D.   less than x.

2. From the information in the passage, which of the following factors most likely plays the greatest role in Zacchini's loss of consciousness during the flight?

   A.   velocity
   B.   height
   C.   acceleration
   D.   momentum

3. Which of the following is true of a projectile in a vacuum when it reaches its maximum height?

   A.   Both its kinetic and potential energies are at a maximum.
   B.   Both its kinetic and potential energies are at a minimum.
   C.   Its kinetic energy is at a maximum and its potential energy is at a minimum.
   D.   Its potential energy is at a maximum and its kinetic energy is at a minimum.

4. What is the vertical component of Zacchini's velocity when he exits the cannon?

   A.   16.2 m/s
   B.   21.6 m/s
   C.   23.8 m/s
   D.   27.0 m/s

5. At which of the following points during the stunt is Zacchini's acceleration the greatest?

   A.   While he is still inside the muzzle of the cannon.
   B.   The moment he exits from the muzzle.
   C.   The moment before he lands in the net.
   D.   Acceleration is constant throughout the stunt.

6. Ignoring the effects of air resistance, Zacchini would have flown farthest if his initial trajectory had been:

   A.   30°
   B.   45°
   C.   53°
   D.   60°

GO ON TO THE NEXT PAGE.

Passage II (Questions 7-13)

Two boys, Tom and Jim, are at the local pool playing a game. They take turns dropping from the diving board and throwing each other a ball. Sometimes the boy dropping from the board throws the ball to the other who is waiting at the edge of the pool. Sometimes the one at the edge of the pool throws the ball to the one dropping from the board. They always drop straight down from the end of the board, and never jump upward.

The diving board is 10 m above the surface of the water and 10 m from the edge of the pool as shown in Figure 1. Tom has a mass of 60 kg and Jim has a mass of 50 kg. The ball has a mass of 1 kg.

Tom is bigger than Jim and is able to throw the ball faster. Tom throws the ball with an initial velocity of 10 m/s, whereas Jim throws the ball with an initial velocity of 8 m/s.

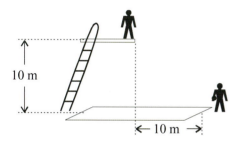

Figure 1

As the boys play the game, they vary the distance that they stand from the edge of the pool. (Note: the gravitational constant $g = 10$ m/s^2. Ignore air resistance unless otherwise indicated.)

7. If Tom throws the ball at the instant Jim leaves the board, in order to hit Jim, Tom should aim:

   A. slightly below Jim.
   B. directly at Jim.
   C. slightly above Jim.
   D. Where Tom should aim will depend upon how fast Tom throws the ball.

8. From the moment he leaves the board, approximately how long will it take Tom to hit the water?

   A. 1 s
   B. 1.4 s
   C. 2 s
   D. 4 s

9. Which of the following accurately describes Tom's fall from the board compared to Jim's fall?

   A. Tom's velocity will change faster and Tom will hit the water with greater velocity.
   B. Tom's velocity will change faster and Tom will hit the water with less velocity.
   C. Jim's velocity will change faster and Jim will hit the water with greater velocity.
   D. Both Tom and Jim will hit the water with the same velocity.

10. Tom throws the ball horizontally the moment he leaves the board. If Jim lets the ball hit the ground, Tom will be in the air:

   A. 1/5 as long as the ball.
   B. the same amount of time as the ball.
   C. 5 times as long as the ball.
   D. 25 times as long as the ball.

11. If Tom throws the ball to Jim releasing it at the moment Jim leaves the board, and Jim catches the ball at the moment he hits the water, approximately what is the maximum height achieved by the ball?

   A. 0 m
   B. 2.5 m
   C. 5 m
   D. 10 m

12. If Tom throws the ball horizontally the moment he leaves the board, approximately how far from the edge of the pool must Jim stand in order to catch it?

   A. 4 m
   B. 10 m
   C. 14 m
   D. 20 m

13. If the boys use a 2 kg ball instead of the 1 kg ball, and Tom wants the ball to follow the same projectile path, Tom must throw the ball with an initial velocity:

   A. half as great as the 1 kg ball.
   B. the same as the 1 kg ball.
   C. twice as great as the 1 kg ball.
   D. four times as great as the 1 kg ball.

GO ON TO THE NEXT PAGE.

Passage III (Questions 14-19)

Students conduct an experiment to study projectile motion. A projectile is launched from a spring-loaded gun. The gun launches the projectile from a hill and with the same speed each time. The gun is aimed so that the initial velocity of the projectile has an angle θ from the horizontal. The angle θ is increased by 15° each time the projectile is launched. The horizontal displacement *d* traveled by the projectile as well as the time *t* spent in flight is measured and recorded. The results are shown in Table 1.

angle θ	displacement d	time t
0°	14.0 *m*	1.4 *s*
15°	16.4 *m*	1.7 *s*
30°	17.3 *m*	2.0 *s*
45°	16.2 *m*	2.3 *s*
60°	12.6 *m*	2.5 *s*
75°	6.9 *m*	2.7 *s*

Table 1 Horizontal displacement and time of flight for a projectile shot from a spring-loaded gun

14. Approximately how high above the ground is the spring-loaded gun held when it releases the projectile?

    A.   1 m
    B.   5 m
    C.   10 m
    D.   14 m

15. Which of the following statements is true concerning the projectile in the experiment?

    A.   The longer the projectile remained in the air, the greater was its horizontal displacement.
    B.   The higher the projectile went, the greater was its horizontal displacement.
    C.   The speed of the projectile was greatest just after it left the spring-loaded gun.
    D.   The speed of the projectile was greatest just before hitting the ground.

16. Each time the projectile is launched, it leaves the spring-loaded gun with an initial speed of:

    A.   1 m/s
    B.   5 m/s
    C.   10 m/s
    D.   20 m/s

17. The projectile would reach its maximum height when fired from which of the following angles?

    A.   30°
    B.   45°
    C.   60°
    D.   90°

18. Which of the following graphs most accurately represents the relationship between the horizontal displacement of the projectile and the angle θ?

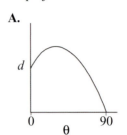
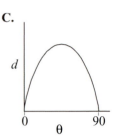
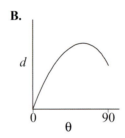
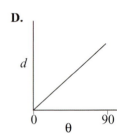

19. Which of the following statements is true concerning the flights of the projectile in the experiment?

    A.   At its maximum height, the speed of the projectile was zero for every flight.
    B.   All projectiles reached maximum acceleration just before hitting the ground.
    C.   The speed of the projectile changed at a constant rate throughout the experiment.
    D.   The distance traveled through the air by the projectile was smallest when launched at 0° from the horizontal.

GO ON TO THE NEXT PAGE.

Questions 20 through 23 are **NOT** based on a descriptive passage.

20. A man takes two strides each second. The same man walks at a rate of 1 m/s. How long are his strides?

A. $^{1}/_{4}$ m
B. $^{1}/_{2}$ m
C. 1 m
D. 2 m

21. The moon has no atmosphere, and has less gravity than earth. How will the path of a golf ball struck on the earth differ from one struck on the moon?

A. Both the earth's atmosphere and gravity will act to lengthen the projectile path of the ball.
B. Both the earth's atmosphere and gravity will act to shorten the projectile path of the ball.
C. The earth's atmosphere will act to shorten the path of the ball but its gravity will act to lengthen the path.
D. The earth's atmosphere will act to lengthen the path of the ball but its gravity will act to shorten the path.

22. All of the following will affect the time of flight for a projectile experiencing no air resistance EXCEPT:

I. the mass of the projectile
II. the initial horizontal velocity of the projectile
III. the initial vertical velocity of the projectile

A. I only
B. III only
C. I and II only
D. I and III only

23. A ball is rolled down a 1 m ramp placed at an angle of 30° to the horizontal. The same ball is rolled down a 1 m ramp placed vertically. Which of the following statements is true? (Note: sin 30° = 0.5, cos 30° = 0.87)

A. The ball required the same amount of time for both trips.
B. The ball had the same displacement at the end of both trips.
C. The ball accelerated at the same rate for both trips.
D. The ball reached approximately 1.4 times the speed on the second trip as it did on the first trip.

STOP. IF YOU FINISH BEFORE TIME IS CALLED, CHECK YOUR WORK. YOU MAY GO BACK TO ANY QUESTION IN THIS TEST BOOKLET.

STOP.

30-MINUTE
IN-CLASS EXAM
FOR LECTURE 2

Statistically speaking, traveling on U.S. highways is more dangerous than airplane travel. At the high speeds achieved by vehicles on the highway, turns must be very gradual. As a safety precaution, highway turns are banked toward the inside. Federal guidelines specify highway curve speed limits based upon the angle of the bank, the average coefficient of friction between a vehicle and the pavement, and the radius of curvature of the turn. The radius of curvature of a turn is the radius of a circle that would be circumscribed by the vehicle if the vehicle were to complete a full circle.

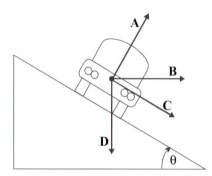

Figure 1

The diagram above shows a vehicle on a highway curve moving in a direction out of the page and turning to the driver's left.

24. Which of the following statements is most likely false concerning the federal guidelines on highway curve speed limits?

    A. The speed limit increases with the radius of curvature.
    B. The bank angle θ increases with the radius of curvature.
    C. A greater bank angle θ allows for a greater speed limit.
    D. A smaller radius of curvature leads to a greater bank angle.

25. If the vehicle in Figure 1 is moving very fast, but not slipping off the bank, the frictional force on the vehicle is most likely:

    A. static and in the direction of vector C.
    B. static and in the direction of vector B.
    C. kinetic and in the direction of vector C.
    D. kinetic and in the opposite direction of vector C.

26. The centripetal force on the vehicle is:

    A. in the direction of B.
    B. in the direction opposite to B.
    C. in the direction of C.
    D. in the direction opposite to C.

27. If the vehicle in Figure 1 were stationary, the net force on the vehicle would be:

    A. zero.
    B. in the direction of A.
    C. in the direction of C.
    D. in the direction of D.

28. If the speed of the vehicle were doubled, the centripetal force required to turn the vehicle would:

    A. decrease by a factor of 2.
    B. remain the same.
    C. increase by a factor of 2.
    D. increase by a factor of 4.

29. If the bank angle θ were increased to 90° and the vehicle did not fall, the frictional force on the vehicle would be:

    A. less than the weight of the vehicle.
    B. equal to the weight of the vehicle.
    C. greater than the weight of the vehicle.
    D. The laws of physics dictate that the vehicle must fall if the bank angle is increased to 90°.

30. Which of the following would require the bank angles which currently exist on highways to be increased?

    A. The average mass of vehicles on the highways increases.
    B. The average mass of the vehicles on the highways decreases.
    C. Curve speed limits are increased.
    D. Curve speed limits are decreased.

Passage II (Questions 31-37)

A student imagines an astronaut sitting in his space vehicle as it orbits an unknown planet sometime in the future. His space vehicle is pressurized so he is able to remove his helmet. The astronaut has a plastic bag of juice. He opens the bag and squeezes the juice out into the air in front of himself. The juice does not pour into his lap but remains as an amorphous blob wiggling in the air in front of him. He puts his mouth to the juice and slurps it in completely. Finished with the juice, he gently tosses the empty bag toward a garbage receptacle. Then the astronaut removes his pen from his pocket and finds that it floats perfectly in the air.

He looks over at his grandfather clock that runs on a pendulum system, and notices that it is time to radio earth. He radios Earth, which is 3×10^{13} km away, that he is done with breakfast. Earth replies that he must change the radius of his orbit. Earth asks him to decrease his present velocity by a factor of four, which he does. Soon afterwards he discovers that he is following the same orbital trajectory as a small moon.

The circular motion of the craft is governed by the equation below:

$$r = \frac{GM}{v^2}$$

where v is the speed of the space ship, r is the orbital radius, M is the mass of the Earth (5.98×10^{24} kg), and G is the gravitational constant (6.67×10^{-11} m^3/kg-s^{-2})

31. The space ship experiences centripetal acceleration while orbiting the planet. According to Newton's laws of motion, if the spaceship encounters no resisting force in the course of its circular orbit, what will be its future path?

    A. It will orbit in a circle forever.
    B. It will gradually spiral inward.
    C. It will gradually spiral outward.
    D. It will break from the orbit to travel in a straight line.

32. If the plastic bag misses the garbage receptacle, from the astronaut's point of view, will it continue straight along its present path at a constant velocity?

    A. Yes, because space is a vacuum.
    B. Yes, because the net force on the bag is zero.
    C. No, because the gravity of the unknown planet will change the trajectory of the bag.
    D. No, because the air molecules in the spacecraft will create air resistance and slow it down.

33. From the astronaut's point of view, along what trajectory should he send his projectile if he wants it to reach the garbage receptacle?

    A. a perfect parabolic path that ends exactly at the receptacle
    B. a parabolic path that ends at the receptacle but is adjusted for air resistance
    C. a perfect parabolic path that ends just above the receptacle
    D. a straight line to the receptacle

34. How many hours will the astronaut's message take to reach earth?

    A. $3 \times 10^{13} \times 3 \times 10^8 \times 60 \times 60$
    B. $(3 \times 10^{16})/(3 \times 10^8) \times 1/60 \times 1/60$
    C. $(3 \times 10^{16})/(3 \times 10^8) \times 60 \times 60$
    D. $(3 \times 10^8)/(3 \times 10^{16}) \times 1/60 \times 1/60$

35. When the astronaut changes his velocity, the radius of his orbit:

    A. increases by a factor of 16.
    B. decreases by a factor of 2.
    C. decreases by a factor of 4.
    D. decreases by a factor of l6.

36. Which of the following is true concerning the spacecraft and the moon when they are in the same orbit? (Assume that neither is using a propulsion system to maintain its orbit.)

    A. They both must be at the same speed.
    B. They both must have the same mass.
    C. They both must have the same mass and speed.
    D. They must have different masses.

37. The passage comes from the imagination of a student. A real pendulum on the clock in orbit would:

    A. swing more slowly than it would if it were on the planet below.
    B. swing more swiftly than it would if it were on the planet below.
    C. swing at the same rate as it would if it were on the planet below.
    D. not swing on the orbiting spacecraft.

Passage III (Questions 38-42)

The earth does not move around the sun in a perfect circle. Not only is the path very slightly elliptical, but the moon creates a wobble in the orbit. It is actually the center of gravity of the earth-moon system, called the *barycenter*, that follows the smooth elliptical path around the sun. Nevertheless, the earth's orbit is so nearly a circle that it can be treated as such for most calculations. The average distance between the earth and the sun is called an astronomical unit, AU.

The moon moves once around the earth every 27.3 days. The moon does not rotate relative to the earth, so the same side of the moon is always facing earth.

Table 1 gives the mass, radius, and orbital radius of the sun, earth, and moon. The universal gravitational constant is: $G = 6.67 \times 10^{-11}$ N m^2/kg^2

	Mass (kg)	Radius (km)	Orbital radius (km)
Sun	1.9×10^{30}	696,000	–
Earth	5.97×10^{24}	6,378	149,600,000
Moon	7.5×10^{22}	1,738	384,400

Table 1 Astronomical statistics

38. A light second is the distance that light moves in one second. How many light seconds is the moon from the earth?

   A. 5.8×10^{-6} light seconds
   B. 1.2×10^{-3} light seconds
   C. 5.8×10^{-3} light seconds
   D.   1.28 light seconds

39. A lunar day is defined as the time that elapses from sunrise to the following sunrise on the moon at a given location. How long is one lunar day?

   A.   12 earth hours
   B.   24 earth hours
   C.   27.3 earth days
   D.   one earth year

40. Which of the following expressions gives the approximate speed of the earth moving through its orbit?

   A. $\sqrt{\dfrac{G \times 1.5 \times 10^{11}}{1.9 \times 10^{30}}}$

   B. $\sqrt{\dfrac{G \times 1.9 \times 10^{30} \times 5.9 \times 10^{24}}{1.5 \times 10^{11}}}$

   C. $\sqrt{\dfrac{G \times 1.9 \times 10^{30}}{1.5 \times 10^{11}}}$

   D. $\sqrt{\dfrac{1.5 \times 10^{11}}{G \times 1.9 \times 10^{30}}}$

41. How much would a 100 kg man weigh on the moon?

   A.   17 N
   B.   100 N
   C.   170 N
   D.   1000 N

42. If F is the gravitational force created on the moon by the earth, which of the following expressions is equal to the gravitational force created on the earth by the moon?

   A. F

   B. $\dfrac{(5.97 \times 10^{24}) \times F}{(7.5 \times 10^{22})}$

   C. $\dfrac{(7.5 \times 10^{22}) \times F}{(5.97 \times 10^{24})}$

   D. $\dfrac{(1,738)^2 \times F}{(5.97 \times 10^{24})(7.5 \times 10^{22})}$

GO ON TO THE NEXT PAGE.

Questions 43 through 46 are **NOT** based on a descriptive passage.

43. In a 'tug of war' two groups of men pull in opposite directions on either end of a rope. Each group applies 2000 N of force. What is the tension in the rope?

  A. 0 N
  B. 1000 N
  C. 2000 N
  D. 4000 N

44. A 50 kg box is moved across the floor at a constant velocity of 5 m/s. The coefficient of friction between the box and the floor is 0.1. What is the net force on the box?

  A. 0 N
  B. 50 N
  C. 250 N
  D. 2500 N

45. The earth spins on its axis flattening its spherical shape from pole to pole and bowing out at the equator. An object is placed on a scale at the equator. How does the centrifugal force and the distance from the center of gravity affect the weight (as measured by the scale) at the equator?

  A. Both the increased distance and the centrifugal force act to decrease the weight of the object.
  B. The increased distance tends to decrease the weight of the object while the centrifugal force tends to increase its weight.
  C. The increased distance tends to increase the weight of the object while the centrifugal force tends to decrease its weight.
  D. The increased distance tends to decrease the weight of the object and the centrifugal force does not affect the weight of the object.

46. A 5 kg mass hangs from a spring distending it 10 cm from its resting point. What is the spring constant k of the spring?

  A. 50 N/m
  B. 100 N/m
  C. 250 N/m
  D. 500 N/m

STOP. IF YOU FINISH BEFORE TIME IS CALLED, CHECK YOUR WORK. YOU MAY GO BACK TO ANY QUESTION IN THIS TEST BOOKLET.

                                                      STOP.

30-MINUTE
IN-CLASS EXAM
FOR LECTURE 3

Puncho was a circus clown whose act consisted of juggling five 0.5 kg balls while riding a unicycle across a tightrope.

Puncho is shown in Figure 1 riding his unicycle while juggling and then riding his unicycle on a tight rope.

Puncho has a mass of 50 kg.

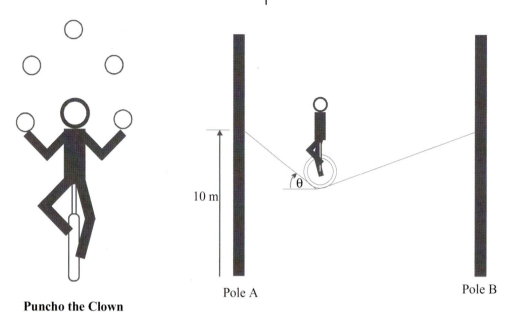

Puncho the Clown

Figure 1

47. If the radius of the wheel on Puncho's unicycle is 0.25 m, and Puncho is riding with a velocity of 10 m/s, how many revolutions does the wheel make each second?

   A. $\pi/20$ revolutions
   B. $\pi/10$ revolutions
   C. $20/\pi$ revolutions
   D. 20π revolutions

48. If the angle θ in Figure 1 is 60°, and Puncho is 2 m from Pole A, what is the net torque on Pole A? (Note: sin 60° = 0.87, cos 60° = 0.5)

   A.   0 N m
   B.   250 N m
   C.   2500 N m
   D.   5000 N m

49. If the distance between Pole A and Pole B in Figure 1 is doubled and the angle θ remains the same, the tension in the tightrope will:

   A.   decrease by a factor of 2.
   B.   remain the same.
   C.   increase by a factor of 2.
   D.   increase by a factor of 4.

50. Puncho throws each ball 5 m into the air. He throws one ball every half second with a velocity of 10 m/s. At any moment when all the balls are in the air, how much greater is their total energy than when all the balls are at rest?

   A.   50 J
   B.   125 J
   C.   250 J
   D.   500 J

51. Why is it easier for Puncho to balance on his unicycle if he carries a long heavy pole centered horizontally at his chest?

   A.   The pole decreases his rotational inertia.
   B.   The pole increases his rotational inertia.
   C.   The weight of the pole increases the frictional force between the unicycle and the tightrope.
   D.   The weight of the pole increases his momentum when he isn't moving.

GO ON TO THE NEXT PAGE.

Passage II (Questions 52-58)

A student performed two experiments to investigate the nature of tension.

Experiment 1

The student used the apparatus shown in Figure 1 to measure the tension in a string when different masses (*M*) were hung from its end. The experimental results showing how the tension changed with *M* are given in Table 1.

Figure 1

Trial	*M* (kg)	*T* (N)
1	0.10	1.0
2	0.15	1.5
3	0.20	2.0
4	0.25	2.5

Table 1

Experiment 2

The student attached one end of a string to a 0.1kg mass resting on a smooth table. The student attached the other end of the string over a pulley to a hanging mass (*m*). The apparatus is shown in Figure 2. The hanging mass was allowed to fall and the tension in the string as it fell was measured. Several different hanging masses were used and the results recorded in Table 2. (Note: Assume massless pulleys for all questions unless otherwise indicated.)

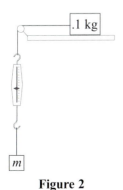

Figure 2

Trial	*m* (kg)	*T* (N)
1	0.10	0.50
2	0.15	0.60
3	0.20	0.67
4	0.30	0.75

Table 2

52. If the smooth table in Experiment 2 is frictionless, during the experiment the mass *m* is:

   A. in static equilibrium.
   B. in dynamic equilibrium.
   C. initially not in equilibrium but may achieve equilibrium if the string and table are long enough.
   D. not in equilibrium and does not achieve equilibrium during the experiment.

53. If the smooth table in Experiment 2 is frictionless, what is the maximum tension that can be achieved?

   A. 0.1 N
   B. 1 N
   C. 10 N
   D. As long as the string does not break, there is no limit to the tension that can be achieved.

54. What is the net force exerted on mass *M* in Experiment 1 Trial 3?

   A. 0 N
   B. 0.1 N
   C. 1 N
   D. 10 N

55. If the string in Experiment 2, Trial 1, were cut, and mass *m* were allowed to fall freely, what would be the tension in the string?

   A. 0 N
   B. 0.1 N
   C. 10 N
   D. 10 N

GO ON TO THE NEXT PAGE.

56. Which of the diagrams below most accurately represents the speed of the block in Experiment 2 after the block begins to slide? (Note: Assume that the tension and friction forces are constant.)

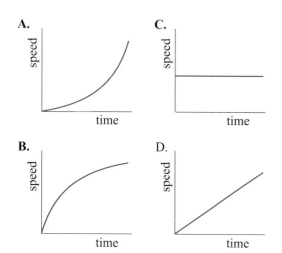

A.

B.

C.

D.

57. How does friction between the 0.1 kg mass and the table in Experiment 2 affect the results of the experiment?

A. The tension in the string is decreased by friction.
B. The tension in the string is increased by friction.
C. Friction decreases as mass *m* increases.
D. Friction increases as mass *m* increases.

58. Based on the results in Table 2, if another trial were attempted in Experiment 2 using a mass *m* of 0.4 kg, what would be the approximate tension in the string?

A. 0.80 N
B. 0.83 N
C. 1.3 N
D. 4.0 N

Passage III (Questions 59-66)

In the early part of World War I (WW I) the science of aeronautics was in its infancy. Primitive propeller planes reached top horizontal speeds of 30 m/s. If a plane didn't come apart, greater speeds were possible in a dive. Initially airplanes were used only for reconnaissance. Enemy pilots would often salute each other with a friendly wave as they passed in the sky. However, as the war progressed, pilots began throwing bricks and other objects at each other. The first bombs were literally dropped from the pilots hands as he flew. In order to hit his target, a pilot would have to take into account his own velocity, wind velocity, and air resistance.

Modern warplanes fire jet-propelled missiles. Such missiles take air in through the front, heat and compress it, and force it out the back along with combusted fuel. Nevertheless, the same factors for dropping a projectile must also be considered when aiming a modern missile. (Note: Ignore air resistance unless otherwise indicated.)

59. If a WW I pilot flying horizontally at top speed dropped a 2 kg bomb from an altitude of 300 m, what would be the kinetic energy of the bomb just before hitting the ground?

A. 900 J
B. 1800 J
C. 6000 J
D. 6900 J

60. If a modern jet-propelled missile with a mass of 300 kg is designed to move vertically upward at 1200 m/s, how much power must be delivered by the propulsion system?

A. 3.6×10^5 W
B. 3.6×10^6 W
C. 2.2×10^{10} W
D. 2.2×10^{14} W

GO ON TO THE NEXT PAGE.

61. If a WW I pilot dropped a 2 kg bomb from an altitude of 300 m, which of the following would result in the greatest kinetic energy for the bomb just before it hit the ground? ($\sin 30° = 0.5$)

   A. The pilot releases the bomb while flying straight up at a velocity of 10 m/s.
   B. The pilot releases the bomb while climbing at an angle 30° above the horizontal at a velocity of 20 m/s.
   C. The pilot releases the bomb while flying straight down at a velocity of 20 m/s.
   D. The pilot releases the bomb while flying horizontally at a velocity of 25 m/s.

62. The gravitational potential energy of WW I propeller planes increased with altitude. Since energy is always conserved, from where did this energy most likely come?

   A. kinetic energy achieved on the runway
   B. kinetic energy of air molecules lifting the plane
   C. chemical potential energy from the airplane's fuel
   D. kinetic energy of the wind

63. When a WW I airplane went into a dive, it might reach a constant terminal velocity due to air resistance. Which of the following is true concerning a diving plane that has reached terminal velocity?

   A. The net force on the plane is zero.
   B. The plane is accelerating at 10 m/s2.
   C. The plane is in static equilibrium.
   D. The air resistance is equal to the force of the propulsive produced by the planes engines.

64. While pulling out of a dive, a pilot's apparent weight:

   A. increases
   B. decreases
   C. remains the same
   D. The pilot is weightless while pulling out of a dive.

65. A WW I pilot increases his altitude at an angle of 30° to the horizontal and a velocity of 20 m/s. If he takes a 2 kg bomb with him, starting from rest on the ground, how much work has been done on the bomb when the plane reaches an altitude of 200 m? (Note: ignore air resistance. $\sin 30° = 0.5$)

   A. 2000 J
   B. 2400 J
   C. 4000 J
   D. 4400 J

66. A WW I pilot flying north at top speed and an altitude of 180 m wishes to drop a bomb on a trench. At how many meters before he is over the trench should he drop the bomb? (Ignore air resistance.)

   A. 60 m
   B. 120 m
   C. 180 m
   D. 360 m

67. A rocket is launched from earth to explore our solar system and beyond. As the rocket moves out of the earth's atmosphere and into deep space, the gravitational constant *g* decreases and approaches zero, and the gravitational potential energy of the rocket:

    A.   also decreases and approaches zero.
    B.   continually increases.
    C.   remains constant.
    D.   increases at first and then decreases and approaches zero.

68. From the right end of a massless, meter stick hangs a 5 kg mass. 20 cm from its left end the meter stick is attached to the ceiling by a string. What downward force *F* should be applied to the left end of the meter stick to balance it horizontally and in rotational equilibrium?

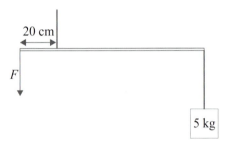

    A.   20 N
    B.   50 N
    C.   100 N
    D.   200 N

69. The earth is approximately 80 times more massive than the moon. The average distance between the earth and the moon is just less than 400,000 km. If the radius of the earth is 6370 km, the center of gravity of the earth-moon system is located:

    A.   at the center of the earth.
    B.   just beneath the earth's surface.
    C.   just above the earth's surface.
    D.   exactly between the earth and the moon.

STOP. IF YOU FINISH BEFORE TIME IS CALLED, CHECK YOUR WORK. YOU MAY GO BACK TO ANY QUESTION IN THIS TEST BOOKLET.

STOP.

30-MINUTE
IN-CLASS EXAM
FOR LECTURE 4

Passage I (Questions 70-76)

Four examples are shown below to demonstrate the properties of collisions. All four examples take place on a frictionless horizontal surface at room temperature. All diagrams are top views looking down from above.

Collision 1

Block A, with mass 2 kg slides towards Block B with a speed of 4 m/s. Block B is at rest and its mass is unknown. After the collision, Block A remains at rest and Block B moves forward at angle θ relative to Block A's original motion with a speed of 4 m/s.

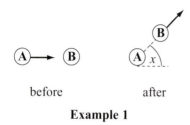

before   after

Example 1

Collision 2

Block A with mass 1 kg slides towards Block B with a speed of 4 m/s. Block B is at rest and has a mass of 1 kg. After the collision, the two blocks stick together and move forward at an angle y relative to Block A's original motion at an unknown speed.

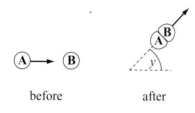

before   after

Example 2

Collision 3

Block A with mass 3 kg is initially at rest. An explosion breaks the blocks into three pieces, each with mass 1 kg. The three pieces each move away at unknown speeds at the angles shown.

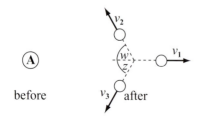

before   after

Example 3

Collision 4

Block A with mass 2 kg slides towards Block B with unknown speed and Block B with mass 1 kg slides towards Block A with unknown speed. After the collision, the two blocks stick together at rest.

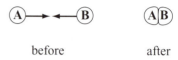

before   after

Example 4

70. Which of the following statements must be true regarding angles *x* and *y* in *Collision 1* and *Collision 2*?

   A. $x = 2y$
   B. $2x = y$
   C. $x = y = 90°$
   D. $x = y = 0°$

71. What is the speed of the combined blocks after *Collision 2*?

   A.   1 m/s
   B.   2 m/s
   C.   4 m/s
   D.   8 m/s

72. What is the mass of Block B in *Collision 1*?

   A.   0.5 kg
   B.   1 kg
   C.   2 kg
   D.   4 kg

73. After *Collision 4*, what has happened to the kinetic energy initially present in the motion of the blocks?

   A.   It remains unchanged.
   B.   It is converted into elastic potential energy.
   C.   It is converted into gravitational potential energy.
   D.   It is converted into heat energy.

74. Which of the following must be true about *Collision 3*?

   A. $v_1 = v_2 + v_3$
   B. $v_2 = v_3$
   C. $v_2\cos(w) = v_3\cos(z)$
   D. $v_2\sin(w) = v_3\sin(z)$

178   GO ON TO THE NEXT PAGE.

75. Which of the collisions is perfectly elastic?

   A.   *Collision 1*
   B.   *Collision 2*
   C.   *Collision 3*
   D.   *Collision 4*

76. If v_A is the speed of Block A and v_B is the speed of Block B before *Collision 4,* which of the following must be true?

   A. $v_A = v_B$
   B. $v_A = 2v_B$
   C. $2v_A = v_B$
   D. $4v_A = v_B$

Passage II (Questions 77-82)

Two small nuclides can join together via nuclear forces to release energy. This process is called *fusion*. However, nuclear forces are only effective at relatively close range, and, in order for this reaction to occur, the particles must overcome the electrostatic repulsion between their positively charged nuclei. These repulsive forces make up the *Coulomb barrier*. For two protons, the height of the Coulomb barrier is about 400 keV.

One way that successful collisions can occur is through high temperatures. This is called thermonuclear fusion. Temperature in thermonuclear studies are reported in terms of the *most probable* kinetic energy K of the interacting particles via the relation:

$$K = kT$$

where k is Boltzmann constant (8.62×10^{-5} eV/K) and T is the temperature in kelvins. Using this method, the temperature at the core of the sun is 1.3 keV; room temperature is approximately 0.03 eV; and the peak temperature for particles to overcome the Coulomb barrier is 400 keV.

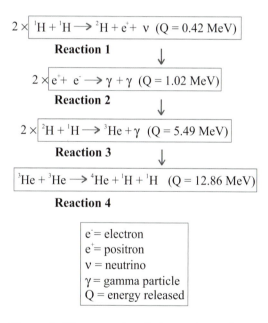

Figure 1 Thermonuclear fusion at the sun's core

Thermonuclear fusion occurs in the sun via the reactions given in Figure 1. Fusion occurs despite the low temperature for two reasons: (1) some particles move at much greater speeds than the most probable speed; (2) some barrier tunneling can occur at temperatures lower than 400 keV. (Note: An electron carries a charge of 1.6×10^{-19} C.)

GO ON TO THE NEXT PAGE.

77. The heat from thermonuclear fusion inside the sun's core comes from:

- A. kinetic energy
- B. chemical energy
- C. mass energy
- D. electrostatic potential energy

78. What is the approximate temperature of the sun's core in kelvins?

- A. 4.6×10^3 K
- B. 1.5×10^4 K
- C. 4.6×10^6 K
- D. 1.5×10^7 K

79. According to Figure 1, the net products of thermonuclear fusion in the sun's core are:

- A. helium, hydrogen, neutrinos, and energy.
- B. helium, neutrinos, and energy.
- C. hydrogen, neutrinos, and energy.
- D. helium, hydrogen, and neutrinos.

80. If an electron and a positron have the same mass, then, according to Reaction 2 in Figure 1 what is the approximate mass of a positron?

- A. 10^{-37} kg
- B. 10^{-30} kg
- C. 10^{-25} kg
- D. 10^{-15} kg

81. In nuclear fission one high-mass nuclide is split into two middle-mass nuclides and energy is released. The nucleons (protons and neutrons) in both nuclides are held together by the nuclear binding energy $Q = \Delta mc^2$. The binding energy per nucleon of the high-mass nuclide:

- A. is greater than the binding energy per nucleon of the middle-mass nuclides.
- B. is less than the binding energy per nucleon of the middle-mass nuclides.
- C. is equal to the binding energy per nucleon of the middle-mass nuclides.
- D. may be either greater or less than the binding energy per nucleon of the middle-mass nuclides.

82. Which of the following is a requirement in order for energy to be released in a fusion reaction?

- A. The resulting nucleus must be at a higher energy state than the colliding nuclides.
- B. The nuclides must collide at a temperature of 400 keV or greater.
- C. The number of nucleons in the fusing nuclides must be large.
- D. The number of nucleons in the fusing nuclides must be small.

GO ON TO THE NEXT PAGE.

Passage III (Questions 83-88)

An important function of many mammalian bones is to act as a lever arm, transmitting an in-force to an out-force via a center of rotation or fulcrum. Three orders of lever arms exist: *first order* where the fulcrum separates the in-force and the out-force; *second order* where the in-force and out-force are on the same side but the out force is nearest to the fulcrum; and *third order* where both forces are also on the same side but the in-force is nearest the fulcrum. In mammalian bone lever systems the in-force is supplied by a muscle, one end of which is attached to the bone at the point where the in-force is applied and the other end anchored to a separate bone closer to the body.

Mammalian bones have evolved divergently to meet the requirements of different mammals. Figures 1 and 2 show the lever system in the forelimbs of two different mammals. Each lever system allows for a ratio of out-force to in-force and velocity of limb movement that best suits its respective user. Swift running mammals take advantage of third order lever systems to reduce bulky limbs and extend limb movements. Large muscles can be kept close to the body requiring less energy expenditure on unnecessary movements; short contractions can be translated into long strides. In order to further maximize velocity the mass of the proximal portion of the limb has been reduced in these swift running mammals.

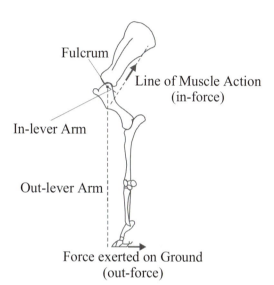

Figure 1

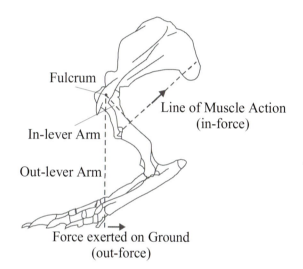

Figure 2

83. What type of lever is shown in Figure 2?

    A.   first order
    B.   second order
    C.   third order
    D.   It can not be determined from the figure.

84. Assuming the figures are drawn to scale, if the same in-force is applied to each lever system, which lever system will have the greatest out-force?

    A.   The lever system in Figure 1.
    B.   The lever system in Figure 2.
    C.   The out-force would be the same in both lever systems.
    D.   The answer cannot be determined from the information given.

85. If the out-lever arm in Figure 1 is 1 m and the in-lever arm is 10 cm, and the mammal applies an in-force of 10 N, what will be the approximate out-force?

    A.   1 N
    B.   l0 N
    C.   40 N
    D.   l00 N

86. The animal in Figure 2 is well adapted for rapid digging. If we assume ideal conditions for the lever system in Figure 2, compared to the in-force supplied by the muscle, the out-force must:

    A.   do less work.
    B.   do more work.
    C.   be less than the in-force.
    D.   be greater than the in-force.

GO ON TO THE NEXT PAGE.

87. According to the passage, which of the following conditions would most likely make the animal in Figure 1 a faster runner?

   A. increasing the length of the in-lever arm and decreasing length of the out-lever arm
   B. decreasing the length of the in-lever arm and increasing length of the out-lever arm
   C. increasing both the length of the in-lever arm and the out-lever arm
   D. decreasing both the length of the in-lever arm and the out-lever arm

88. Which position has the greatest in-lever arm?

A.

C.

B.

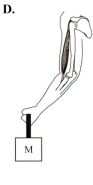

D.

Questions 89 through 92 are **NOT** based on a descriptive passage.

89. The rate at which the thyroid gland absorbs iodine can be measured using the radio nuclide ^{128}I. The half-life of ^{128}I is 25 min. A patient is administered 800 μg of ^{128}I. If no ^{128}I is absorbed by the thyroid, approximately how much will remain in the patient's blood after 2 hours?

   A. 0 μg
   B. 27 μg
   C. 55 μg
   D. 800 μg

90. ^{218}Po undergoes two alpha decays and four beta decays to become:

   A. ^{210}Bi
   B. ^{226}Ra
   C. ^{210}Pb
   D. ^{210}Po

91. A pulley system is attached to a massless board as shown below. The board pivots only at the pivot point. A 10 kg mass M sits exactly in the middle of the board.

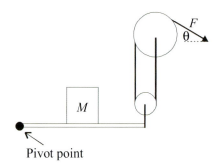

Pivot point

If the angle θ is 30°, what is the force F necessary to lift the 10 kg mass? (Note: sin30° = 0.5)

   A. 12.5 N
   B. 25 N
   C. 50 N
   D. 100 N

182   GO ON TO THE NEXT PAGE.

92. If the two objects shown below collide and remain together without spinning, what will be their final velocity? (sin 60° = 0.87; cos 60° = 0.5)

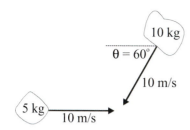

A. 5 m/s
B. 5.8 m/s
C. 8.7 m/s
D. 10 m/s

STOP. IF YOU FINISH BEFORE TIME IS CALLED, CHECK YOUR WORK. YOU MAY GO BACK TO ANY QUESTION IN THIS TEST BOOKLET.

STOP.

30-MINUTE
IN-CLASS EXAM
FOR LECTURE 5

Because heating a solid increases the vibrational energy of its molecules resulting in an increase in space required by each molecule, a typical solid will expand when heated. For such solids, the fractional change in their length per unit temperature is given by a *coefficient of linear expansion*, which is specific for each solid. Although the change in length varies slightly with temperature for any solid, The following equation gives a good approximation.

$$\Delta L = L\alpha\Delta T$$

where L is the original length of the solid, ΔL is the change in length, α is the coefficient of linear expansion for the particular substance, and ΔT is the change in temperature.

Of course, any solid that increases in length when heated will also expand in both other directions. The change in volume V for such a solid is given by:

$$\Delta V = V\beta\Delta T$$

where β is the coefficient of volume expansion which is exactly 3 times the coefficient of linear expansion. The equation for the change in volume can be applied to most liquids as well as solids. Water, however, has a maximum density at 4°C.

A list of the coefficients of linear expansion for some common substances is provided in Table 1.

Substance	α $(10^{-6}/°C)$
Ice (at 0°C)	51
Aluminum	23
Brass	19
Steel	11
Glass (ordinary)	9

Table 1

93. What is the coefficient of volume expansion for glass?

    A. $9 \times 10^{-18}/°C$
    B. $27 \times 10^{-18}/°C$
    C. $9 \times 10^{-6}/°C$
    D. $2.7 \times 10^{-5}/°C$

94. A bimetal strip consisting of brass and steel is welded together lengthwise as shown.

    As the temperature increases:

    A. the brass will contract and the steel will expand, bending the rod to the left.
    B. the steel will contract and the brass will expand, bending the rod to the right.
    C. the brass will expand faster than the steel, bending the rod to the right.
    D. the steel will expand faster than the brass, bending the rod to the left.

95. If a piece of brass is slowly heated from 25°C to 35°C, by approximately what percent will its length be increased?

    A. 0.0019 %
    B. 0.019 %
    C. 0.19 %
    D. 1.9 %

96. Which of the following substances contracts the most when cooled?

    A. aluminum
    B. brass
    C. steel
    D. glass

97. A bottle is half filled with water at 4°C and sealed shut. The bottle is placed on a scale and put into a freezer. As the water nears 0°C, the water level in the bottle:

    A. falls and the reading on the scale remains constant.
    B. rises and the reading on the scale remains constant.
    C. rises and the reading on the scale decreases.
    D. rises and the reading on the scale increases.

GO ON TO THE NEXT PAGE.

98. Which of the following is true concerning an aluminum buoy that floats in a lake all year round? (Note: The volume coefficient of expansion for water is $2 \times 10^{-3}/°C$.)

  A. The buoy floats *higher* in the winter because the density of water changes *more* than the density of aluminum.

  B. The buoy floats *higher* in the winter because the density of water changes *less* than the density of aluminum.

  C. The buoy floats *lower* in the winter because the density of water changes *more* than the density of aluminum.

  D. The buoy floats *lower* in the winter because the density of water changes *less* than the density of aluminum.

Passage II (Questions 99-105)

The pipe shown in Figure 1 holds a fluid with a specific gravity of 5.0. The top of the pipe at end A is sealed so that only a negligible amount of vapor pressure exists above the fluid surface. A narrow flexible section extends as shown from end A and is sealed at end D. Both ends of the pipe can be opened so that fluid flows from point A to D.

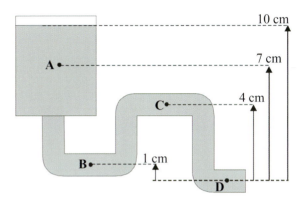

Figure 1 Pipe with unknown fluid

The points A, B, C, and D and the surface of the liquid are measured from an arbitrary point as shown. Assume that the unknown fluid behaves ideally unless otherwise indicated.

99. When both ends are sealed shut, the pressure is the greatest at point:

  A. A
  B. B
  C. C
  D. D

100. When both ends are open, the flow rate is the greatest at point:

  A. A
  B. B
  C. D
  D. The flow rate is the same at all points.

101. What is the pressure at point C when the pipe is closed and the fluid is at rest?

  A. 2000 Pa
  B. 3000 Pa
  C. 2000 Pa + 1 atm
  D. 3000 Pa + 1 atm

102. What is the approximate velocity of the fluid at point D when the pipe is opened at both ends?

- **A.** 0.9 m/s
- **B.** 1.1 m/s
- **C.** 1.4 m/s
- **D.** 2.0 m/s

103. A 2 kg object submerged in the unknown fluid has an apparent loss of mass of 0.5 kg. What is the specific gravity of the object?

- **A.** 1
- **B.** 1.25
- **C.** 5
- **D.** 20

104. If both ends of the pipe were opened, all of the following would decrease significantly at point B as the unknown fluid drained from the pipe EXCEPT:

- **A.** volume flow rate
- **B.** fluid velocity
- **C.** fluid density
- **D.** fluid pressure

105. The pipe is closed at both ends and the fluid is at rest. Compared to the pressure at point A, the pressure at point C is:

- **A.** half as great.
- **B.** twice as great.
- **C.** $^4/_7$ as great.
- **D.** $^7/_4$ as great.

GO ON TO THE NEXT PAGE.

The flight of a golf ball does not strictly follow the rules of projectile motion. The reason for this deviation is that the golf ball experiences a force called "lift" F_L. The lift force is directly proportional to the difference in pressure above and below the ball caused the ball's rotation during its flight. Lift can be roughly explained using Bernoulli's theorem.

$$\Delta P = \frac{1}{2}\rho v_2^2 - \frac{1}{2}\rho v_1^2$$

where ΔP is the pressure difference, ρ is the density of the air surrounding the golf ball ($\rho = 1.2$ kg/m^3), and v_2 and v_1 are the effective airspeeds above and below the ball.

As the golf ball flies through the air, air moves past the ball at speed u. But as the ball spins, it drags some air along its surface. If the surface of the ball is moving at speed w, then the *effective airspeed* above the ball is $u + w$ and the *effective airspeed* below the ball is $u - w$.

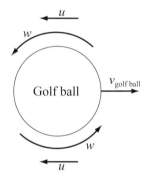

Golf ball manufacturers are continually experimenting with different surface patterns to improve lift properties. The mass of a typical golf ball is 45 grams and the diameter is 4.3 cm. The volume of a golf ball is 42 cm^3.

106. Assuming the spin on a golf ball has no effect on its horizontal acceleration, how does the flight of a ball undergoing the lift force compare to the flight of a ball that experiences no lift?

   A.   The ball that experiences lift will go higher, but not as far horizontally.
   B.   The ball that experiences lift will go higher and farther horizontally.
   C.   The ball that experiences lift will not go as high but will travel farther horizontally.
   D.   The ball that experiences lift will not go as high or as far horizontally.

107. The air very close to the surface of the ball is dragged along by a golf ball's spinning motion so that it moves at the same speed as the surface of the ball. If a golf ball in flight spins with a frequency of 60 Hz, what is the approximate speed w of the air at its surface?

   A.   1 m/s
   B.   4 m/s
   C.   8 m/s
   D.   20 m/s

108. Which of the following changes would NOT serve to increase the lift force F_L exerted on a golf ball in flight?

   A.   Weather conditions cause an increase in the density of air.
   B.   A golf ball with a lower density is used.
   C.   The golf ball is struck harder, causing it to move with greater speed.
   D.   The golf ball is struck with an angled club, causing it to spin more rapidly.

109. When a golf ball like the one described in the passage lands in a lake, which of the following will be true?

   A.   The ball will sink.
   B.   The ball will float with 96% of its volume submerged.
   C.   The ball will float with 93% of its volume submerged.
   D.   The ball will float with 87% of its volume submerged.

110. If a golf ball in flight spins in the direction opposite the one shown in Figure 1, the ball will experience:

   A.   a downward force because the pressure will be greater below the ball.
   B.   a downward force because the pressure will be greater above the ball.
   C.   an upward force because the pressure will be greater below the ball.
   D.   an upward force because the pressure will be greater above the ball.

111. Which of the following expressions is equal to the difference between the *effective airspeeds* above and below a golf ball while it is in flight?

   A. u
   B. w
   C. $2u$
   D. $2w$

GO ON TO THE NEXT PAGE.

Questions 112 through 115 are **NOT** based on a descriptive passage.

112. A 5 liter container weighing 2 kilograms is thrown into a lake. What percentage of the container will float above the water? (1 L = 1 dm^3)

    A.   10%
    B.   40%
    C.   60%
    D.   90%

113. A brick sits on a massless piece of Styrofoam floating in a large bucket of water. If the Styrofoam is removed and the brick is allowed to sink to the bottom:

    A.   the water level will remain the same.
    B.   the water level will fall.
    C.   the water level will rise.
    D.   the density of the brick must be known in order to predict the rise or fall of the water level.

114. A water tower is filled with water to a depth of 15 m. If a leak forms 10 m above the base of the tower, what will be the velocity of the water as it escapes through the leak?

    A.   10 m/s
    B.   14 m/s
    C.   17 m/s
    D.   20 m/s

115. What is the approximate absolute pressure 5 m below the surface of a lake that is 20 meters deep?

    A.   50,000 Pa
    B.   150,000 Pa
    C.   200,000 Pa
    D.   300,000 Pa

STOP. IF YOU FINISH BEFORE TIME IS CALLED, CHECK YOUR WORK. YOU MAY GO BACK TO ANY QUESTION IN THIS TEST BOOKLET.

STOP.

30-MINUTE
IN-CLASS EXAM
FOR LECTURE 6

Passage I (Questions 116-122)

Due to the large volume of traffic between Manhattan and Boston, a group of engineers proposed a tunnel that would allow a train to carry passengers along a perfectly straight path between the two cities. The engineers reasoned that the train could operate without consuming any energy because the force of gravity would pull the train down the first half of the tunnel. As the train accelerated during the first half of the journey, it would acquire exactly enough momentum to carry through the second half of the journey against the gravitational force. If friction is neglected and the graviational constant g is assumed to be constant throughout the trip, a one-way trip would be one-half of a cycle of simple harmonic motion similar to the swinging of a pendulum from one side to the other. (The radius of the earth is 6370 km. $g = 10$ m/s^2. Assume ideal conditions unless otherwise instructed.)

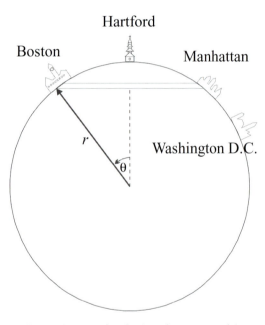

Figure 1 Tunnel train (not drawn to scale)

116. Which of the following equations gives the acceleration of the train at the beginning of the trip?

A. $g \sin\theta$
B. $g \cos\theta$
C. Gm_{earth}/r^2
D. g

117. A similar tunnel was proposed to be built from Boston to Washington DC. Based upon Figure 1 compared to the travel time for the trip from Boston to Manhattan, the travel time for the trip from Boston to Washington DC would be:

A. greater because the distance is greater.
B. the same because the distance is greater but the train would go faster.
C. shorter because the train would go faster.
D. shorter because the trip would be downhill all the way.

118. Given ideal conditions, which of the following expressions most closely represents the time necessary for a trip from Boston to Manhattan?

A. $2\pi\sqrt{\dfrac{r}{g}}$

B. $\pi\sqrt{\dfrac{r}{g}}$

C. $2\pi\sqrt{\dfrac{g}{r}}$

D. $\pi\sqrt{\dfrac{g}{r}}$

119. Which of the following diagrams shows the change in the speed of a train as it travels on a one-way trip from Boston to Manhattan?

A.

C.

B.

D.

GO ON TO THE NEXT PAGE.

120. Which of the following best describes the net force and the acceleration on the train during the trip?

- **A.** The net force and acceleration are zero when the train is directly beneath Hartford.
- **B.** The net force and acceleration are at a maximum when the train is directly beneath Hartford.
- **C.** The net force is at a minimum when the train is directly beneath Hartford but the acceleration is constant throughout the trip.
- **D.** The net force and acceleration are constant throughout the trip.

121. Because the train goes downhill, then uphill, the shape of the track must be:

- **A.** a smooth constant curve along the entire length.
- **B.** a straight track along the entire length.
- **C.** a straight track with one bend exactly beneath Hartford where the train turns uphill.
- **D.** a successive series of straight track and curved track.

122. The engineers assumed that acceleration of gravity would remain constant during the trip. If we consider that the force of gravity gets smaller as the train nears the center of the earth, how will this affect the trip?

- **A.** The trip will require more energy than calculated by the engineers.
- **B.** The trip will require less energy than calculated by the engineers.
- **C.** The trip will require more time than calculated by the engineers.
- **D.** The trip will require less time than calculated by the engineers.

Passage II (Questions 123-127)

Because bats are nocturnal hunters they rely upon sound waves to locate their prey. A horseshoe bat emits ultrasonic waves from its nostrils that reflect off its prey and return to the bat. When a horseshoe bat detects flying prey, it adjusts the frequency of the waves until the frequency of the waves rebounding off the prey is 83 kHz, the frequency at which the bat hears best. From the difference in the frequencies, the bat can judge the position of its prey and capture it.

The frequency at which the moth receives and reflects the waves emitted by the bat is given by the Doppler effect equation:

$$\frac{f_m}{f_b} = \frac{340 \pm v_m}{340 \pm v_b}$$

where f_b is the frequency of the waves emitted by the bat, f_m is the frequency at which the waves reflect off the moth, v_b is the velocity of the bat, v_m is the velocity of the moth. The sign conventions are chosen in accordance with the Doppler effect.

Certain moths can avoid being captured by bats by either flying directly away from the ultrasonic waves, or *clicking* to create a jamming frequency and confuse the bat.

A horseshoe bat flies at approximately 10 m/s. Assume that the moth flies at 5 m/s. The velocity of an ultrasonic wave in air is 340 m/s.

123. By flying directly away from the ultrasonic waves, the moth most likely avoids capture because:

- **A.** the sound waves reflect away from the bat.
- **B.** the frequency of the reflected waves is decreased so that it approaches the frequency of the emitted waves and the bat may not detect the moth.
- **C.** the frequency of the reflected waves is increased so that it approaches the frequency of the emitted waves and the bat may not detect the moth.
- **D.** the frequency of the reflected waves is increased so that it separates from the frequency of the emitted waves and the bat may not detect the moth.

GO ON TO THE NEXT PAGE.

124. If the bat and moth fly directly toward each other, and the bat sends ultrasonic waves at 66 kHz, at what frequency do the waves reflect off the moth?

- **A.** 63 kHz
- **B.** 65 kHz
- **C.** 67 kHz
- **D.** 69 kHz

125. Which of the following will decrease the frequency of the waves detected by the bat?

- **I.** The moth flies toward the bat.
- **II.** The bat flies toward the moth.
- **III.** The moth flies away from the bat.

- **A.** I only
- **B.** III only
- **C.** I and II only
- **D.** II and III only

126. As the humidity of air is increased, there is less time between the moment when a bat sends a signal and the moment when the bat receives the signal from its prey. This is most likely because the addition of water vapor to air:

- **A.** increases the speed of sound in air by decreasing the density of the air.
- **B.** increases the speed of sound in air by increasing the density of the air.
- **C.** decreases the speed of sound in air by decreasing the density of the air.
- **D.** decreases the speed of sound in air by increasing the density of the air.

127. Which wavelength does the horseshoe bat hear best?

- **A.** 2×10^{-3} m
- **B.** 4×10^{-3} m
- **C.** 2 m
- **D.** 4 m

GO ON TO THE NEXT PAGE.

Passage III (Questions 128-134)

A piano creates sound by gently striking a taught wire with a soft hammer when a key on the piano is pressed. All piano wires in a given piano are approximately the same length. However, each wire is tied down at two points, the *bridge* and the *agraffe*. The length of the wire between the the bridge and the agraffe is called the *speaking length*. The speaking length is the part of the wire that resonates. The point of the wire struck by the hammer is displaced perpendicularly to the wire's length. A standing wave described by Equation 1 is generated by the hammer strike, where *v* is the velocity, *T* is the tension in the wire, and μ is the mass per unit length of the wire.

$$v = \sqrt{\frac{T}{\mu}}$$

Equation 1 Velocity of a wave on a piano wire

Different notes are created by using wires of different lengths, and masses. Most piano strings are actually three parallel wires; however, some lower notes are made by two or even a single wire.

Tuning a piano involves adjustment of the tension in the wires until just the right pitch is achieved. Correct pitch is achieved by listening to the beat frequency between the piano and a precalibrated tuning fork.

128. A piano wire with a *speaking length* of 120 cm is displaced 0.5 cm when struck by the piano hammer. What is the length of the first harmonic resonating through the wire?

    A. 60 cm
    B. 120 cm
    C. 180 cm
    D. 240 cm

129. A piano with which of the following properties would deliver a note with the lowest pitch?

    A. 100 cm speaking length; 800 N tension;
    B. 120 cm speaking length; 800 N tension;
    C. 100 cm speaking length; 700 N tension;
    D. 120 cm speaking length; 700 N tension;

130. The following are characteristics of a wave on a piano wire. Doubling which one will have the LEAST effect on the intensity of the sound produced?

    A. μ
    B. period
    C. speaking length
    D. amplitude

131. A piano note is compared to a tuning fork vibrating at 440 Hz. Three beats per second are discerned by the piano tuner. When the tension in the string is increased slightly, the beat frequency increases. What was the initial frequency of the piano wire?

    A. 434 Hz
    B. 437 Hz
    C. 443 Hz
    D. 446 Hz

132. Sound waves move through air at approximately 340 m/s. A piano wire with a 90 cm speaking length resonates at a frequency of 360 Hz. What is the wavelength of the resulting sound wave?

    A. 0.94 m
    B. 1.06 m
    C. 4 m
    D. 40 m

133. The wave on a piano wire is NOT an example of a:

    A. transverse wave.
    B. longitudinal wave.
    C. standing wave.
    D. a harmonic wave.

134. If, when the hammer strikes the piano wire, the displacement of the wire increases, which of the following properties of the wave on the wire also increases?

    A. the frequency
    B. the wavelength
    C. the amplitude
    D. the velocity

GO ON TO THE NEXT PAGE.

135. A 5 kg mass bounces in simple harmonic motion at the end of a spring. At which point is the acceleration of the mass the greatest?

A. When the spring is fully compressed and when the spring is fully extended.
B. When the spring is at its rest length.
C. When the spring is halfway between its rest length and its fully extended or compressed length.
D. The acceleration is constant.

136. Two waves are traveling toward each other on the same string. If wave A has an amplitude of 3 cm and a wavelength of 10 cm, and wave B has an amplitude and wavelength twice that of wave A, what will be the maximum displacement of the string when the waves interfere with each other?

A. 0 cm
B. 3 cm
C. 6 cm
D. 9 cm

137. The period T of a pendulum is given by:

$$T = 2\pi\sqrt{\frac{L}{g}}$$

where L is the length and g is the free fall acceleration near the surface of the earth. In order to increase the period of a pendulum by 42%, the length must be:

A. decreased by 51%
B. decreased by 20%
C. increased by 42%
D. increased by 102%

138. Identical wine glasses A and B contain water. If gently struck with a spoon the water and the glass will vibrate at the same frequency. Which glass will ring at the higher pitch when struck?

A B

A. glass B because more air in the glass will create resonance at a longer wavelength
B. glass B because less water in the glass results in less inertia which allows the glass to vibrate at a higher frequency
C. glass A because less air in the glass will create resonance at a shorter wavelength
D. glass A because more water in the glass lowers the frequency at which the glass can vibrate

STOP. IF YOU FINISH BEFORE TIME IS CALLED, CHECK YOUR WORK. YOU MAY GO BACK TO ANY QUESTION IN THIS TEST BOOKLET.

30-MINUTE
IN-CLASS EXAM
FOR LECTURE 7

If the velocity of a charged particle moving through a uniform magnetic field has a component parallel to that field the particle will move in a helical path as shown in Figure 1. The net force F on the particle can be described by the equation:

$$F = qvB\sin\theta$$

where q is the charge on the particle, v is the velocity of the charge, B is the magnetic field strength, and θ is the angle between the velocity and the magnetic field. The pitch p of the helix is the distance between adjacent turns. The radius r of the helix is determined by the component of velocity of the charge perpendicular to the magnetic field and is independent of the component of the velocity parallel to the magnetic field.

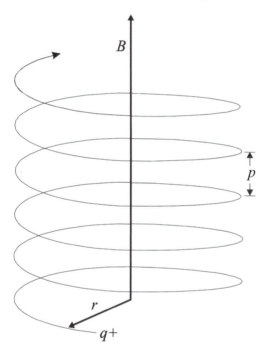

Figure 1 Path of a charged particle moving through a uniform magnetic field

A nonuniform magnetic field that is stronger at its ends than at its middle can trap a charged particle by reflecting it back and forth between its ends. Such a situation is shown in Figure 2.

In a similar phenomenon electrons and protons above the atmosphere are reflected back and forth between the north and south poles of the earth's magnetic field forming the two *Van Allen belts* high above the atmosphere. Occasionally a solar flare shoots additional electrons and protons into the *Van Allen belts* creating an electric field at the point where the electrons normally reflect. The electric field drives the electrons along the earth's magnetic field lines into the atmosphere where they collide with the electrons of air molecules forcing them to a higher energy level. The energized electrons quickly drop back to their lower energy level emitting photons. Oxygen atoms emit green light and nitrogen atoms emit pink light. This light forms the curtain of lights in the sky known in the northern hemisphere as the *aurora borealis* and in the southern hemisphere as the *aurora australis*.

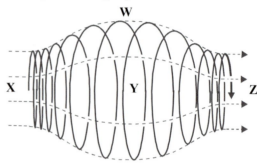

Figure 2 Path of a charged particle trapped in a changing magnetic field

139. If the magnetic field in Figure 2 represents a portion of the Earth's magnetic field, at which labelled point would you expect to find the aurora borealis?

    A. W
    B. X
    C. Y
    D. Z

140. Which of the following most accurately describes the change in the pitch and period of the helical path traveled by a negatively charged particle moving through a magnetic field that is gradually strengthening?

    A. The pitch increases and the period decreases.
    B. The pitch increases and the period increases.
    C. The pitch decreases and the period remains the same.
    D. Both the pitch and the period decrease.

GO ON TO THE NEXT PAGE.

141. The diagram below shows five paths travelled by charged particles through a uniform magnetic field. If path X is the path of a proton, which path would most closely represent the path of an electron moving with the same speed?

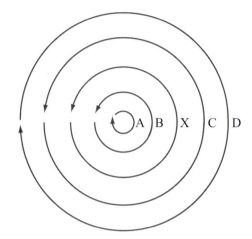

A. A
B. B
C. C
D. D

142. If the following particles move at the same speed and travel a helical path through a magnetic field which one is likely to experience the greatest net force?

A. a proton with a pitch p
B. an electron with a pitch $2p$
C. an alpha particle with a pitch p
D. an alpha particle with a pitch $2p$

143. The electrons and protons caught in the Van Allen belts reflect from one pole to the other. Looking up from the North pole, electrons rotate counterclockwise. Protons rotate:

A. counterclockwise both when looking up from the North Pole or when looking up from the South Pole.
B. clockwise both when looking up from the North Pole or when looking up from the South Pole.
C. clockwise when looking up from the North Pole but counterclockwise when looking up from the South Pole.
D. counterclockwise when looking up from the North Pole but clockwise when looking up from the South Pole.

144. Which of the following most accurately describes the work done by the Earth's magnetic field on an electron trapped in the Van Allen belts?

A. No work is done because the force is always perpendicular to the motion of the electron.
B. Work is done only by the component of the field that is parallel to the velocity of the electron.
C. Work is done only by the component of the magnetic field that is perpendicular to the velocity of the electron.
D. The work done is equal to the force on the electron times the distance traveled by the electron.

145. In order for the Van Allen belts to form, the magnetic field created by the earth must be:

A. weakest near the North Pole.
B. weakest near the South Pole.
C. weakest around the equator.
D. the same strength throughout.

199

GO ON TO THE NEXT PAGE.

Passage II (Questions 146-151)

Under normal conditions an electric field exists in the air near the surface of the Earth with an average strength of approximately 100 V/m. Since the human body is a relatively good conductor of electricity it remains at the same potential as the ground and the electric field in the air adjusts around the body accordingly as shown in Figure 1.

The atmosphere is about 50,000 m deep and the total potential difference between the ground and the top of the atmosphere is approximately 400,000 V. Air is a poor conductor and thus the average current is only about 10^{-12} A/m².

A lightning strike occurs when the bottom of a cloud has a negative electric charge that is greater than the negative charge below it on the ground. This temporarily reverses the electric field between the ground and the cloud, allowing electrons to flow from the cloud to the ground. The current in a lightning strike is about 10,000 amperes and a typical strike will deliver a charge of 20 coulombs.

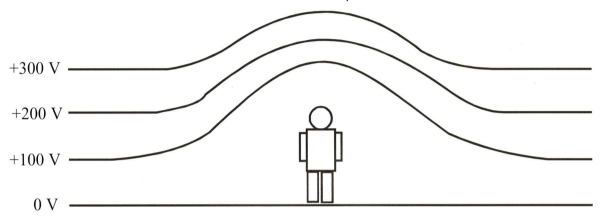

Figure 1 Potential gradient near the surface of the earth

146. The electric potential of the ground was measured at the top of a hill. If the height of the hill is 20 meters above the level of the surrounding plain, what will be the measured voltage?

   A.   0 V
   B.   5 V
   C.   200 V
   D.   2000 V

147. 147. What is the approximate duration of the lightning strike described in the passage?

   A.   2 seconds
   B.   0.5 seconds
   C. 2×10^{-3} seconds
   D. 5×10^{-6} seconds

148. What is the average resistance of the atmosphere?

   A.   0 Ω/m²
   B.   4 Ω /m²
   C. 4×10^{7} Ω /m²
   D. 4×10^{17} Ω /m²

149. Which of the following best describes the electric field vectors above a flat plain at the Earth's surface?

   A.   perpendicular to the ground and pointing upward
   B.   perpendicular to the ground and pointing downward
   C.   parallel to the ground and pointing north
   D.   parallel to the ground and pointing south

150. If the total electric current reaching the Earth's surface is nearly constant at 1800 A, approximately how much electrical energy is dissipated each second by the atmosphere?

   A. 4×10^{-7} J
   B. 4×10^{5} J
   C. 7.2×10^{8} J
   D. 1.3×10^{24} J

151. Which of the following describes the direction of current flow during a lightning strike?

   A.   From a cloud at high potential to the ground at lower potential.
   B.   From a cloud at low potential to the ground at higher potential.
   C.   From the ground at high potential to a cloud at lower potential.
   D.   From the ground at low potential to a cloud at higher potential.

GO ON TO THE NEXT PAGE.

Passage III (Questions 152-157)

In 1879 Edwin Hall demonstrated that conducting electrons in a copper wire are deflected by a magnetic field. This phenomenon is now known as the Hall effect. The Hall effect also predicts the charge of the conduction carriers inside the copper wire.

To demonstrate the Hall effect a copper strip carrying a current i is placed in a magnetic field with field strength B directed into the page as shown in Figure 1. The magnetic field and the average velocity of the electrons v result in a force which pushes the electrons to one side of the copper strip. This in turn creates an electric field E inside the strip which pushes the electrons in the opposite direction. An equilibrium quickly builds up to where the force on the electrons due to E and B are equal and in opposite directions. The Hall potential difference V is proportional to the strip width d and can be measured with a voltmeter.

When the electric and magnetic forces are in balance the number density of charge carriers n (number of electrons per unit volume) is given by the following equation:

$$n = (Bi)/(Vle)$$

where e is the charge on one electron and l is the thickness of the strip and equals the cross-sectional area divided by the strip width; $l = A/d$.

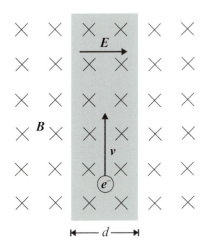

Figure 1 Electrons moving through a copper strip in a magnetic field

The average velocity of the electrons can also be measured using the Hall effect. If the copper strip is moved in a direction opposite to the electron velocity, the Hall potential difference will be zero when the strip velocity equals the electron velocity. ($e = 1.60 \times 10^{-19}$ C)

152. In Figure 1, the force on the moving electron due to the magnetic field is in which direction?

    A.   to the left
    B.   to the right
    C.   into the page
    D.   toward the top of the page

153. Which of the following will be true if the direction of the magnetic field in Figure 1 is reversed and the system is allowed to establish equilibrium?

    A.   The electric field E will be reversed.
    B.   The electron velocity v will be reversed.
    C.   The Hall potential difference will be zero.
    D.   The magnetic field in Figure 1 cannot be reversed because the current creates a magnetic field directed into the page.

154. Which of the following is true when the copper strip in Figure 1 is moved in the direction opposite to the elctrons with a velocity greater than the average electron velocity v?

    A.   The electric field E is equal to the magnetic field B.
    B.   The electric field E is in the opposite direction of the electric field in Figure 1.
    C.   The magnetic field B is in the opposite direction of the magnetic field in Figure 1.
    D.   The Hall potential difference will be zero.

155. If the copper strip is held stationary, the net force on the copper strip is:

    A.   zero.
    B.   directed into the page.
    C.   directed to the right.
    D.   directed to the left.

GO ON TO THE NEXT PAGE.

156. If an electron were to break free from the surface of the copper strip, which of the following would most accurately represent its path from the moment it breaks free?

A.   C.

B.   D.

157. Which of the following describes the Hall potential difference where R is the effective resistance of the copper strip?

A. evB
B. iR
C. evR
D. Ed

Questions 158 through 161 are **NOT** based on a descriptive passage.

158. The capacitor shown below is fully charged. Both resistors have a 2Ω resistance. When the switch is opened, what is the initial current through resistor A?

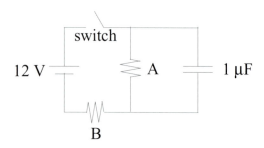

A. 2 A
B. 3 A
C. 6 A
D. 12 A

159. What is the charge on the capacitor in the circuit below after the circuit has been on a long time?

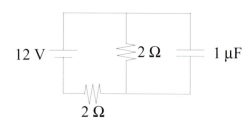

A. 1.2×10^{-5} C
B. 2.5×10^{-6} C
C. 6.0×10^{-6} C
D. 1.7×10^{-7} C

160. Charges A, B, C, and D are charged particles forming a square as shown. A and D have a charge of +2 C; B and C have a charge of –4 C. If q is a particle with a charge of +1 sitting directly in the middle of the square, what is the net force on q due to the other particles?

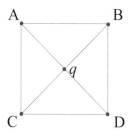

A. 0 N
B. 1 N
C. 1.4 N
D. 4 N

161. A particle possessing a charge of +2 C and a mass of 1 g is exposed to an electric field with strength 5 N/C. How far will the particle move in 10 seconds?

A. 1×10^3 m
B. 2×10^5 m
C. 5×10^5 m
D. 1×10^6 m

STOP. IF YOU FINISH BEFORE TIME IS CALLED, CHECK YOUR WORK. YOU MAY GO BACK TO ANY QUESTION IN THIS TEST BOOKLET.

STOP.

30-MINUTE
IN-CLASS EXAM
FOR LECTURE 8

Passage I (Questions 162-167)

A physicist performed the following experiments to investigate the wave nature of light.

Experiment 1: Single Slit

Monochromatic light with frequency f is incident on a diaphragm in which there is a single slit of width W. The light shining through the slit falls on a detector located a distance D to the right of the slit. D is much greater than W. The detector measures the energy delivered by the scattered wave as a function of the distance x. The entire apparatus is shown in Figure 1.

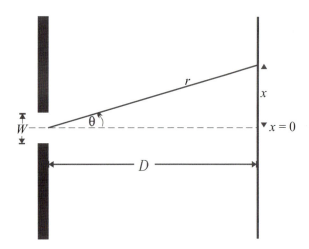

Figure 1 Single slit apparatus
(not drawn to scale)

The light falling on the detector reveals a series of dark and light fringes. These results are shown in Figure 2.

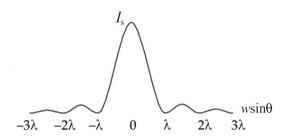

Figure 2 Intensity vs. $w \sin\theta$ for Experiment 1

The intensity at any given point near the center of the detector is a function of the phase difference ϕ between the rays at the top and bottom of the slit the moment they strike the same point on the detector. The intensity is given by the following equation:

$$I_s = I_m \, (\sin \tfrac{1}{2}\phi)/\tfrac{1}{2}\phi$$

where I_m is the intensity of light striking the detector directly across from the slit.

Experiment 2: Double Slit

In Experiment 2 another slit also of width W is made in the diaphragm at a distance s from the first slit and the diaphragm is recentered as shown in Figure 3. s is large compared to the wavelength of light λ. Again the physicist shines a monochromatic beam of light of frequency f on the diaphragm. This time a different fringe pattern forms. The results of Experiment 2 are shown in Figure 4.

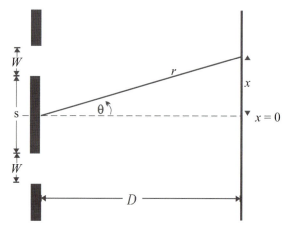

Figure 3 Double slit apparatus
(not drawn to scale)

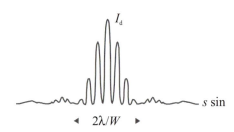

Figure 4 Intensity vs. $s \sin\theta$ for Experiment 2

The intensity striking near the center of the diaphragm in Experiment 2 is given by the following equation:

$$I_d = 4I_s \cos^2(\tfrac{1}{2}\psi)$$

where ψ is the phase difference between rays of light from the different slits the moment they strike the detector at the point in question.

GO ON TO THE NEXT PAGE.

162. What wave phenomenon or phenomena are demonstrated by the two experiments?

    A. Experiment 1 demonstrates only interference and Experiment 2 only diffraction.
    B. Experiment 1 demonstrates only diffraction and Experiment 2 only interference.
    C. Both experiments demonstrate interference and diffraction.
    D. Neither experiment demonstrates interference or diffraction.

163. In Experiment 1 which of the following equations represents the time necessary for light to travel from the slit to any point on the detector? (c = speed of light)

    A. $x/c\sin\theta$
    B. x/c
    C. $D/c\sin\theta$
    D. D/c

164. If light were purely a particle phenomenon which of the following would best describe the results the physicist could expect from either experiment?

    A. The graph in Figure 2 would have more peaks.
    B. The graph in Figure 4 would have more peaks.
    C. The graph in Figure 2 would have 1 peak.
    D. The graph in Figure 4 would have 1 peak.

165. If white light were used in Experiment 1 the outermost fringes of light on the detector would appear:

    A. blue
    B. red
    C. white
    D. green

166. If the same light source is used for both experiments, the brightest fringe in Experiment 2 will have an intensity:

    A. half as great as the brightest fringe in Experiment 1.
    B. equal to the brightest fringe in Experiment 1.
    C. twice as great as the brightest fringe in Experiment 1.
    D. four times as great as the brightest fringe in Experiment 1.

167. If the amplitude of the light wave in Figure 1 were doubled, which of the following would be true?

    A. I_s would increase by a factor of 2.
    B. I_s would increase by a factor of 4.
    C. The distance between the peaks in Figure 2 would increase by a factor of 2.
    D. The distance between the peaks in Figure 2 would decrease by a factor of 2.

_____

GO ON TO THE NEXT PAGE.

The compound microscope (Figure 1) uses two convex lenses in order to magnify small objects at short distances. The lens nearest the object is called the *objective*; the lens nearest the observer is called the *ocular* or *eyepiece*. The distance between the two lenses minus the sum of the magnitudes of their focal lengths is called the *tube length L*.

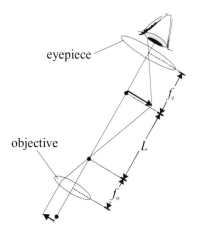

Figure 1 A compound microscope

If a small object is placed just outside the focal point of the objective, an enlarged image is formed just inside the focal point of the eyepiece. The lateral magnification m_o of this image is given by the equation:

$$m_o = -\frac{L}{f_o}$$

where f_o is the focal length of the objective.

The eyepiece acts as a simple magnifier on the image formed by the objective. The angular magnification of the eyepiece M_e is given by the equation:

$$M_e = -\frac{25\text{cm}}{f_e}$$

where f_e is the focal length of the eyepiece, and 25 cm is the closest point to the eye for which a sharp image may be formed; this distance is called the *near point* or the *distance of most distinct vision*.

The total magnification of the microscope is given by the product of the lateral magnification of the objective and the angular magnification of the eyepiece.

$$M_{\text{total}} = m_o M_e$$

168. A certain compound microscope magnifies an image 1200 times. If the eyepiece is replaced with a lens with twice the power, the image will be magnified by a factor of:

    A.   600
    B.   1800
    C.   2400
    D.   4800

169. The image of the object in Figure 1 created by the objective is:

    A.   virtual and inverted
    B.   virtual and upright
    C.   real and upright
    D.   real and inverted

170. If the eyepiece on a compound microscope has a power of 25 diopters, what is the focal length of the eyepiece?

    A.   0.25 cm
    B.   −0.25 cm
    C.   4 cm
    D.   −4 cm

171. A 2 mm object is magnified 500 times by a compound microscope. The magnitudes of the focal lengths of the eyepiece and the objective are 1 cm and 0.5 cm respectively. What is the distance between the two lenses when the object is in focus?

    A.   8.5 cm
    B.   10.0 cm
    C.   11.5 cm
    D.   15.0 cm

172. What would happen if the object were placed just inside the focal point of the objective?

    A.   The objective would form a virtual, upright image of the object on the object side of the lens.
    B.   The objective would form a virtual, upright image of the object on the side of the lens opposite to the object.
    C.   The objective would form a real, inverted image of the object beyond the eyepiece.
    D.   The objective would form a real, inverted image of the object behind the object.

GO ON TO THE NEXT PAGE.

173. The word 'READ' is placed under the microscopic in the upright position. Which of the following represents the word when viewed through the microscope?

   A. READ
   B. ꓤƎAꓷ
   C. ꓷAƎꓤ
   D. ꓷAƎꓤ

174. Which of the following describes how a compound microscope magnifies an image?

   A. Light reflects off an object and diffracts through the lenses.
   B. Light disperses off an object and reflects through the lenses.
   C. Light reflects off an object and refracts through the lenses.
   D. Light refracts off an object and reflects through the lenses.

Passage III (Questions 175-180)

A refracting telescope can be made from two convex lenses separated by a tube length *s*. The focal points of the two lenses must coincide in order for the telescope to focus on distant objects. Although Figure 1 shows two simple lenses, in practice, each lens is usually a compound lens. The lens nearer the observer is called the eyepiece, and the other lens is called the objective.

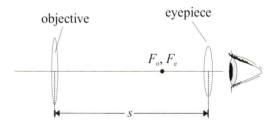

Figure 1 A telescope

The angular magnification of a telescope is given by the following equation:

$$M = -\frac{f_{obj}}{f_{eye}}$$

where *f* is the focal distance of the respective lenses.

Since a telescope is used to view distant objects, it requires *light-gathering power*. Light-gathering power determines how bright the image will be, and is increased by increasing the diameter of the objective. *Resolving power*, the ability to distinguish between two distant points, is also important for a telescope.

Refracting telescopes may have two flaws, *spherical and chromatic aberration*. Spherical aberration results in a blurred image because true spherical lenses do not focus all parallel light rays exactly on the focal point. This can be fixed by using parabolic lenses. Chromatic aberration occurs because different wavelengths refract at different angles.

175. Which of the following must be true in order for a refracting telescope to magnify distant images?

   A. The focal length of the eyepiece must be greater than the focal length of the objective.
   B. The focal length of the objective must be greater than the focal length of the eyepiece.
   C. Only the eyepiece must be a compound lens.
   D. Both the eyepiece and the objective must be compound lenses.

176. Where will the objective form the image of a very distant object?

    A.   in front of the objective
    B.   behind the objective but in front of the focal point of the objective
    C.   at the focal point of the objective
    D.   behind the eyepiece

177. If all lenses shown below are made from the same type of glass, which lens will have the greatest positive power in diopters?

    A.   **C.**

    B.   **D.**

178. Which of the following helps to explain chromatic aberration in a refracting telescope?

    A.   When light enters the lens, the frequency is lowered in a greater proportion for blue light than for red light.
    B.   When light enters the lens, the wavelength is shortened in a greater proportion for red light than for blue light.
    C.   When light enters the lens, the wavelength is lengthened in a greater proportion for blue light than for red light.
    D.   When light enters the lens, the wavelength is shortened in a greater proportion for blue light than for red light.

179. If the eyepiece of the telescope shown in Figure 1 has a power of 100 diopters, and the magnification of the telescope is –9, what is the focal length of the objective?

    A.   9 cm
    B.   –9 cm
    C.   10 m
    D.   –10 m

180. If the space between the lenses in the telescope in Figure 1 were filled with water, which of the following changes to the tube length would bring the image back into focus. (index of refraction for glass = 1.5, index of refraction for water = 1.3, index of refraction for air = 1)

    A.   increasing the tube length to compensate for the longer focal lengths of the lenses in water
    B.   increasing the tube length to compensate for the increased power of each lens
    C.   decreasing the tube length to compensate for the decrease in focal lengths of the lenses in water
    D.   decreasing the tube length to compensate for the decreased power of each lens

GO ON TO THE NEXT PAGE.

Questions 181 through 184 are **NOT** based on a descriptive passage.

---

181. Although waves in the open ocean propagate in all directions, waves washing into any shore usually move nearly perpendicular to the shore. Which of the following best explains the reason for this phenomenon?

   A. The shallow water decreases the speed of the waves causing them to refract.

   B. The shallow water increases the speed of the waves causing them to refract.

   C. The shallow water decreases the speed of the waves causing them to diffract.

   D. The shallow water increases the speed of the waves causing them to diffract.

182. A mirror has a radius of curvature of 8 cm and makes a real inverted image 20 cm from its surface. Where is the object?

   A. 4 cm
   B. 5 cm
   C. 10 cm
   D. 20 cm

183. A 3 cm object is placed 15 cm in front of a convex mirror. The image forms 5 cm behind the mirror. How big is the image?

   A. 1 cm
   B. 3 cm
   C. 5 cm
   D. 9 cm

184. On a hot day, a driver on the highway may see a *mirage* that appears as a puddle of water far ahead on the hot pavement. The mirage is actually a virtual image of the sky caused by light rays bending as shown below. Which of the following helps to explain the formation of the *mirage*?

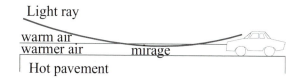

   A. Hot pavement is an efficient reflector.

   B. The thin layer of warmer air acts as an aperture through which light diffracts.

   C. As air warms the speed of light decreases.

   D. As air warms the speed of light increases.

STOP. IF YOU FINISH BEFORE TIME IS CALLED, CHECK YOUR WORK. YOU MAY GO BACK TO ANY QUESTION IN THIS TEST BOOKLET.

GO ON TO THE NEXT PAGE.

ANSWERS & EXPLANATIONS

FOR

30-MINUTE IN-CLASS EXAMS

ANSWERS FOR THE 30-MINUTE IN-CLASS EXAMS

Lecture 1	Lecture 2	Lecture 3	Lecture 4	Lecture 5	Lecture 6	Lecture 7	Lecture 8
1. D	24. B	47. C	70. D	93. D	116. A	139. D	162. C
2. C	25. A	48. A	71. B	94. C	117. B	140. D	163. A
3. D	26. A	49. B	72. C	95. B	118. B	141. A	164. C
4. B	27. A	50. B	73. D	96. A	119. A	142. C	165. B
5. A	28. D	51. B	74. D	97. B	120. A	143. C	166. D
6. B	29. B	52. D	75. A	98. A	121. B	144. A	167. B
7. B	30. C	53. B	76. C	99. D	122. C	145. C	168. C
8. B	31. A	54. A	77. C	100. D	123. B	146. A	169. D
9. D	32. D	55. A	78. D	101. B	124. D	147. C	170. C
10. B	33. D	56. D	79. B	102. C	125. B	148. D	171. C
11. B	34. B	57. B	80. B	103. D	126. A	149. B	172. A
12. A	35. A	58. A	81. B	104. C	127. B	150. C	173. C
13. B	36. A	59. D	82. D	105. B	128. D	151. C	174. C
14. C	37. D	60. B	83. C	106. B	129. D	152. B	175. B
15. D	38. D	61. D	84. B	107. C	130. A	153. A	176. C
16. C	39. C	62. C	85. A	108. B	131. C	154. B	177. A
17. D	40. C	63. A	86. C	109. A	132. A	155. A	178. D
18. A	41. C	64. A	87. B	110. B	133. B	156. B	179. A
19. D	42. A	65. D	88. A	111. D	134. C	157. D	180. A
20. B	43. C	66. C	89. B	112. C	135. A	158. B	181. A
21. B	44. A	67. B	90. D	113. B	136. D	159. C	182. B
22. C	45. A	68. D	91. B	114. A	137. D	160. A	183. A
23. D	46. D	69. B	92. B	115. B	138. B	161. C	184. D

MCAT PHYSICS	
Raw Score	**Estimated Scaled Score**
23	15
22	14
21	13
19–20	12
18	11
16-17	10
15	9
13-14	8
12	7
10-11	6
9	5
7-8	4

EXPLANATIONS TO IN-CLASS EXAM FOR LECTURE 1

Passage I

1. **D is correct.** The value x in the equation gives the distance the projectile would travel in the absence of air resistance. Like all frictional forces, air resistance creates a force in the opposite direction of motion, so Zacchini should expect to fly a shorter distance than x.

2. **C is correct.** The passage says that it is the "propulsion" that causes the loss of consciousness. In other words, the force on Zacchini causes him to accelerate at a rate so great that he loses consciousness.

3. **D is correct.** Total energy is conserved throughout the flight. At maximum height gravitational potential energy mgh is maximized, so kinetic energy $\frac{1}{2}mv^2$ is minimized.

4. **B is correct.** The vertical component is $v\sin\theta$ or 27×0.8.

5. **A is correct.** While in the cannon the acceleration is so great that it makes him unconscious. While in the cannon muzzle, Zacchini goes from zero velocity to maximum velocity. This is the greatest change in velocity in the shortest distance or time. Acceleration is rate of change in velocity.

6. **B is correct.** For a projectile without air resistance, the range is maximized at 45°. This is a fact that you should memorize for the MCAT. Subtracting or adding to the angle of trajectory from 45° by equal amounts results in equal ranges. For instance, 30° and 60° are both 15° from 45° and result in the same range.

Passage II

7. **B is correct.** Without air resistance, both Jim and the ball will accelerate downward at the same rate, 10 m/s^2. This is the same situation as if Tom and Jim were two astronauts in a spaceship orbiting earth. An orbiting spaceship and everything inside it fall toward earth at the same rate. Everything in the spaceship appears to float from the perspective of the two astronauts, Tom and Jim. In this case, it is obvious that Tom should throw the ball directly at Jim. In the diagram shown on the left, the ball moves with a constant horizontal velocity, and both Jim and the ball accelerate downward at the same rate. Notice that the ball moves along a straight line with respect to Jim, but moves in a parabolic path with respect to Tom. At every moment, the ball appears to Jim as if it were coming straight toward him along the dotted line. This effect is independent of the speed of the ball, and independent of where Jim catches the ball.

8. **B is correct.** The equation is $x = \frac{1}{2}gt^2$. x equals 10 m. You should probably know without calculating that an object starting from rest falls 5 m in one second and 20 meters in two seconds.

9. **D is correct.** The velocity of a projectile experiencing no air resistance is independent of its mass.

10. **B is correct.** Only vertical velocity dictates the time of flight for a projectile. When Jim throws the ball from the board, both Jim and the ball have an initial vertical velocity of zero. Again, the velocity of a projectile experiencing no air resistance is independent of its mass.

11. **B is correct.** Look at the diagram for question 7. Jim will travel a vertical distance of 10 m starting from zero m/s and constantly accelerating. The ball will start with an initial vertical velocity upward, slow to zero, and then reverse direction to arrive at the same point and at the same time as Jim. Thus the ball could not possibly travel as far as Jim. 10 m and 5 m are out. The ball definitely rises above 0 m. Thus B is correct. Another way to figure this out is to recognize that Jim's trip requires 1.4 seconds (see question 8). This means that the ball must reach its peak at 0.7 seconds due to the symmetry of projectile motion. From the formula $x = \frac{1}{2}gt^2$ we have approximately 2.5 m.

12. **A is correct.** Since Tom's fall lasts 1.4 seconds, the ball's flight also lasts 1.4 seconds. (See question 8. Tom's flight time is the same as Jim's. Mass is irrelevant; they have the same initial vertical velocity.) The distance traveled by the ball is its horizontal velocity (10 m/s from the passage) times its flight time. This is 14 m. Notice that the edge of the pool is already 10 m from the board, so the answer is four meters.

13. **B is correct.** Mass is irrelevant to the path of a projectile experiencing no air resistance. Now, in order to achieve that velocity, Tom must use more force on the 2 kg ball, but that's a different question.

Passage III

14. **C is correct.** This can be deduced from any trial, but the easiest is from the 0° trial. Since the vertical velocity is zero in this trial, the height is found from the equation $x = \frac{1}{2}gt^2$. This gives $x = 10$ m.

15. **D is correct.** Since the projectile starts from a height of 10 meters, it reaches a maximum velocity just before it strikes the ground: potential energy turns to kinetic energy. Table 1 shows us that A is wrong. B is wrong because if we fire the projectile straight up, it will have zero horizontal displacement but maximum height.

16. **C is correct.** Again, the first trial is the easiest to examine. From the first trial, we have $d = vt$, which gives us $v = 10$ m/s.

17. **D is correct.** This should be intuitive. $v\sin\theta = \sqrt{2gh}$. Sin 90° is 1, so h is maximized at 90 degrees.

18. **A is correct.** This is the only graph that isn't zero when θ is zero.

19. **D is correct.** The distance through the air is not the horizontal displacement. This is best solved by process of elimination: A is wrong because only vertical velocity is zero at maximum height. B is wrong because acceleration was constant for all projectiles. C is wrong because only the velocity changed at a constant rate; as the projectile climbed, speed decreased; as it fell, speed increased.

Stand Alones

20. **B is correct.** Use units. 1 m/s 2 strides/s = $\frac{1}{2}$ m/stride

21. **B is correct.** The atmosphere will create air resistance, shortening the path of the ball, and the gravity will reduce the time of flight, also shortening the path of the ball.

22. **C is correct.** Only the vertical velocity affects the time in flight of a projectile experiencing no air resistance.

23. **D is correct.** The velocity is proportional to the square root of the initial height of a ball rolling down an inclined plane: $v^2 = 2ax$ or $v = \sqrt{2gh}$. The ball falls twice as far in the second trial. Thus the ball has √2 times the velocity. Eliminate A by taking the example to extremes. If the ball falls straight down, it will obviously take less time to travel one meter than if the ball rolls down at a very slight angle. Displacement is a vector; direction matters, so B is wrong. C is wrong because the acceleration down an inclined plane is $g\sin\theta$. You also should have known C is wrong because if A is wrong, speed is distance over time, so C would be wrong as well.

EXPLANATIONS TO IN-CLASS EXAM FOR LECTURE 2

Passage I

24. **B is correct.** B and D are opposites so one must be the false statement. The larger the radius of curvature, the straighter the curve. A straight line would require no bank angle. (Radius of curvature is discussed in Physics Lecture 8)

25. **A is correct.** Friction is always parallel to the surfaces that create it, and it always opposes sliding motion between the two surfaces. In this case, the car is going very fast and, if the bank were made of ice (had no friction), the car would slide up the bank. The friction is static because the vehicle has no motion relative to the bank in the direction of friction (i.e., the tires do not slide along the pavement).

26. **A is correct.** If we were to draw a circle circumscribing the path of the car, arrow B would point to the center of that circle. The centripetal force always points to the center of the circle.

27. **A is correct.** A stationary object experiences no net force. We will discuss this more in Physics Lecture 3.

28. **D is correct.** Centripetal force is given by $F_c = mv^2/r$. Doubling v requires that F quadruples.

29. **B is correct.** Since there is no vertical acceleration, the net vertical force would have to be zero ($F = ma$). The only vertical force downward would be the weight of the vehicle, so the frictional force would have to be equal and opposite. The normal force is the centripetal force of the wall on the vehicle. The car must be moving fast enough for the frictional force to be equal to gravity. So $f_s = \mu_s N = \mu_s mv^2/r$. $\mu_s mv^2/r = mg$.

30. **C is correct.** The mass of the vehicles will not affect the required bank angle because the centripetal force, the frictional force and the force down the incline due to gravity are all proportional to mass. A greater speed limit on the curves would require a greater bank angle in order to keep the cars from sliding off the road.

Passage II

31. **A is correct.** As long as there are no resisting forces like friction, the centripetal force will always have the same magnitude and will always be perpendicular to the spaceship's motion, so the speed of the spaceship will never change. The ship will continue to travel with the motion dictated by the equation in the passage unless another force causes it to change.

32. **D is correct.** The passage says the ship is pressurized, thus there are air molecules in the ship. The passage also says that there is air in the cabin. The man has his helmet off and is still alive so there must be air in the ship. Air molecules create air resistance, which will slow any projectile. The gravity of the planet acts equally on the ship, the astronaut, and the projectile, so relative to the astronaut, the bag will move along a straight line.

33. **D is correct.** The bag will move in a straight line relative to the astronaut. (See question 32.)

34. **B is correct.** $t = d/v$. Convert seconds to hours. You must know that radio waves are electromagnetic, and electromagnetic waves move at the speed of light or 3×10^8 m/s.

35. **A is correct.** Centripetal force equals gravitational force. $GmM/r^2 = mv^2/r$. Thus v^2 is inversely proportional to r.

36. **A is correct.** Their orbits are related only to their velocities because both gravitational and centripetal force are proportional to mass. (See the equation in question 35.)

37. **D is correct.** A pendulum is propelled by gravity. Since the clock is in free fall the entire apparatus is propelled by gravity and the pendulum would not fall faster than the apparatus from which it is hanging.

Passage III

38. **D is correct.** Light travels 3×10^8 m each second, so a light second is equal to 3×10^8 m. The distance in light seconds is the orbital radius of the moon (found in Table 1), converted to meters (384,400,000 m), divided by meters per light second (3×10^8 m/light second). Using scientific notation, this comes out to something slightly greater than 1.

39. **C is correct.** The passage states that the same side of the moon always faces the earth and that the moon moves around the earth once every 27.3 days. Thus the moon revolves once on its axis every 27.3 days. Yes, you probably would be expected to know what defines a day on a given planet.

40. **C is correct.** These are not lengthy calculations, so use your pencil! To solve this problem we set the gravitational force of the sun on the earth equal to the centripetal force.

$$F = G\frac{M_{sun}\, m_{earth}}{r^2_{orbital}} = m_{earth}\frac{v^2}{r}$$

solving for v we get:

$$v = \sqrt{\frac{G M_{sun}}{r}}$$

41. **C is correct.** The quickest way to solve this problem is by proportions. The radius of the earth is a little less than 4 times as large as the radius of the moon. According to $F = Gmm/r^2$, this would lead to an *increase* in relative gravity on the moon by a factor of something less than 16. From Table 1 we see that the earth is about 80 times more massive than the moon. This would lead to a *decrease* in relative gravity on the moon by a factor of 80. Multiplying the man's weight on the earth (1000 N) by 16 and dividing by 80 we get: 16,000/80 = 200 N. This is easily closest to 170. Don't be afraid to round off. **OR,** you can solve this problem the long way: From Table 1, plug into $F = Gmm/r^2$ for the moon and solve.

42. **A is correct.** This is Newton's 3rd law: For every force there is an EQUAL and opposite force.

Stand Alones

43. **C is correct.** Just as if we suspended a 200 kg mass from the rope, the ceiling would pull upward with a force of 2000 newtons and the mass would pull downward with 2000 newtons, but the tension in the rope would still be *mg* or 2000 newtons.

44. **A is correct.** Since there is no acceleration, the net force is zero.

45. **A is correct.** From the $F = Gmm/r^2$ equation, we know that the weight is reduced by increasing r. The flattened shape of the earth makes the equator further from the center of gravity of the earth. Secondly, if there were no gravity, objects along the equator would be thrown away from the earth by the centrifugal force. More precisely, they would continue straight in the direction of their present velocity instead of turning with the earth's surface. Thus, some of the force of gravity is used up as centripetal force to turn the direction of the velocity of the objects. This results in a decrease in the weight of the object.

46. **D is correct.** $F = -kx$ and $F = mg$. Thus $mg = -kx$. Ignore the negative which only indicates that the force is in the opposite direction of the displacement. $5 \times 10 = 0.1k$.

EXPLANATIONS TO IN-CLASS EXAM FOR LECTURE 3

Passage I

47. **C is correct.** Each revolution moves Puncho $2\pi r$ meters, which equals 0.5π m/revolution. If we examine the units, we see that dividing the velocity 10 m/s by 0.5π m/rev gives us $20/\pi$ revolutions/second. The question asks for revolutions in one second, so the answer is $20/\pi$ revolutions.

48. **A is correct.** Since the pole is stationary, the net torque must be zero Newton meters.

49. **B is correct.** As shown by the equations below, the angle is related to the mass of Puncho and the tension in the rope, and is not related to the length of rope.

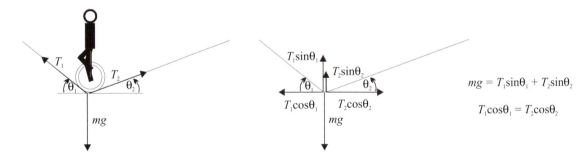

50. **B is correct.** Since gravity is the only force acting on a ball while it is in the air, and because gravity is a conservative force, while in the air, the total energy of each ball remains constant. Each ball has an energy equal to the initial kinetic energy given to it by Puncho, $\frac{1}{2}mv^2 = 25$ J. Five balls gives a total energy of 125 J. Or each ball has an energy equal to the maximum potential energy which is P.E. = $mgh = 0.5 \times 10 \times 5 = 25$ J. Five balls gives a total energy of 125 J.

51. **B is correct.** When Puncho is on his unicycle, he doesn't want to move laterally. Inertia is the tendency for an object to resist change in its present state of motion. Mass is a measure of inertia, so a massive pole increases inertia. As an object's mass is spread from its center of gravity, more torque is required to rotate that object; its rotational inertia is increased.

Passage II

52. **D is correct.** There is an initial net force, and all the forces involved are constant, so the acceleration is constant. Acceleration means no equilibrium. The mass does not achieve equilibrium regardless of how long it falls; it always accelerates.

53. **B is correct.** Think of the extreme case. If the mass m is much, much larger than 0.1 kg, the greatest acceleration is still only equal to $g = 10$ m/s^2. In order to accelerate 0.1 kg at the rate of g, we would only need 1 N of tension in the string. ($F = ma$)

54. **A is correct.** The mass in Experiment 1 is in static equilibrium; there is no net force.

55. **A is correct.** Mass m would fall at a rate of $g = 10$ m/s^2. Any tension in the string would slow this rate and mass m would no longer be in free fall. The tension in the string must be zero.

56. **D is correct.** The forces on the block are constant, so, from $F = ma$, so is the acceleration. The block does accelerate because tension had to overcome static friction to move the block initially. Kinetic friction is weaker than static friction, so the tension must be greater than kinetic friction.

57. **B is correct.** Friction is a force opposing motion, which is in the opposite direction of tension, increasing the tension. Changing mass m does not change the friction. The friction is given by $f = \mu N$, where N is the normal force which in this case is the weight of the 0.1 kg block.

58. **A is correct.** You should use Table 2 to figure this out quickly. You can see from the table that there is not a linear relationship between mass m and tension T. From trial 1 to 3 the mass was doubled increasing the tension by 0.17 N; from trial 2 to 4 the mass was doubled increasing the tension by 0.15 N. Thus, you would expect that if we double the mass of trial 3 we would get an increase in tension of less than 0.15 N. A is the only answer that satisfies this criterion.

Trial	m (kg)	T (N)
1	0.10	0.50
2	0.15	0.60
3	0.20	0.67
4	0.30	0.75

0.17 N increase
0.15 N increase
Increase should be less than 0.15 N so T should be less than 0.83.

The long way to figure this out is as follows: Assuming no friction, first look at the 0.1 kg mass. $T = ma \Rightarrow T = 0.1a$. For the other block $mg = T + ma \Rightarrow 0.4(10) = T + 0.4a$. Putting both equations together we get $0.4(10) = T + 0.4(T/0.1) \Rightarrow 4 = 5T \Rightarrow T = 4/5 = 0.8$.

Passage III

59. **D is correct.** Once the bomb is in the air, gravity is the only force acting upon it. Since gravity is a conservative force, total mechanical energy is conserved. Just before the bomb hits the ground, all the energy would be kinetic. The initial potential energy of the bomb is $P.E. = mgh = 2 \times 10 \times 300 = 6000$ J. The initial kinetic energy of the bomb is $K.E. = \frac{1}{2}mv^2 = \frac{1}{2} \times 2 \times 30^2 = 900$ J. The total energy is the sum of these two.

60. **B is correct.** The power required is $P = Fv$. Where the force is the weight of the rocket mg, and v is the velocity of the rocket. Thus, $1200 \times 300 \times 10 = 3.6 \times 10^6$ W.

61. **D is correct.** Energy is a scalar and is conserved. The total initial energy will equal the final energy in every case. Also, in every case gravitational potential energy will be completely converted to kinetic energy. Since energy is a scalar, the direction of the plane does not affect its initial energy. (Notice that in question 59 we were not concerned with the direction in which the plane was flying.) The initial potential energy is the same in each case. Thus the initial energy and the final energy are greatest where the initial velocity is the greatest.

62. **C is correct.** The plane is not a glider. It receives its energy from fuel.

63. **A is correct.** Terminal velocity is constant velocity, so the net force must be zero. The forces acting on the plane are its propulsive force, the air resistance, and gravity. The sum of these forces is zero.

64. **A is correct.** The apparent weight of the pilot is the reading on a scale if he were sitting on the scale during his dive. When he pulls out of the dive, he is decelerating. This means that the scale underneath him would have to push up with more force than his weight. His apparent weight increases.

65. **D is correct.** Don't use vectors to solve this problem. The work done is equal to the change in potential and kinetic energy. $W = \Delta K.E. + \Delta P.E.$ $W = \frac{1}{2}mv^2 + mgh = \frac{1}{2} \times 2 \times 400 + 2 \times 10 \times 200 = 400 + 4000$.

66. **C is correct.** The time for the bomb to reach the ground is found from the equation $x = \frac{1}{2}gt^2$. $t = 6$ seconds. The horizontal velocity of the bomb is the same as the plane, 30 m/s. In 6 seconds, the bomb will move 180 meters horizontally.

Stand Alones

67. **B is correct.** Energy is required to separate attracting bodies. The rocket is attracted to earth by gravity. Gravity is a conservative force so the added energy goes into potential energy.

68. **D is correct.** The left end is 4 times closer to the balancing point than the right end, and thus has a lever arm four times smaller. A lever arm four times smaller requires a force four times greater or $4mg$.

69. **B is correct**. Finding the center of gravity can be done like a torque problem. To find the center of gravity, we find the balancing point. The lever arm for the moon must be 80 times longer than the lever arm for the earth because the earth is 80 times heavier. We should divide the distance from the earth to the moon into 81 equal parts, but it is easier to use 80. 400,000/80 = 5,000. Thus 400,000/81 < 5,000. The center of gravity is less than 5,000 km from the center of the earth, which is just beneath the surface of the earth.

EXPLANATIONS TO IN-CLASS EXAM FOR LECTURE 4

Passage I

70. **D is correct.** In order for momentum to be conserved, the horizontal and vertical components must be equal before and after the collision. There is no vertical momentum before either *Collision 1* or *Collision 2*, so there can be none afterwards. In order to have zero vertical momentum, angles x and y must be equal to zero.

71. **B is correct.** In order for momentum to be conserved, The momentum m_1v_1 (before) must equal $(m_1 + m_2)v$ (after). So, (1 kg)(4 m/s) = (2 kg)(v). Thus, $v = 2$ m/s.

72. **C is correct.** To conserve momentum, m_Av_A (before) must be equal to m_Bv_B (after). Therefore (2 kg)(4 m/s) = m(4 m/s). So $m = 2$ kg.

73. **D is correct.** There is no motion after the collision, so there is no kinetic energy. The blocks are permanently deformed and all of the collisions take place on a horizontal surface, so there is no elastic or gravitational potential energy. So the kinetic energy must be converted into heat energy during the collision.

74. **D is correct.** The vertical momentum before the explosion is zero, so it must be zero after the explosion. The momentum going up the page is (1 kg)$v_2\sin(w)$, and the momentum down the page is (1 kg)$v_3\sin(z)$. These two must be equal if they are to add up to zero. The other particle moves horizontally, so it has no effect on the vertical momentum.

75. **A is correct.** In order for a collision to be perfectly elastic, mechanical energy must be conserved. Mechanical energy is not conserved in explosions or in collisions where the colliding objects stick together, so only *Collision 1* can be perfectly elastic.

76. **C is correct.** The two blocks come to a stop after the collision, so their momenta must have been equal and opposite before the collision. Therefore (2 kg)v_A = (1 kg)v_B. So $2v_A = v_B$.

Passage II

77. **C is correct.** Energy from a fusion reaction comes from rest mass energy: $E = mc^2$

78. **D is correct.** The equation is given in the passage. The temperature at the sun's core is given as 1.3 keV. We divide this by Boltzmann's constant to get D. Don't forget the *kilo* in keV.

79. **B is correct.** The net reaction found by adding all the reactions together is: $4\,^1H + 2e^- \rightarrow\,^4He + 6\gamma + 2\nu$

80. **B is correct.** The energy for the reaction came from the annihilation of an electron and a positron. This energy equals mc^2, where m represents the mass of both the electron and positron. But first we must convert to joules by multiplying 1.02 MeV (don't forget that Mega = 10^6) times coulombs/electron (given at the end of the passage). This is the energy in $E = mc^2$. We divide energy by the speed of light squared to get the mass of the electron and the positron. We divide by two for the mass of the positron. The answers are given to the nearest magnitude of 10, so, as usualy, round your numbers and do calculations quickly: $10^6 \times 10^{-19} = m \times 9 \times 10^{16} \Rightarrow m = 10^{-13}/10^{17} = 10^{-30}$. The true mass of a proton or electron is 9.1×10^{-31} kg.

81. **B is correct.** If energy is released then stronger bonds must be formed. As stated in the question, the strength of the bonds comes completely from the binding energy.

82. **D is correct.** Choice A is a violation of the conservation of energy. B is contradicted twice in the passage. C is contradicted in the passage and you should know that large nuclei undergo fission and small nuclei undergo fusion.

Passage III

83. **C is correct.** Both forces act on the same side of the fulcrum and the in-force is nearer to the fulcrum. From the passage, this is a third order lever system. The passage also states that running mammals take advantage of a third order lever system. Although Figure 1 shows a running mammal, and Figure 2 a digging mammal, the two lever systems are the same.

84. **B is correct.** The lever in Figure 2 has a greater in-lever arm to out-lever arm ratio and thus applies greater leverage and more force.

85. **A is correct.** The out-lever arm is 10 times greater than the in-lever arm, so the force applied by the out-lever arm must be 10 times smaller. As stated in the passage, the advantage to this system is speed not strength.

86. **C is correct.** The same formula as the previous question applies. The shorter lever arm requires the greater force. Work is not changed by an ideal machine.

87. **B is correct.** Decreasing the in-lever arm while increasing the out-lever arm creates greater relative velocity between the fulcrum and the point of out-force application. The animal in figure 2 is a digger and the animal in Figure 1 is a runner; notice the lever arm proportions. The passage also explains this. The passage tells us that swift runners take advantage of third order lever systems. In other words, swift runners take advantage of having the in-force closer to the fulcrum and the out-force further away.

88. **A is correct.** The elbow is the fulcrum. The distance from the elbow to the point where the force due to the muscle is 90° is greatest in A. This is the in-lever arm.

Stand Alones

89. **B is correct.** 2 hours is approximately 5 half-lives. $2^5 = 32$. $800/32 = 25$. But you should just count on your fingers.

90. **D is correct.** Two alpha decays indicate a loss of 8 in mass number and four in atomic number. 4 beta decays indicates an increase of four in atomic number. The element remains the same and the mass number goes to 210.

91.   **B is correct.** The angle is irrelevant. Both the lever and the pulley system reduce the force necessary by a factor of 2 each. The total reduction is by a factor of 4.

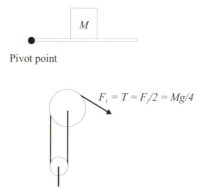

92.   **B is correct.** The horizontal momentum of the two rock system equals zero so there will be no horizontal velocity. The vertical momentum is 87 kg m/s. We divide this by 15 kg to get 5.8 m/s.

EXPLANATIONS TO IN-CLASS EXAM FOR LECTURE 5

Passage I

93.   **D is correct.** The passage states that the coefficient of volume expansion is 3 times α. Use the value of α from the table. Don't forget that the table gives α in magnitudes of 10^{-6}.

94.   **C is correct.** Steel has a lower α than brass and increases more slowly to temperature change.

95.   **B is correct.** Plug in 19×10^{-6} for α, 10 for ΔT, and solve for $\Delta L/L$. $\Delta L/L$ is the fractional change in length. Multiply this times 100 to get the percent change in length.

96.   **A is correct.** Aluminum has the highest α, and thus has the greatest change in length or volume per change in temperature.

97.   **B is correct.** Since the density of water is greatest at 4 °C, water expands when cooled below 4 °C. The weight does not change with expansion or contraction. There are the same number of water molecules; only the space between them has changed.

98.   **A is correct.** The easy way to solve this problem is to take things to the extremes: Since the aluminum has a much smaller volume coefficient of expansion, imagine that the aluminum doesn't change volume at all. The buoy must displace enough water to equal its mass. The mass of the buoy doesn't change with temperature. So in our extreme example only the volume of water is changing with temperature. When the water gets warm, it expands. The same mass of water fills more volume. The buoy sinks in the summer, in order to displace enough water to equal its weight.

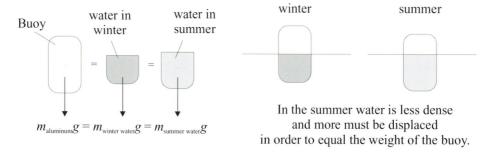

In the summer water is less dense and more must be displaced in order to equal the weight of the buoy.

$$m_{aluminum}g = m_{winter\ water}g = m_{summer\ water}g$$

The more difficult way to solve this problem is as follows: $\rho_{buoy}V_{buoy}g = \rho_{water}V_{water\ displaced}g \Rightarrow \rho_{water\ displaced}g = \rho_{buoy}g(V_{buoy}/V_{water\ displaced})$. Because aluminum changes volume much more slowly than water when heated, V_{buoy}/V_{water} gets smaller as temperature increases.

Passage II

99. **D is correct.** This is a fluid at rest. The pressure is greatest where the depth is the greatest. $P = \rho g y$; where y is measured from the surface.

100. **D is correct.** In an ideal fluid, flow rate is the same at all points.

101. **B is correct.** $P = \rho g y$. ρ is 5 times that of water, thus ρ is 5000 kg/m³. Measure y from the surface of the fluid: 6 cm. $P = 5000 \times 10 \times 0.06 = 3000$ Pa. The pipe is sealed shut so there is no atmospheric pressure.

102. **C is correct.** Choose $h_0 = 0$ to be point D, so $h = 0.1$ m, and we have $v = v = \sqrt{2gh} = 1.4$ m/s. **Important:** Notice that the velocity at C and B will also be 1.4 m/s because $Q = Av$. We can only use $v = \sqrt{2gh}$ at point D because the pressure is the same at point D as at the surface of the fluid.

103. **D is correct.** The volume of fluid displaced by the object is equal to the volume of the object. The mass of the fluid displaced by the object is equal to the apparent loss of mass of the object (weight = 5 N). Since the specific gravity of the fluid is 5, the same volume of water would weigh 1 N. Thus, the object weighs 20 times more than water giving it a specific gravity of 20.

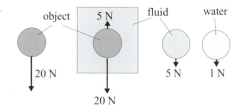

104. **C is correct.** As y decreases, the pressure ($P = \rho g y$) decreases, velocity ($v = : h = y$ in this case) decreases, and flow rate ($Q = Av$ [since v decreases, Q decreases) decreases, but not the density. At first glance, this appears to violate the rule that Q is constant everywhere in an ideal fluid. The reason that it doesn't violate this rule is because the rule says Q is constant everywhere in space, not in time. In other words, Q can change with time, but not with position; at any given moment, Q is constant in any given cross-section of an ideal fluid.

105. **B is correct.** Point C is twice the depth as point A, so the pressure is twice as great. ($P = \rho g y$) This question is really just asking "Do you measure y from the top, or from the bottom?" Of course, you measure y from the top.

Passage III

106. **B is correct.** Since lift acts against gravity, the ball will undergo less downward acceleration, so it will go higher and stay in the air longer. The horizontal distance is given by the horizonatl velocity times the time in the air. Since time in the air increases, it will also go farther horizontally.

107. **C is correct.** The speed of a point on the surface of a rotating object can be found by multiplying the frequency of rotation by the circumference. Don't forget to convert centimeters to meters. So $w = (3.14)(0.043 \text{ m})(60 \text{ Hz}) = 8.1$ m/s. 60 Hz has one significant digit, so the answer can have only one significant digit. The answer is 8 m/s.

108. **B is correct.** The density of the ball has nothing to do with the force exerted on it. A less dense ball might experience greater acceleration for a given force, but it will not change the actual lift force. All of the other choices will increase the pressure difference as shown in the equation in the passage.

109. **A is correct.** The density of the ball is (45 g)/(42 cm³). Since the density is greater than 1 g/cm³ (the density fo water), the specific gravity is greater than 1 and the ball will sink in water.

110. **B is correct.** If the spin is reversed, the relative airspeed will be decreased above the ball, causing the pressure above the ball to be greater than the pressure below.

111. **D is correct.** Subtract the airspeed below the ball $u - w$ from the airspeed above the ball $u + w$ to get the difference $2w$.

Stand Alones

112. **C is correct.** The density of the container is 2 kg/ 5 × 10⁻³ m³ = 400 kg/m³. The specific gravity is 0.4 which means that 60% floats above the water. Or even simpler, the bottle weighs 2 kg, while 5 liters of water would weight 5 kg, so the specific gravity of the bottle is 2/5 = 0.4.

113. **B is correct.** When the brick is on the Styrofoam, the water that is displaced is equal to the weight of the brick. When the brick is submerged, the water that is displaced is equal to less than the brick. More water is displaced by the floating brick-Styrofoam combination and thus the water level falls when the brick is submerged.

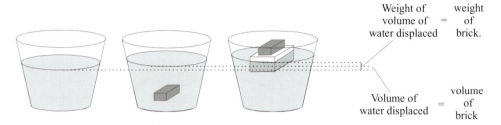

114. **A is correct.** The leak is 5 m below the surface. We use $v = \sqrt{2gh}$ where $h = 5$ m.

115. **B is correct.** 10 meters of water produces approximately 1 atm or 10⁵ Pa of pressure ($P = \rho gh$). 5 m produces half of that. Add atmospheric pressure (10⁵ Pa) to get 150,000 Pa.

EXPLANATIONS TO IN-CLASS EXAM FOR LECTURE 6

Passage I

116. **A is correct.** As shown in the diagram below, this is an inclined plane. The acceleration of any object down an inclined plane with no friction is $g \sin\theta$.

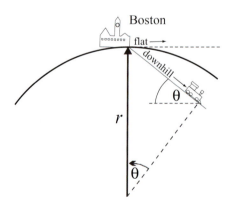

117. **B is correct.** The motion duplicates a pendulum with a length equal to the radius of the Earth. One period is equal to a round trip on the train. The equation for the period of a pendulum is $T = 2\pi\sqrt{(L/g)}$. Notice that the period is independent of the distance that the pendulum swings. Since the periods are equal, the top speed must be greater for the longer trip.

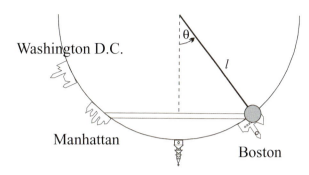

118. **B is correct.** The passage says that the motion is similar to a pendulum. The period of a pendulum is given by $T = 2\pi\sqrt{(L/g)}$. Here, L is the same as r, and we only want half the period because it is a one way trip. See the diagram above.

119. **A is correct.** Simple harmonic motion can be graphed as a sine curve. Since a trip from Boston to Manhattan is half a cycle, Choice A is correct answer.

120. **A is correct.** At the midpoint in the trip, the train is on a flat plane perpendicular to the radius of the earth. The forces on the train are gravity acting straight toward the center of the earth, and the normal force acting straight away from the center of the earth. Since the train is obviously not accelerating in either or these directions, these two forces are equal, and the net force is zero. Newton's second law, $F = ma$, tells us that the acceleration must also be zero.

121. **B is correct.** See Figure 1. The track is straight. It is our perception of *uphill* and *downhill* that is the problem. We perceive *downhill* as any vector with some component in the direction toward the center of the earth, and *uphill* as any vector with some component in the direction away from the center of the earth. Because we are so small compared to the earth, we are accustomed to thinking of the direction of the center of the earth as being constant. This is not the case. In the example of the tunnel train, it is the direction toward the center of the earth that changes and not the direction of the track.

122. **C is correct.** Gravity decreases as we move toward the center of the earth from the surface, so acceleration decreases, and maximum velocity will be less. The trip will require more time.

Passage II

123. **B is correct.** Only B gives the correct prediction of change in frequency when the moth flies away from the bat. The Doppler effect predicts that when the source moves away from the observer, the observed frequency goes down. In this case, the bat is observing the frequency reflected off the moth.

124. **D is correct.** The waves reflect off the moth at the same frequency that it receives them. This is the Doppler effect. Don't use the equation in the passage. To find the frequency at which the bat receives the waves use $\Delta f/f = v/c$ where $f = 66$ kHz, $v = 15$ m/s (the relative velocity), and $c = 340$ m/s. Since they are moving toward each other, the frequency will increase. Thus, to find the frequency at which the waves reflect off the moth we add Δf to 66 kHz.

125. **B is correct.** Only movement that separates the pair will decrease the frequency.

126. **A is correct.** If the signal takes less time, then it must be going faster. The speed of sound in a medium increases with decreasing density. You may think that humid air is heavier, but this is incorrect. There is a decrease in density as water vapor is added to air that occurs because the molecular mass of water (18 g/mol) is less than that of nitrogen (28 g/mol) or oxygen (32 g/mol) gases, the main constituents of air.

127. **B is correct.** This is just $v = \lambda f$. The numbers from the passage are: $f = 83$ kHz; $v = 340$ m/s. Don't forget the <u>kilo</u>hertz.

Passage III

128. **D is correct.** The length of the first harmonic is the longest possible standing wavelength, which is simply twice the length between the fastened ends of the wire.

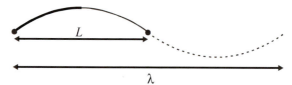

129. **D is correct.** Pitch correlates with frequency; $f\lambda = v$. We can set this equation equal to the one in the passage to see that increased tension raises frequency, and increased length lowers frequency. (From question 128 we know that speaking length L is proportional to wavelength λ.)

130. **A is correct.** Intensity is given by $I = \frac{1}{2}\mu\omega^2A^2v$. Doubling μ increases intensity by a factor of only 2. Since w = $2\pi f = 2\pi/T$, doubling T would decrease intensity by a factor of 4. The speaking length is directly proportional to the fundamental wavelength. From $v = f\lambda$, doubling the speaking length doubles λ and reduces f by a factor of 2, reducing intensity by a factor of 4. Doubling amplitude increases intensity by a factor of 4. Thus, changing μ has the least effect.

131. **C is correct.** 3 Hz is the beat frequency. The beat frequency is the difference between the frequency of the tuning fork and the frequency of the piano, so we know that the original frequency must be 3 Hz away from 440. We just don't know which direction. Tightening the string increased the beat frequency. This means that tightening the string moved us away from the tuning fork. Tightening the string increases the frequency, so when we increase the frequency we are moving away from 440 Hz. The original frequency of the piano note must be 443 Hz.

132. **A is correct.** This is just $v = \lambda f$. The speaking length is extraneous information.

133. **B is correct.** The piano wire moves up and down, while the wave moves along the string; the medium is moving perpendicular to the propagation of the wave. This is a transverse, not a longitudinal, wave.

134. **C is correct.** This is the definition of amplitude. The velocity is dictated by the medium. The wavelength is dictated by the speaking length. The frequency is dictated by the velocity and wavelength. How hard or far you strike the string only affects the amplitude.

Stand Alones

135. **A is correct.** When the spring is fully compressed or fully extended is when the Hooke's law forces are the greatest, and this indicates that the acceleration is the greatest. $F = ma$.

136. **D is correct.** The maximum amplitude will result from constructive interference. This is the sum of the amplitudes.

137. **D is correct.** The period is increasing by 1.42 or about the square root of 2. From $T = 2\pi\sqrt{(L/g)}$ we see that the square of the period is proportional to the length. L increases by a factor of 2, or a 100% increase.

138. **B is correct.** Only B and C allow for a higher frequency, which would explain a higher pitch. Heavier objects vibrate more slowly. The water in the glass increases the inertia of the system and creates a lower frequency.

EXPLANATIONS TO IN-CLASS EXAM FOR LECTURE 7

Passage I

139. **D is correct.** The Earth's magnetic field points from the geographic South to the geographic North. From the passage, the aurora borealis is in the north.

140.   **D is correct.** The easy way to answer this question is to look at Figures 1 and 2. From the passage and Figure 1 we see that pitch is the distance between the spirals. From Figure 2, we see that pitch is decreasing as the spirals move toward the stronger magnetic field. (The magnetic field lines are the horizontal lines. Closer field lines indicate a stronger field.) This leaves answer choice C or D. The period is the length of time necessary for the particle to make one rotation. You should know that the force on a moving particle due to a magnetic field is perpendicular to the velocity of the charge. This means that a magnetic field can do no work on a moving charge, which, in turn, means that it cannot change its kinetic energy or its speed. If the speed is the same, and from Figure 2 we see that the spirals are getting smaller, then the length of time to make each spiral is also decreasing. Thus, the period is decreasing.

141.   **A is correct.** The electron has a negative charge, so it will be turned by the magnetic field in the opposite direction of the positively charged proton. The electron has less mass than the proton, so it will turn in a smaller circle than the proton. You can use the equation for centripetal force: $F = mv^2/r$. When m increases, r must also increase.

142.   **C is correct.** From $F = qvB$ we know that charge increases force, so the alpha particle will experience the greatest force. Only the velocity perpendicular to the magnetic field will create a force on a charged particle. Any velocity in the direction of the pitch does not increase the force. Thus the smaller the pitch, the greater the force.

143.   **C is correct.** The protons rotate in the opposite direction to the electrons because they have an opposite charge. As per Figure 2, the particles continue rotating in the same direction when they reflect from one pole to the other. However, the perspective from one pole to another. Imagine a two headed coin. The noses on either side point in opposite directions. When the coin spins, if we view the front side and the head appears to tilt downward, the head on the opposite side would appear to tilt upward. If the coin continued spinning in the same direction as it followed the magnetic field lines from the North Pole to the South Pole, we would see the opposite side of the coin. From our point of view at the south pole, the opposite side would appear to be spinning counter-clockwise.

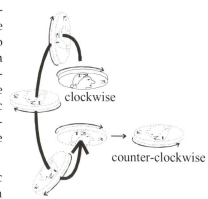

clockwise

counter-clockwise

144.   **A is correct.** The force on any moving charged particle due to a magnetic field can only be perpendicular to the movement of the particle, and can therefore do no work. This is why the speed of the electron doesn't change.

145.   **C is correct.** According to Figure 2, in order for the particles to bounce from pole to pole, the magnetic field at the poles must be stronger than at the equator.

Passage II

146.   **A is correct.** Use the same logic as that used in the passage to explain why the human body remains at the same potential as the ground. The ground is a conductor, so it will be at the same potential at any height.

147.   **C is correct.** Use the definition of current. A = C/sec. So sec = C/A = 20/10,000 = 2×10^{-3} seconds.

148.   **D is correct.** $V = IR$: From the passage: $400,000 = 10^{-12} \times R$.

149.   **B is correct.** An electric field vector points from positive to negative potential. Figure 1 shows the electric field gets more positive as we move upward.

150.   **C is correct.** This question concerns the rate of energy transfer or power. $P = IV$. The answer is given in joules because the question asks for energy.

151.   **C is correct.** Current always flows from high potential to low potential, so B and D are wrong. During a lightning strike, electrons flow from the cloud to the ground, so current must flow in the opposite direction, from the ground to the cloud.

Passage III

152. **B is correct.** The passage states that the electric field force is in opposition to the magnetic force. Electrons want to move against an electric field. The electric field pushes the electron to the left. You can also use the right hand rule: Point your thumb in the direction of the current, down the page (opposite to movement of electrons), point your fingers in the direction of the magnetic field, and push in the direction of your palm. Your palm should be facing to the right. This is the force on the electrons due to the magnetic field.

153. **A is correct.** The passage states that at equilibrium "the force on the electrons due to E and B are equal and in opposite directions." Thus the direction of B creates the direction of E and reversing B will reverse E. B and D concern the current which can be adjusted independently of the magnetic field. A Hall potential difference will be established regardless of the direction of current, so C is wrong.

154. **B is correct.** Moving the strip in the direction of the current is the same as moving the strip in the opposite direction to the electrons. If the strip is moved at the same speed as the electrons, the electrons are stationary with respect to the magnetic field and there is no Hall Effect. (This is explained in the passage.) When the strip is moved faster than the electrons, the relative velocity of the electrons with respect to the magnetic field is reversed. Thus the force on the electrons due to the magnetic field is also reversed. The Hall Effect is established in the opposite direction from the original.

155. **A is correct.** If the copper strip is held stationary then the sum of the forces or the net force must be zero. No acceleration; no net force.

156. **B is correct.** The electric field E created by the magnetic field pushing the electrons to the right demonstrates the direction of force on the electrons due to the magnetic field B. Also, right hand rule applies for the same result. Since the force is constant and perpendicular to the velocity, the magnitude of the velocity cannot change but the direction changes at a constant rate. The particle follows a circular path.

157. **D is correct.** The potential difference is the electric field times the distance. Choice B is the potential difference along the length of the strip, not the Hall effect, which is the potential difference across the width of the strip.

158. **B is correct.** The voltage across the capacitor is 6 volts. $IR = V$ so 3 amps = 6 V/ 2 Ω. See the diagram below.

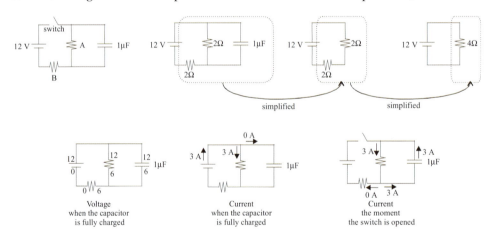

159. **C is correct.** The charge is equal to the voltage times the capacitance. See the diagram above for the solution of the circuit.

160. **A is correct.** According to Coulomb's law ($F = kqq/r^2$), A and D apply equal and opposite forces on q, and so do C and B.

161. **C is correct.** First set the force equal to mass times acceleration $Eq = ma$. Then use the uniform accelerated motion equation $x = \frac{1}{2}at^2$

EXPLANATIONS TO IN-CLASS EXAM FOR LECTURE 8

Passage I

162. **C is correct.** Diffraction is demonstrated by the light waves bending as they move through the opening. This happens in both experiments. Interference is demonstrated in both experiments where the path length traveled by light rays differs creating alternating high and low intensity bands due to constructive and destructive interference.

163. **A is correct.** From Soh Cah Toa, $x/\sin\theta$ is equal to r. From distance divided by velocity equals time, r/c is the time light takes to travel to any given point on the detector.

164. **C is correct.** There would be no diffraction. In experiment 1, all the light would go directly to the detector at the level of the slit to form 1 peak on the graph. In experiment 2, two peaks would be formed.

165. **B is correct.** Longer wavelengths are diffracted the most. Red has the longest wavelength.

166. **D is correct.** The equations show that I_d max is 4 times greater than I_s.

167. **B is correct.** Intensity is proportional to energy, and energy is proportional to the square of the amplitude.

Passage II

168. **C is correct.** From the passage we know that $m_o m_e = M_{total}$ and $m_e = -25\text{cm}/f_e$. Thus, the focal length is inversely proportional to the magnification. Since power is inversely proportional to the focal length, doubling the power doubles the magnification.

169. **D is correct.** The object is outside the focal length of a converging lens and thus creates a real inverted image.

170. **C is correct.** The focal length of a converging lens is positive. A diopter is the reciprocal of the focal length in <u>meters</u>. Thus, 1/25 equals 0.04 meters.

171. **C is correct.** Just plug and chug. $M_{total} = m_o m_e = 500 \times 0.01 \times 0.005/ 0.25 = L$. $L = 10$ cm. Then add the focal lengths.

172. **A is correct.** An object inside the focal point of a converging lens makes a virtual upright image on the same side as the object.

173. **C is correct.** The objective inverts the first image. This first image is within the focal point of the eyepiece so the eyepiece creates a virtual image WITHOUT changing the orientation. The final image is an inverted image of the object. An inverted image is inverted up and down, and left and right. When you push the slide left, it looks to be moving to the right under the microscope. When you push the slide up, it looks to be moving down. So, left is right and up is down on an inverted image. Answer choice C has these characteristics. Choice C is the inverted image.

174. **C is correct.** Go back to lecture 8 for an explanation of refraction and reflection.

Passage III

175. **B is correct.** From the equation in the passage we can see that this is true.

176. **C is correct.** Although this is an approximation, it is the best answer. Light rays from distant objects will be approximately parallel and thus converge on the focal point. Since the rays aren't truly parallel, they would form slightly behind the focal point but this is not an answer choice.

177. **A is correct.** A thicker center converges more. Only converging lenses have positive power.

178. **D is correct.** When light enters the lens, velocity slows, frequency remains constant, and wavelength must shorten. This effect is greater on blue light than red light. This is called chromatic dispersion.

179. **A is correct.** $P = 1/\text{focal length}$. This means the focal length of the eyepiece is 0.01 m. The focal length of the objective must be nine times greater, or 9 cm. It is positive by the equation or because converging lenses have positive focal lengths.

180. **A is correct.** Light bends less moving from glass to water and thus the focal lengths of the lenses would lengthen. The tube length must be increased so that the two new focal points will coincide as per the passage.

Stand Alones

181. **A is correct.** The waves are not moving through an aperture, so they are refracted, not diffracted. Since the waves are moving nearly perpendicular to the shore they must be turning toward the normal, which means their speed must be decreasing. Waves refract toward the normal when a new medium slows their progress. The new medium is water that is more shallow.

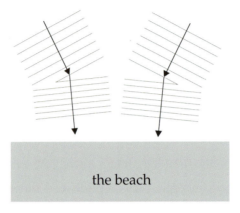

182. **B is correct.** The mirror is concave since it makes a real inverted image. The focal length is positive, and half the radius of curvature. From the thin lens equation ($1/f = 1/d_i + 1/d_o$) we get $d_o = 5$ cm.

183. **A is correct.** Magnification $= -d_i/d_o$

184. **D is correct.** The mirage is created by refraction of light. The light enters the warmer air and speeds up causing it to turn upward. The diagram below shows how the lower portion of the wave speeds up as it enters the warmer air causing the wave to turn.

ANSWERS & EXPLANATIONS

TO

QUESTIONS IN THE LECTURES

ANSWERS TO THE LECTURE QUESTIONS

Lecture 1	Lecture 2	Lecture 3	Lecture 4	Lecture 5	Lecture 6	Lecture 7	Lecture 8
1. C	25. C	49. D	73. D	97. D	121. A	145. C	169. A
2. A	26. C	50. C	74. A	98. C	122. C	146. B	170. D
3. B	27. D	51. B	75. B	99. C	123. C	147. A	171. A
4. D	28. A	52. A	76. D	100. D	124. B	148. C	172. D
5. C	29. D	53. C	77. C	101. C	125. B	149. B	173. C
6. C	30. B	54. D	78. A	102. B	126. C	150. A	174. D
7. B	31. A	55. B	79. A	103. A	127. A	151. A	175. B
8. C	32. A	56. A	80. D	104. D	128. A	152. B	176. A
9. C	33. A	57. A	81. B	105. D	129. B	153. A	177. B
10. C	34. D	58. C	82. B	106. B	130. D	154. B	178. D
11. B	35. D	59. A	83. B	107. A	131. C	155. D	179. B
12. B	36. C	60. B	84. A	108. D	132. D	156. A	180. A
13. A	37. C	61. D	85. C	109. D	133. B	157. C	181. B
14. A	38. B	62. C	86. C	110. B	134. B	158. D	182. C
15. C	39. D	63. C	87. B	111. C	135. B	159. D	183. A
16. D	40. A	64. C	88. C	112. A	136. D	160. C	184. C
17. C	41. D	65. A	89. C	113. D	137. B	161. C	185. D
18. D	42. C	66. A	90. B	114. A	138. C	162. B	186. B
19. A	43. C	67. C	91. D	115. B	139. C	163. D	187. A
20. A	44. C	68. A	92. D	116. D	140. D	164. A	188. D
21. B	45. B	69. C	93. B	117. B	141. D	165. C	189. D
22. B	46. A	70. D	94. B	118. A	142. C	166. D	190. D
23. A	47. B	71. C	95. A	119. D	143. B	167. A	191. B
24. B	48. C	72. B	96. A	120. B	144. B	168. B	192. C

EXPLANATIONS TO QUESTIONS IN LECTURE 1

1. **C is correct.** The balloon travels in three perpendicular directions. These can be considered three displacement vectors. The total displacement is the vector sum of the three. If you notice, two of the vectors have lengths of 8 and 6, multiples of 4 and 3 respectively. These are the components of a 3-4-5 triangle. Thus, the displacement from the tail of the 6 km vector to the head of the 8 km vector is 10 kilometers. This 10 km vector is perpendicular to the other 10 km vector. Using the Pythagorean theorem on the two 10 km vectors gives a total displacement of approximately 14 km.

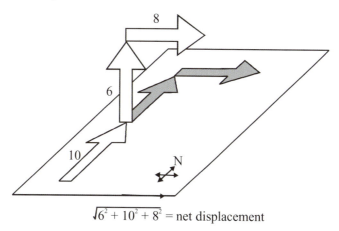

$$\sqrt{6^2 + 10^2 + 8^2} = \text{net displacement}$$

2. **A is correct.** Since the runner is on a circular track of ? km, the runner will end up where he/she began. This is zero displacement and zero velocity.

3. **B is correct.** The man is making a 30-60-90 triangle. Where he turns represents the 30° angle in the triangle. The distance back to the entrance is half the hypotenuse or 100 sin30°. You can either recognize the proportions of a 30-60-90 triangle or, if you have a lot of extra time on your hands while taking the MCAT, use the law of cosines: $A^2 = B^2 + C^2 - 2BC\cos(a)$.

4. **D is correct.** Acceleration is the rate of change of velocity. Since velocity is a vector it specifies direction. The direction of the earth's motion is constantly changing.

5. **C is correct.** Since the beginning and starting points are the same, the displacement is the same.

6. **C is correct.** If the car is slowing down, the velocity and acceleration must have opposite signs. Since the car is moving forward, it's safe to assume that the velocity is positive.

7. **B is correct.** The direction for a vector must specify a straight line at a specific point. You couldn't draw an arrow to represent "in a circle."

8. **C is correct.** You need to convert your units.

$$\left(\frac{36 \text{ km}}{1 \text{ hr}}\right)\left(\frac{1000 \text{ m}}{1 \text{ km}}\right)\left(\frac{1 \text{ hr}}{3600 \text{ sec}}\right) = 10 \text{ m} / \text{s}$$

In 10 seconds, the elephant can run 100 m.

---

9. **C is correct.** Velocity is the slope on a d/t graph. Constant velocity requires only a straight line on a d/t graph. Any acceleration represents a change in velocity and so can not represent constant velocity.

10. **C is correct.** Since we are looking for distance and not displacement, we add up the total area between the line and the x-axis. We could also use our linear motion equations since there is constant acceleration.

11. **B is correct.** The graph shows an object moving in one direction at a constant velocity and suddenly changing directions. There is no gradual acceleration. The baseball is the only object that suddenly changes direction. A is wrong because the description describes gradual acceleration, and there is no gradual acceleration in the graph. C is constantly changing velocity. D is a gradual change in velocity.

12. **B is correct.** This problem may be tricky because the question only implies a necessary variable. That variable is initial velocity. The initial velocity is zero. The average velocity of any constantly accelerating object that starts with zero velocity is the final velocity divided by two. This from $v_{avg} = (v + v_o)/2$. Then the average velocity times time equals displacement, $v_{avg}t = x$. Thus, $25/12.5 = 2$. Or, by Salty's method:

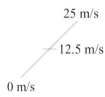

25 m/s

12.5 m/s

0 m/s

Average velocity times time equals distance: $12.5 \times 2 = 25$.

13. **A is correct.** This is a plug and chug problem. The correct formula is $v = v_o + at$. Which results in $25 = 50 + a2$. Thus $a = 12.5$. You also could reason that if it had taken only one second to slow from 50 to 25 m/s then the acceleration would have been -25 m/s^2. But it took more than one second so the acceleration must be less.

14. **A is correct.** The graph clearly shows that displacement increases with time. Since the displacement graph is a straight line, the particle must be moving at constant velocity, so neither velocity nor acceleration are increasing.

15. **C is correct.** Acceleration is 5 m/s^2 so the velocity is reduced by 5 m/s each second. Starting from 20 requires 4 seconds. Average velocity is between 20 and 0 which is 10 m/s. 10 m/s for 4 seconds gives 40 meters. Or use the equation that doesn't include time.

$$v_f^2 = v_o^2 + 2ax$$

The car comes to a stop, so $v_f = 0$. If we plug in $v_o = 20$ and $a = -5$, we'll get $x = 40$ m.

16. **D is correct.** In order for the particle to move backwards, the velocity graph would have to dip below zero. Between 10 and 15 seconds, the particle is slowing down, but not going backwards.

---

17. **C is correct.** The best way to answer this question is to plug 4 seconds into the linear motion equations $s = s_o + v_ot + \frac{1}{2}at^2$. This results in $s = \frac{1}{2}at^2$. The distance traveled by the apple is 80 m so it reaches 20 m in altitude. You could solve this problem using proportions. The square of the time is proportional to the distance. If we double the time, we multiply the distance by 4.

18. **D is correct.** Since both the ball and the skydivers are accelerating at the same rate, each skydiver should aim for the other's chest.

19. **A is correct.** You should use Salty's system in every single physics problem. However, sometimes the problem is easy enough for you to imagine the diagram in your head. This problem probably requires actually drawing a diagram. Once you have your diagram, you may notice that the antelope needs to be in the air for 2 seconds at 10 m/s to clear 20 meters. So now you have t. You know that the upward trip equals the downward trip, so the downward trip lasts one second. You also know that the downward trip starts at zero because a projectile at its peak has zero velocity. The question is now simplified to "How far does a free falling body starting from rest travel in one second". At the end of one second the body is traveling at 10 m/s, thus its average velocity is 5 m/s. The object travels 5 meters. Alternatively, once you have 2 seconds, you can plug 2 seconds into $s = s_o + v_ot + \frac{1}{2}at^2$, with s and s_o as zero. Doing the math gives you the initial velocity of 10 m/s. The velocity at the top is zero. Using $v^2 = v_o^2 + 2ax$ gives you $x = 5$.

20. **A is correct.** This is a proportions question. The correct equation is $v_o\sin\theta = \sqrt{(2gh)}$. Remember, due to the symmetry of projectile motion, the velocity in this equation can be initial or final depending upon the direction of motion. Multiplying the height by four only doubles the velocity.

21. **B is correct**. You can use $v_o\sin\theta = \sqrt{(2gh)}$. The sine of 30° is $\frac{1}{2}$. Thus the vertical velocity is 50 m/s. 50^2 is 2500. Divide this by $g = 10$, and by 2 gives 125. Practice doing problems like this in your head to save time, build your confidence, and most of all, to sharpen your skills. The initial vertical velocity is 50 m/s; the final at max height is zero. This is a change in velocity of 50 which takes 5 seconds at 10 m/s². Draw your line and multiply the average velocity by 5 seconds.

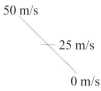

22. **B is correct.** At terminal velocity, acceleration is zero. The force of air resistance counters gravity exactly so the force is equal to the weight for both balls. Ball X requires more collisions with air molecules to compensate for the larger force of gravity. More collisions means greater air resistance.

23. **A is correct.** The horizontal speed has no effect on the length of time that a projectile is in the air, so you don't need it here. Because the initial vertical speed is zero, you can use the equation below.

$$x = (1/2)gt^2 \text{ with } x = 40 \text{ and } g = 10$$

$$t = \sqrt{8} = 2.8$$

Since there is only one significant figure in the numbers in the problem we round the answer up to 3.

24. **B is correct.** The horizontal distance traveled for a projectile is given by $vt\cos\theta$. In this case, $v = 30$, $t = 6$, and $\theta = 40°$.

EXPLANATIONS TO QUESTIONS IN LECTURE 2

25. **C is correct**. This is a straight forward $F = ma$ plug-n-chug problem. The moon is thrown in to confuse you. The gravitational force of the moon acts perpendicularly to the horizontal force and is countered by a normal force. It has no effect on the motion.

26. **C is correct**. Since the mass of the rocket is decreasing, and the force remains constant, the rate of change in velocity (acceleration) must be increasing.

27. **D is correct**. The downward force is $mg = 100$ N. The first 100 N upward counters this to give a net force of zero and thus a constant velocity. We want a net force of $mg = 100$ N upwards. This requires adding 100 more newtons for a total of 200 N.

28. **A is correct**. Since both skydivers are at constant velocity, they must both experience a net force of zero.

29. **D is correct**. Since the projectile is at constant velocity when the force of air resistance is F, The force propelling the projectile must have a magnitude F as well. When the air resistance is reduced by a factor of 4, the net force must be $F - \frac{1}{4}F = \frac{3}{4}F$. Thus $\frac{3}{4}F = ma$.

30. **B is correct**. Because the masses are all on a line, you can just average the distance of the masses from the origin to get the central point. The average distance is $(2 + 3 + 7)/3 = 4$.

31. **A is correct**. The net force on the plane is 2500 N – 500 N = 2000 N to the east. The mass of the plane will be the weight divided by g. That's $40,000/10 = 4000$ mg. Acceleration is $F/m = 2000/4000 = 0.5$ m/s² to the east.

32. **A is correct.** If the car is moving in a straight line at a constant speed, then it is not accelerating. From Newton's second law, you know that if there is no acceleration, then there is no net force. Friction is irrelevant.

---

33. **A is correct.** This question requires setting the gravitational force between the earth and the moon equal to the centripetal force.

$$F = G\frac{Mm}{r^2} = m\frac{v^2}{r}$$

34. **D is correct.** The work done will remain the same. $W = Fd$. The distance is increased from $^1/_2$ to 4. This is an increase by a factor of 8. Since work remains constant, force must decrease by a factor of 8.

35. **D is correct.** This question uses misdirection by introducing the concept of circular motion. Gravitational force is not affected by movement. The gravitational force is inversely proportional to the square of the radius.

36. **C is correct.** The acceleration is $g\sin\theta$; however, θ is constantly decreasing and with it the sine of θ. Thus, the acceleration is decreasing. Since there is some acceleration throughout the drop, the velocity is increasing.

37. **C is correct.** The force down the incline is $mg\sin\theta$. The acceleration down the incline is $g\sin\theta$. The sine of θ is opposite over hypotenuse which is $20/40 = ?$. Thus the acceleration is $^1/_2 g$ or 5 m/s². If we plug this into our linear motion equation we have $x = ^1/_2(^1/_2 g)t^2$. x is the length of the incline. Thus $40 = ^1/_2(^1/_2 g)t^2$. $16 = t^2$. $t = 4$ seconds.

38. **B is correct.** Set the weight equal to Newton's law of universal gravitation.

$$mg = \frac{GMm}{R^2}, \; m \text{ cancels, so } g = \frac{GM}{R^2}$$

39. **D is correct.** $v = d/t$. Once around a circular track is the same as the circumference, so $d = 2\pi r$. So $v = 2\pi r/t = (6.28)(30)/63 = (0.1)(30) = 3$ m/s.

40. **A is correct.** The force parallel to the ramp is the same as the net force, $mg\sin\theta$. As θ increases, $\sin\theta$ increases and so does the net force. The force perpendicular to the ramp is the same as the normal force, $mg\cos\theta$. As θ increases, $\cos\theta$ decreases, and so does the normal force.

---

41. **D is correct.** If we look at the point on the tire that makes contact with the road, that point does not move relative to the road or else the tires would spin in place. Since there is no relative movement, the friction must be static. The force of friction is in the direction opposite to the way the tires are trying to slide against the road. This is the force that accelerates the vehicle. So the only way that the truck can move forward is if the force on the tires is in this direction.

42. **C is correct.** Tension in a static system is defined by the force in one direction. The rope will also experience a force from the right, but that does not double the tension. That force is necessary to make the tension equal to 900 N.

43. **C is correct.** The force changes with the displacement of the tires. The greater the displacement, the greater the force, the greater the magnitude of acceleration as per the formula $F = k\Delta x = ma$.

44. **C is correct.** Since the frictional force is constant, this is a linear motion problem with constant acceleration. The normal force is mg, so the frictional force is $mg\mu$. The acceleration is just $g\mu$. Using $v^2 = v_0^2 + 2ax$ and plugging in $g\mu$ for the acceleration, gives us answer C.

45. **B is correct.** The tension could only be as great as the force at one end. Thus, the tension could not be greater than the force applied by the first team.

46. **A is correct.** On an inclined plane $F_n = mg\cos\theta$. So the force of friction is equal to $\mu mg\cos\theta$.

47. **B is correct.** The difference in mass between the two situations is 0.5 kg, so the difference in force is 5 N. The difference in displacement is 1 cm. These are the numbers we plug into Hooke's law. $k = F/x = (5 \text{ N})/(1 \text{ cm}) = 5$ N/cm. By the way, we can do this because we are really subtracting one equation from the other.

$$F_{1.5} = -k\Delta x_{1.5}$$

$$-F_1 = -k\Delta x_1$$

$$F_{1.5} - F_1 = -k\Delta x_{1.5} - -k\Delta x_1 \Rightarrow \Delta F_{1.5} = -k(\Delta x_{1.5} - -\Delta x_1)$$

48. **C is correct.** If the elevator is moving at constant speed, then there is no acceleration and no net force, so the tension in the cable must exactly balance the weight of the elevator.

EXPLANATIONS TO QUESTIONS IN LECTURE 3

49. **D is correct.** When the tightrope walker stands in the middle of the rope, he is in static equilibrium. The vertical and the horizontal net force must equal zero. The force downward is the weight of the tightrope walker, 750 N. The force upward must also equal 750 N. The upward force must come from the vertical component of the tension in the rope. If the rope is perfectly straight, there is no vertical component.

50. **C is correct.** If we begin by examining the problem as a static equilibrium problem, the tension in the rope with no acceleration would be 500 N. If we want to pull the climber upward, we must increase the tension by *ma*, which is 250 N.

51. **B is correct.** The force upwards is defined by the question to be 200 N. The force on either end of a massless rope must be the same. The tension in the rope must be 200 N. This question answers itself and then attempts to confuse the issue by discussing a rusted pulley.

52. **A is correct.** The skydiver has a constant velocity so the net force must be zero, and by definition, this means the skydiver is in dynamic equilibrium.

53. **C is correct.** You don't have to look at the diagram for this problem. C is the only answer that could be false and still have all the rest be true. Form a triangle with the vectors to prove to yourself that they sum to zero.

54. **D is correct.** The third force must have equal components pulling to the south and west to counter the other two forces. Since the two components are equal, the third force will be directed exactly to the southwest.

55. **B is correct.** The bucket is moving at constant speed, so there is no acceleration. If there is no acceleration, then the system is in dynamic equilibrium. All of the other situations described include accelerated motion.

56. **A is correct.** The block is accelerating across the floor so the force applied by the child must be greater than any force that is resisting the motion. The weight of the block acts vertically, so it is not directly involved in the horizontal motion. It is true that the frictional force is likely to be less than the weight, but that doesn't indicate whether the force applied by the child is greater or less than the weight.

57. **A is correct.** The pole is not rotating, so the net torque must be zero.

58. **C is correct.** The sign is in static equilibrium. Since the wall is frictionless, there is no torque in this problem. The vertical component of the force must be equal to the weight of the sign. The vertical component is equal to the tension times sin30°. *mg* = *T*sin30°. If we double *mg*, we double the tension.

59. **A is correct.** The longest lever arm is on A. The entire wrench is the lever arm on A.

60. **B is correct.** This is a straight forward torque problem. If we choose our point of rotation to be the point on the board where the string attaches to the board, and we understand that the weight of the board acts at the center of gravity which is the center of the board in this case, the counter-clockwise torque is 3 kg × 0.2 m. The clockwise torque is the weight of the board times 0.3 m. Setting these equal, we have the mass of the board at 2 kg.

61. **D is correct.** The net torque must be zero. If we choose the rotation point to be the end of board Y, then $1 \text{ m} \times F = 4 \text{ m} \times 4 \text{ N}$.

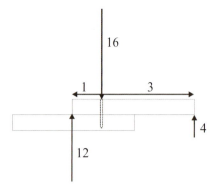

A little tip for torque problems: Find a force that is neither known nor asked for, and choose the point where this force acts to be your rotational point.

62. **C is correct.** If you push on the edge farthest from the hinges, you'll have the greatest lever arm, which will give you the greatest torque.

63. **C is correct.** For the best balance, the torques should be equivalent. $(400 \text{ N})(5 \text{ m}) = (500 \text{ N})(x)$. So $x = 4 \text{ m}$

64. **C is correct.** Increasing the diameter of the screwdriver handle increases the lever arm for the force applied by his grip. Increased lever arm gives more torque to turn the screw.

---

65. **A is correct.** The frictional force applied by Jupiter's atmosphere times the distance along which it is applied equals the change in mechanical energy of the meteor. If we ignore the gravitational force of Jupiter, the change in the mechanical energy is a loss of all kinetic energy which equals $\frac{1}{2}mv^2$. We set this equal to force times distance and solve for force.

66. **A is correct.** The potential energy increases as you go up the stack. This may seem obvious if you are thinking about 'mgh'; however, you would be thinking about this problem incorrectly because g does not remain constant. If you use Newton's law of gravitation to solve for g at any altitude and then plugged it into 'mgh' ($g = Gm/r^2$, $r = h$), you would get the reverse answer that potential energy decreases to zero. A fast and easy way to understand this problem is to think of work. Your system is the stack of blocks. Each time you add a block, you do work on the system. In other words, you transfer energy to your system.

67. **C is correct.** A simple technique for solving this and many other physics problems is to "take the examples to extremes". Here the examples are reasonably close in mass. What if object A were one million times as massive as object B? In other words, imagine that object A is a piano and object B is a dime. Now we place them on a spring and propel the piano one inch into the air. Will the dime be propelled one million inches into the air at the same time? Of course not. Thus we know that mass is not proportional to the height. Since all the answers are given as such, only C can be correct. We could also look at this problem and ask ourselves, "When do the masses become projectiles? They must become projectiles the moment the spring stops pushing. From $F = ma$, we know that this is the moment the spring stops accelerating. This means that the masses become projectiles at the same moment and with the same velocity. As we learned in Lecture 1, mass is irrelevant to projectile paths.

68. **A is correct.** This is a proportions problem. We set the initial elastic potential energy equal to the final energy, $\frac{1}{2}kx^2 = mgh$, and we see that the square of the displacement of the spring is proportional to the height, $x^2 = h$. Thus, to increase the height by a factor of four, we must increase the displacement of the spring by a factor of 2.

69. **C is correct.** The horizontal component of the force is 87 N. To find the acceleration we use $F = ma$. $a = 8.7 \text{ m/s}^2$. We use $v = v_o + at$ and arrive at $v = 17.4 \text{ m/s}$.

70. **D is correct.** The rock starts out with gravitational potential energy. As it falls, it loses gravitational potential energy and gains kinetic energy. As the rubber band stretches, the rock slows to a stop and kinetic energy is transferred to the elastic potential energy of the rubber band.

71. **C is correct.** $1 \text{ kW-hour} \left(\dfrac{3600 \text{ sec}}{1 \text{ hour}} \right) = 3600 \text{ kW-sec} = 3,600,000 \text{ W-sec}$

A Watt is a J/sec, so a W-sec = (J/sec)(sec) = Joule

So 3,6000,000 W-sec = 3,600,000 J

72. **B is correct.** $P = W/t$. If the power is increased, more work can be done in less time. Choice B says the reverse of this.

EXPLANATIONS TO QUESTIONS IN LECTURE 4

73. **D is correct.** Impulse is equal to change in momentum, $F\Delta t = \Delta mv$. We know the change in momentum but not F or t. We do not have enough information to solve for F.

74. **A is correct.** This is easily visualized if we take the example to extremes. If the boy were somehow able to make himself nearly weightless, would he travel at some extremely high velocity? This is actually similar to a projectile problem. The boy receives his kinetic energy from his initial potential energy. When he drops his coat and boots, he is leaving that potential energy unused at the point where he dropped them.

75. **B is correct.** The initial and final momentums must be equal. The initial vertical momentum is $mv\cos60°$. Since ball B has no vertical momentum, all the vertical momentum remains in ball A. Ball A has no horizontal momentum after the collision, so all of its momentum is represented by $mv\cos60°$.

76. **D is correct.** To answer this question, we simply compare the total energy of the car at zero, 30, and 60 km/h. All the energy is kinetic energy. $K = \frac{1}{2}mv^2$. Without doing too much math we can see that if you double the velocity you increase energy by four times. The question asks for the difference in the energies, $4 - 1 = 3$.

77. **C is correct.** The initial momentum of the cat-cardboard system is zero, so the final momentum must be zero. Since the cat has twice the mass as the cardboard, the cardboard will have twice the velocity.

78. **A is correct.** Choice I represents conservation of momentum, which is always true. Choice II is conservation of kinetic energy. In an inelastic collision, kinetic energy is not conserved. As for Choice III, if the masses are different before and after the collision and momentum is conserved, then the velocities before and after must be different.

79. **A is correct.** Momentum is a vector quantity, so the two vectors with the same magnitude and opposite directions will add up to zero both before and after the collision.

80. **D is correct.** From the impulse equation $Ft = mv$. The trapeze artist is brought gradually to a stop in the safety net, so the change in momentum takes place over a longer time than if the person hit the floor. The increase in time means that less force is required to achieve the same change in momentum, which makes the fall less dangerous.

---

81. **B is correct.** The pulley does not change the work, so it does not change the rate at which work is done. The power is work/time or mgh/t.

82. **B is correct.** The eccentric pulley does not work on the principles of a normal pulley but, instead, works on the same principle as a lever. The lever arm for the string at point A in position 1 is greater than that for point B in position one. In position 2, the reverse is true. The lever is stationary, so the sum of the torques must equal zero, or the clockwise torque equals the counter-clockwise torque. Where the lever arm is greater, the tension force must be less.

83. **B is correct.** Machines are used because they decrease the force required to perform a task. An ideal machine requires the same work as would be done without the machine, but a non-ideal machine requires more work because frictional forces must be overcome.

84. **A is correct.** By zigzagging, she is basically using a ramp. Her path is not as steep, but it is longer. The work remains the same, but the force is lessened.

85. **C is correct.** The work cannot be decreased by a machine. Therefore, $Fd = mgh$. $d = 300/25 = 12$.

86. **C is correct.** For a lever $F_1 l_1 = F_2 l_2$. The radii of the two pulleys act as the lever arms for the system, so increasing the diameter of pulley A will decrease the force required to pull rope A. Changing the lengths of the ropes will have no effect on the machine.

87. **B is correct.** The formula for machines is $F_{input} d_{input} = F_{output} d_{output}$, where d is the distance over which the forces act. If mechanical advantage is equal to (output force)/(input force) , then it must also be equal to (input distance)/(output distance).

88. **C is correct.** For an inclined plane, $Fd = mgh$, so $(50 \text{ N})d = (1000 \text{ N})(1 \text{ m})$ and $d = 20 \text{ m}$.

---

89. **C is correct.** Since Y is not normally found in the meteorite, we assume that all the Y came from the decomposition of X. The total amount of X originally, then, must have been 15%. The amount left is 10% of 15%, or 1.5%. We count on our fingers to find the half-lives. 50%, 25%, 12.5%. A little more than 3 half-lives. 3 times 45 is 135 plus a little more is 140.

90. **B is correct.** This is a reverse collision. The initial momentum is zero; so, the final momentum must be zero. The momentum of the alpha particle is approximately $mv = 4 \times 10^7$. The momentum of the other particle, Rn-220 must be equal in magnitude and opposite in direction. Thus, the velocity of Rn equals $(4 \times 10^7)/220$. This quickly rounds to $4 \times 10^7/2.2 \times 10^2$ whichis slightly less than 2×10^5 or choice B.

91. **D is correct.** This is a simple exercise in plug-n-chug. Whenever there is some mysterious missing mass, $E = mc^2$.

92. **D is correct.** First count the change in protons in order to discover the identity of the final atom. In this case, each alpha decay results in the loss of 2 protons, and each beta decay results in the gain of one proton. (Remember, create a negative, create a positive.) Thus, we have a net loss of 2 protons, and we know that our atom is Pb. Now we track the change in the mass number. Each alpha decay loses 4 mass units and each beta results in no change in the mass units. (Beta decay is an exchange of a proton for a neutron.) This means a total loss of 8 mass units for a new mass number of 208.

93. **B is correct.** This is a half-life curve, for equal units of time the amount divides by 2.

94. **B is correct.** The half life is the amount of time it takes for half of the isotope to decay. The graph decreases from 60 g to 30 grams in 2.5 hours, so the half life must be 2.5 hours.

95. **A is correct.** ${}^{210}_{83}\text{Bi} \rightarrow {}^{206}_{82}\text{Pb} + {}^{4}_{2}\alpha + {}^{0}_{-1}\beta$.

96. **A is correct.** In alpha decay, a particle identical to a helium nucleus is released, so the mass number will change by 4. None of the other processes will change the mass number.

EXPLANATIONS TO QUESTIONS IN LECTURE 5

97. **D is correct.** Atmospheric pressure supports the column of fluid. The pressure at the bottom of the column must be equal to atmospheric pressure. The pressure is equal to ρgh. If ρ is decreased by a factor of 13.6, the height must be increased by the same factor. Notice that, given the choices, there is no need to do the math. Every other answer is less than 10 times as tall.

98. **C is correct.** The only difference between the two discs is what they are covering. Ignore everything else. The first disc has atmospheric pressure pushing upward; the second disc does not. This is the difference between the forces necessary to lift them.

99. **C is correct.** The brick displaces a volume of water equal to its own weight. Since its density is 1400 kg/m^3, its density is 1.4 times that of water, and it must displace a volume of water 1.4 times its own volume. Since this

is only $^1/_2$ the volume of the Styrofoam, the full volume of the Styrofoam must be 2.8 times larger than the volume of the brick.

100. **D is correct.** The balloon rises because the buoyant force is greater than the weight. When these forces are equal, the balloon will stop rising. Thus the balloon stops rising when: $\rho_{air}Vg = \rho_{helium}Vg$. The volumes are always equal because the balloon is always fully submerged in the atmosphere. Another way to look at this problem is to see that the balloon is fully submerged in the fluid atmosphere. We want the balloon to float, not rise or sink, so we use the floating equation: Fraction submerged = $\rho_{object}/\rho_{fluid}$. The entire balloon is submerged, so the fraction submerged is equal to one.

101. **C is correct.** If you have forgotten the floating equation, the quickest way to do this problem is to take the example to the extremes. If the specific gravity of the toy were 0.999, the toy would be almost the same weight as water and, of course, only a very small part would float above the water; $0.001/1 = 0.1\%$. The specific gravity must be how much is under the water. Now we look at the example in the question. 45% must be under water so 55% must be above. To solve this problem mathematically, we set the buoyant force equal to the weight of the toy,

$$\rho_{water}V_{submerged\ fraction\ of\ the\ toy}g = \rho_{toy}V_{toy}g.$$

We end up with the ratio:

$$V_{submerged\ fraction\ of\ the\ toy}/V_{toy} = \rho_{toy}/\rho_{water}$$

The right side of this equation is the specific gravity, and the left side is the fraction of the toy submerged. To find the fraction of the toy above water, subtract the submerged fraction from 1.

102. **B is correct.** The pressure on both sides is the same. Force is equal to the product of pressure and area, so the force will be larger on the side with the greater area.

103. **A is correct.** The formula for fluid pressure is $P = \rho gh$. If the density is changed, the pressure will change by the same ratio. Since the specific gravity of ethyl alcohol is 0.8, the pressure will decrease by a factor of 0.8.

104. **D is correct.** Pressure depends only on depth and density, not on the shape of the container.

_____

105. **D is correct.** The cross sectional area A is increased by a factor of 4 when r is doubled: $A = \pi r^2$. Since Q remains constant, the velocity decreases by a factor of 4, $Q = Av$. From Bernoulli's equation, we see $K = P + ^1/_2\rho v^2$. We know that the $^1/_2\rho v^2$ term decreases by a factor of 16, however, we don't know the amount and thus we don't know by how much P increases.

106. **B is correct.** The fluid at A, C, and D is at atmospheric pressure. The fluid at B is at atmospheric pressure plus ρgh.

107. **A is correct.** Since the molecules of water are more attracted to the soil than to other water molecules, the shape of the meniscus is concave. The surface tension creates a net force which pulls the water upward.

108. **D is correct.** Increasing the length increases resistance to flow, $\Delta P = QR$. All other factors mentioned decrease the resistance to flow. Notice that this question is concerned with a real fluid. For an ideal flow, there is no viscosity, and the radius and length of the pipe do not affect flow rate of an ideal fluid.

109. **D is correct.** The equation for velocity of fluid from a spigot is derived from Bernoulli's equation The relationship is $h = v^2$.

110. **B is correct.** The drop with stronger intermolecular forces will have greater surface tension, which will cause it to bead up more.

111. **C is correct.** For ideal flow, volume flow rate is constant at all points, so the volume flow rate will be equal at points A and B.

112. **A is correct.** The equation governing the speed is $v = \sqrt{2gh}$. As h decreases, so does v.

113. **D is correct.** The pressure at the bottom of the column is given by ρgh. Setting this equal to maximum pressure we get $12 \times 10^5 = 4000 \times 10 \times h$.

114. **A is correct.** The Young's modulus for any substance is a constant.

115. **B is correct.** Using the formula for Young's modulus we have:

$$\text{strain} = (5.4 \times 10^3 / 6 \times 10^{-4}) / 9 \times 10^9.$$

Thus strain equals 10^{-3}. This is 0.1%.

116. **D is correct.** The weight per unit area cannot exceed one fifth of the yield strength. Convert 1.5×10^8 kg to 1.5×10^9 N. Divide the yield strength by 5 and set this equal to the weight per unit area.

$$(0.5 \times 10^8 \text{ N/m}^2) = (1.5 \times 10^9 \text{ N}) / A$$

$$A = (1.5 \times 10^9 \text{ N}) / (0.5 \times 10^8 \text{ N/m}^2) = 30 \text{ m}^2$$

117. **B is correct.** The strain must remain the same. The deformity of the shoe will double with the height vecause F/A does not change. This keeps the strain ($\Delta x / h_o$) the same.

118. **A is correct.** Copper has the largest value for Young's modulus, so it will undergo the least strain for a given stress.

119. **D is correct.** Young's modulus for lead is one-fourth the modulus for glass. So the fractional change in lead will be four times the change for glass.

120. **B is correct.** The bulk modulus describes a substance's resistance to pressure applied from all sides, which is the same as the stress encountered under water.

EXPLANATIONS TO QUESTIONS IN LECTURE 6

121. **A is correct.** The period of each wave is 4 seconds so the frequency is $\frac{1}{4}$ Hz. The wavelength is 12 meters. $v = f\lambda$.

122. **C is correct.** The formula for this problem is $v = \sqrt{(\beta/\rho)}$. Although densities of solids are usually greater than the density of gases, this would make waves move more slowly. Thus, the answer must be that solids are less compressible than gasses. This means that they have a higher bulk modulus β.

123. **C is correct.** The frequency of the waves being sent is equal to the frequency of waves being received. Everything else is irrelevant information. Every second one wave is sent. In 10 seconds, 10 waves are sent.

124. **B is correct.** Sound level (β) is related to intensity (I) by $\beta = 10 \log (I/I_o)$, so a change of 20 dB in sound level means that I is 100 times greater at 5 meters. The intensity of a sound wave is proportional to the square of the amplitude, so to change the intensity by a factor of 100 requires a change in amplitue by a factor of only 10. This question requires you to consider two relationships. Although you should know both relationships for MCAT, that's probably one step more than a real MCAT question would require.

125. **B is correct.** By definition. (See the first page of this lecture)

126. **C is correct.** Frequency is related to both wavelength and period by inverse relationships. There is no direct mathematical relationship between amplitude and frequency.

127. **A is correct.** If it takes 1 second for the wave to go to the bottom and back, it must take 0.5 seconds for the wave to reach the bottom. We know that $vt = x$, and x is the depth in this case. So, (1500 m/s)(0.5 sec) = 750 m.

128. **A is correct.** A 10 dB increase means that the intensity is increasing by a factor of 10, so if the intensity is only doubled, there will be less than a 10 dB increase (actually, it's about a 3 dB increase).

---

129. **B is correct.** The pattern repeats twice between the dotted lines.

130. **D is correct.** This is the definition of interference. The displacements of two superimposed waves are summed all along the wave.

131. **C is correct.** An audible beat frequency requires that the two sound waves have close frequencies.

132. **D is correct.** When energy is added to a structure at one of its natural frequencies, the amplitude reaches some maximum value. At this point, damping effects create an energy loss at the same rate at which energy is absorbed, and the total energy of the structure is constant. A standing wave is produced.

133. **B is correct.** The formula for the third harmonic closed on both sides is $L = 3\lambda/2$. Here, L is 0.5 m. Thus $\lambda = 0.33$ m.

134. **B is correct.** When two slightly different frequencies are sounded at the same time, they will create beats with a frequency equal to the difference. So 883 Hz – 879 Hz = 4 Hz.

135. **B is correct.** The first and second harmonics are the only consecutive harmonics that have a ratio of 1 to 2. The second harmonic is the length of the string. Alternatively, use the harmonic series formula, $L = \dfrac{n\lambda_n}{2}$, to find n. $\dfrac{n(4.0)}{2} = \dfrac{(n+1)(2.0)}{2}$ From this you can find that $n = 1$. Now plug $n = 1$ back in to find L. $L = \dfrac{(1)(4.0)}{2} = 2.0$.

136. **D is correct.** If there is perfect constructive interference, the amplitudes will add (6 + 3 = 9). If there is perfect destructive interference, they will subtract (6 – 3 = 3).

___

137. **B is correct.** The period of a pendulum is not related to the mass of the bob. It is similar to projectile motion in this respect. It is possible to think of a pendulum like a 'guided' body in free fall.

138. **C is correct.** As shown earlier in the lecture, kinetic energy of a pendulum can be described by a sine wave with energy fluctuating between zero and some maximum.

139. **C is correct.** The square of the amplitude is proportional to the intensity.

140. **D is correct.** For the frequency to increase, the relative velocity must move the source and observer toward each other. Be careful. The relative velocity does not dictate at what frequency the sound is heard. A wind can also change the frequency by changing the velocity of the sound, but, even with a wind, the source and the observer must have a relative velocity.

141. **D is correct.** The velocity of the wave on a string is a function of the properties of the string, so it will remain constant. The wavelength of a standing wave is determined by the length of the string, so it will remain constant. If the velocity and wavelength are constant, then frequency is constant too.

142. **C is correct.** The pendulum is at its greatest speed at point A, so it will be at it's greatest kinetic energy. All of the other quantities are at zero at this point.

143. **B is correct.** Remember, frequency of a pendulum is related to the square root of g/l. High above the earth, the acceleration due to gravity will decrease. If g decreases, the frequency will decrease. If the frequency of the time-keeper decreases, the clock will slow down.

144. **B is correct.** Harmonic motion is motion that is repeated over and over again. There is no repeated action in the fall of a skydiver.

___

EXPLANATIONS TO QUESTIONS IN LECTURE 7

145. **C is correct.** This is a units question. 100 N/C is equivalent to 100 V/m. The one coulomb experiences 100 Newtons of force. This is a measure of the strength of the electric field: 100 N/C. Another way to say 100 N/C is 100 V/m. The plates are one meter apart, so they must have a 100 volt potential difference.

146. **B is correct.** The forces are conservative so if we turn the picture 90°, this is just like gravity, *mgh*; the vertical distance *h*, and not the horizontal distance, is what matters. Similarly, in the question, only the distance against the electric field matters. The work required is the force times the distance parallel to the field or *Eqd*.

147. **A is correct.** The force is given by Coulomb's law, $F = k\, qq/r^2$. The electrostatic force changes with the square of

the distance between the centers of charge.

148. **C is correct.** The electric field above an infinitely large electric plate remains constant with distance. You can visualize this by imagining the electric field lines. The lines are perpendicular to the plate and have nowhere to spread. By bending in one direction or another, they would increase their distance from one line, only to decrease their distance from another line. Since the lines would remain at an equal distance from one another, the electric field would remain constant.

149. **B is correct.** This problem is about energy. The system has a total electric potential energy of $U = kqq/r$. Remember, the forces acting are conservative so mechanical energy is conserved. Thus, as the first particle is propelled away from the second, electric potential energy is converted to kinetic energy. When the first particle moves 25 cm, it has doubled its distance of separation. From $U = kqq/r$, we know that the first particle has lost half of its potential energy to kinetic energy when r is doubled.

$$\frac{U}{2} = k\, \frac{qq}{r \cdot 2}$$

When the first particle is infinitely far from the second particle, it will have lost the rest of the electric potential energy to kinetic. In other words, it will have twice the kinetic that it had at 25 cm. We know from $K.E. = \frac{1}{2}mv^2$ that if we multiply the $K.E.$ by 2, we must multiply the velocity by the square root of 2 or approximately 1.4. 1.4 times 10 equals 14 m/s.

$$K.E. = \frac{1}{2}mv^2$$

150. **A is correct.** The field lines are directed away from both charges, so by definition they are both positively charged.

151. **A is correct.** Doubling both masses will increase the attractive gravitational force. Choice C is wrong because doubling both charges will increase the repulsive electrical force. Choices B and D will not change the forces at all.

152. **B is correct.** Electrostatic forces are conservative, so the work done by a force against them is conserved in potential energy. A volt is a joule/coulomb, so you can get voltage by dividing work by charge. (90 J)/(10 C) = 9 J/C = 9 V.

---

153. **A is correct.** The electric field inside a capacitor is constant. By definition, a dipole has equal but opposite charges on either end. The force on each end of the dipole is Eq and in opposite directions. The net force is zero.

154. **B is correct.** The effective resistance is 3 Ω. The voltage divided by the effective resistance gives 4 amps coming out of the battery. The 4 amps split evenly at the node before A and B; 2 amps through each resistor.

155. **D is correct.** Increasing the voltage across the plates would increase the amount of charge on the capacitor but not the capacitance of the capacitor. Capacitance is defined by $C = Q/V$.

156. **A is correct.** The energy for the light comes from the battery. The rate at which the energy is released is the power. $P = i^2R$. Since the voltage remains constant, the change in the current will produce the greatest change in the power. Where more light bulbs are attached, the resistance goes up and the current goes down; thus the power goes down and less light is produced.

157. **C is correct.** This is Kirchoff's first rule: current flowing into a node must also flow out. Since the resistors have equal resistances, the current is the same in both parallel branches. Thus 4 amps flow into the node from both branches. Therefore 8 amps must flow out of the node.

158. **D is correct.** A Watt is a joule/sec. So you can get Joules by multiplying power and time. Don't forget to convert time to seconds. So (60 W)(60 sec) = 3600 J.

159.   **D is correct.** Adding a resistor in parallel decreased the overall resistance, which will increase the current and the power. The voltage of the battery is not affected by changes in the circuit.

160.   **C is correct.** Choice A comes from $V = IR$, with I replaced by C/sec. Choice B comes from $P = I^2R$. Choice D comes from $P = V^2/R$.

---

161.   **C is correct.** The maximum voltage is given by $V_{max} = \sqrt{2}\ V_{rms}$.

162.   **B is correct.** A magnetic field runs from magnetic north to magnetic south. The north pole of a compass needle points to the south pole of the earth's magnetic field, which is near the geographic North Pole.

163.   **D is correct.** You must remember that the force is perpendicular to both the velocity and the magnetic field. You may recall from Lecture 1 that since velocity and the magnetic field are both vectors, and their product, force, is a vector, the product will always be perpendicular to the other two vectors.

164.   **A is correct.** We can either memorize the Bio-Savart law, $B = \mu_o i/2\pi r$, or visualize how the energy of the field is spread from the wire. As we move away from the wire, the energy spreads out over a cylinder surrounding the wire. The circumference of this cylinder increases directly with the radius. In other words, if we double the radius, or distance from the wire, there is twice as much room over which to spread the energy.

165.   **C is correct.** The electric field between the plates will push a positive charge to the right, so the magnetic field must push the drop to the left to counter the force. The right hand rule shows that a magnetic field coming out of the page will push a falling positively charged drop to the left.

166.   **D is correct.** A charged particle moving parallel to magnetic field lines experiences no force. Remember, $F = qvB\sin\theta$. If θ is zero, then F is zero.

167.   **A is correct.** Lenz's law says that current will flow in a loop of wire to oppose the changes in magnetic field inside the loop. If the field strength is decreasing, then current will flow to try to increase field strength. Using the right hand rule, you can see that a clockwise current will create a magnetic field inside the loop.

168.   **B is correct.** Since the path is circular, the particle must be traveling at 90 degrees to the magnetic field (otherwise the path would be helical). The centripetal force is equal to the magnetic force. So, $qvB = mv^2/r$. If you solve for q, you get mv/Br.

EXPLANATIONS TO QUESTIONS IN LECTURE 8

169.   **A is correct.** The ray will turn toward the normal as it enters the glass and away from the normal as it exits the glass.

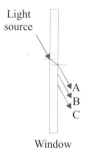

170.   **D is correct.** Blue has the highest frequency of the given choices. Remember, ROY G. BIV.

171.   **A is correct.** We are given 'km'; we want 'years'. We work with the units as follows: km x s/m x min/s x hrs/min x days/hrs x yrs/days x m/km. Everything cancels but years.

172.   **D is correct.** Reflection is indicative of either wave or particle theory.

173.   **C is correct.** Light passes through the piece of glass as shown below. Only the thicker glass directs the light toward A.

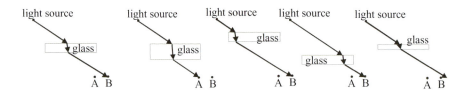

174.   **D is correct.** As the light is dimmed, less and less energy is available to the light bulb until, at the last moment, there is only enough energy to produce red light.

175.   **B is correct.** We can find the speed of light through glass by using the index of refraction. $n = c/v$, or $v = c/n = (3 \times 10^8)/1.5 = (2 \times 10^8)$. Once we know the speed of light in glass, we can use $x = vt$. Rearrange the equation to solve for t and change cm into meters. $t = (1 \times 10^{-2})/(2 \times 10^8) = 0.5 \times 10^{-10} = 5 \times 10^{-11}$

176.   **A is correct.** Choice A describes refraction, not diffraction. Roughly speaking, diffraction occurs when waves bend around corners.

---

177.   **B is correct.** Focal distance is equal to one half the radius of curvature, $f = \frac{1}{2}r$.

178.   **D is correct.** $m = d_i/d_o$.

179.   **B is correct.** According to the lens maker's equation, as the refractive indices of the lens and the surrounding medium approach one another, the lens will lose its effect. However, you don't need the lens maker's equation to visualize this. If we use our technique of taking examples to their extremes, we can imagine a lens made out of water. When we use the lens in the air, it acts as a magnifying glass; when we use it in water, it doesn't work. If the water were at a slightly different temperature to change the index only slightly, the water lens would bend light only slightly under water.

180.   **A is correct.** Virtual images are called 'virtual' because they are not really there, so they cannot be projected on to a screen. Real images can be seen if they are focused into the eye or projected onto a screen. Diverging lenses and convex mirrors, by themselves, can only create virtual images.

181.   **B is correct.** The light ray is bending in the wrong direction. This is a diverging lens, it should diverge parallel light rays.

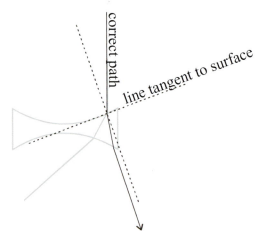

182.   **C is correct.** The light rays that bounce off a flat mirror do not intersect in front of the mirror, so to create an image, you follow them back to their implied source behind the mirror. That's where the virtual image appears.

183.   **A is correct.** An increase in the index of refraction of a lens will increase the bending of the light rays, which will increase the power of the lens. Alternatively, you can look at the lens maker's equation to see that increasing n_1 will increase $1/f$. Increasing the radius of curvature of one side will flatten the lens and reduce the amount that it refracts light, thus decreasing its power. Since $P = 1/f$, an increase in f will decrease the power.

184.   **C is correct.** $f = r/2$. So if f is 4, then r is 8.

185. **D is correct.** The thin lens equation is $^1/_1 = ^1/_4 + ^1/d_i$. The object distance is always positive. This results in a value of $4/3$ for d_i. Since this value is positive, the image is behind the lens where the 'eye' is. Remember, I (eye) am positive that real is inverted.

186. **B is correct.** This one is tricky. First of all, a convex mirror can't make an inverted image so A and C are out. Secondly, The focal point on a concave mirror is positive. Thus, from the thin lens equation, $1/f = 1/5 + 1/d_i$. Since the image and the focal distance are positive, the focal distance must be less than 5 (which is the same as saying $1/f$ must be greater than $1/5$).

187. **A is correct.** The object is outside the focal distance of a converging mirror; the image will be positive, real, and inverted. The thin lens equation gives $^1/_2 = ^1/_4 + 1/d_i$. The image distance is four, so the magnification is negative 1. The negative means that the image is inverted.

188. **D is correct.** The focal distance is negative so the lens is diverging and the power is $1/f$.

189. **D is correct.** See question 187. If the lens is diverging then the image and the object cannot be at the same distance, $1/f = 1/d_i + 1/d_o$. Since d_i is negative, the focal distance would have to be infinite; a flat lens.

190. **D is correct.** When an object is placed at the focal point of a lens, the rays will emerge parallel on both sides of the lens. If the rays never intersect, then no image is formed. If you use the thin lens equation, you'll get an image distance of infinity.

$$\frac{1}{f} = \frac{1}{f} + \frac{1}{\infty}$$

191. **B is correct.** If an object is placed at a very large distance from a lens, we can think of it as being placed at infinity. For an object placed an infinite distance from a lens, the image will appear at the focal point.

$$\frac{1}{f} = \frac{1}{\infty} + \frac{1}{f}$$

192. **C is correct.** A converging lens is the only one of the choices that produces an inverted image on the side opposite the object.

Lecture Question Expls.

INDEX

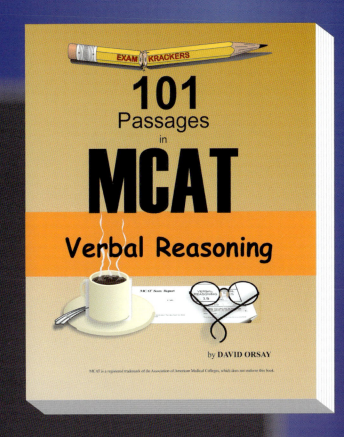

An Unedited Student Review of This Book

The following review of this book was written by Teri R—. from New York. Teri scored a 43 out of 45 possible points on the MCAT. She is currently attending UCSF medical school, one of the most selective medical schools in the country.

"The Examkrackers MCAT books are the best MCAT prep materials I've seen-and I looked at many before deciding. The worst part about studying for the MCAT is figuring out what you need to cover and getting the material organized. These books do all that for you so that you can spend your time learning. The books are well and carefully written, with great diagrams and really useful mnemonic tricks, so you don't waste time trying to figure out what the book is saying. They are concise enough that you can get through all of the subjects without cramming unnecessary details, and they really give you a strategy for the exam. The study questions in each section cover all the important concepts, and let you check your learning after each section. Alternating between reading and answering questions in MCAT format really helps make the material stick, and means there are no surprises on the day of the exam-the exam format seems really familiar and this helps enormously with the anxiety. Basically, these books make it clear what you need to do to be completely prepared for the MCAT and deliver it to you in a straightforward and easy-to-follow form. The mass of material you could study is overwhelming, so I decided to trust these books—I used nothing but the Examkrackers books in all subjects and got a 13-15 on Verbal, a 14 on Physical Sciences, and a 14 on Biological Sciences. Thanks to Jonathan Orsay and Examkrackers, I was admitted to all of my top-choice schools (Columbia, Cornell, Stanford, and UCSF). I will always be grateful. I could not recommend the Examkrackers books more strongly. Please contact me if you have any questions."

Sincerely,
Teri R—

About the Author

Jonathan Orsay is uniquely qualified to write an MCAT preparation book. He graduated on the Dean's list with a B.A. in History from Columbia University. While considering medical school, he sat for the real MCAT three times from 1989 to 1996. He scored in the 90 percentiles on all sections before becoming an MCAT instructor. He has lectured in MCAT test preparation for thousands of hours and across the country for every MCAT administration since August 1994. He has taught premeds from such prestigious Universities as Harvard and Columbia. He was the editor of one of the best selling MCAT prep books in 1996 and again in 1997. Orsay is currently the Director of MCAT for Examkrackers. He has written and published the following books and audio products in MCAT preparation: "Examkrackers MCAT Physics"; "Examkrackers MCAT Chemistry"; "Examkrackers MCAT Organic Chemistry"; "Examkrackers MCAT Biology"; "Examkrackers MCAT Verbal Reasoning & Math"; "Examkrackers 1001 questions in MCAT Physics", "Examkrackers MCAT Audio Osmosis with Jordan and Jon".